THE ‹‹‹
LONG LIFE
COOKBOOK

Also by Anne Casale

Italian Family Cooking:
Like Mama Used to Make

THE ❧ LONG LIFE COOKBOOK

Delectable Recipes for Two

Anne Casale

FOREWORD BY
ROBERT N. BUTLER,
SERIES EDITOR

*Published with the cooperation of the Gerald and May Ellen Ritter
Department of Geriatrics and Adult Development,
Mount Sinai School of Medicine,
Mount Sinai Hospital*

A LONG LIFE BOOK

BALLANTINE BOOKS

NEW YORK

LIBRARY OF CONGRESS CATALOGING-IN-PUBLICATION DATA
Casale, Anne.
The long life cookbook.
Includes index.
1. Low-salt diet—Recipes.   2. Low-fat diet—Recipes.
3. Low-sugar diet—Recipes.   4. Aged—Nutrition.
I. Title.   II. Title: Recipes for two.
RM237.8.C37   1988   641.5'63   86-48014
ISBN 0-345-33377-2

Book design by Beth Tondreau Design

Manufactured in the United States of America

10   9   8   7   6   5   4   3

THE LONG LIFE COOKBOOK
is dedicated to
my two grandsons

John Paul and Colin Edward Murphy

*The greatest legacy I can offer is a heart filled with love and the
wherewithal to lead a happy and healthy life.*

‹‹‹‹-

CONTENTS

≪≪-

⋘

ACKNOWLEDGMENTS

My personal gratitude to Joëlle Delbourgo, my editor, for requesting that I write this book; Dr. Andrea P. Boyar, for her guidance with the nutritional development of recipes; and to David Wald, a very dear friend, my deepest appreciation for the many hours spent helping me put my thoughts into words.

FOREWORD

In the late 1960s and early 1970s, the hippies—the baby-boomer generation—chanted, "You are what you eat!" and unwittingly started a small revolution in the American kitchen. Scientists in the laboratory, respected chefs, and consumers in the supermarkets began to voice their concerns about how the foods we eat affect our health and well-being. While the youth movement may have been responsible for starting to raise our food consciousness, the older set has furthered the cause because it is they who are most susceptible to heart disease and other health problems that can be exacerbated by poor nutritional habits.

On a regular basis, researchers are providing us with eye-opening reports about the detrimental effects of foods low in fiber and high in salt content and cholesterol—in other words, the traditional American diet—on the health and longevity of our population. It's pretty clear at this point that a diet consisting of moderate amounts of protein, high-fiber foods, and plenty of fruits and vegetables will lessen the risk of heart disease in healthy people, particularly when such a diet is combined with moderate exercise. Consumers have taken the cue from these scientific insights and are demanding healthier food products on their grocers' shelves and in restaurants. But while more people are now more interested in healthier eating habits, they're not at all willing to sacrifice good-tasting food and variety in their menus. The community of food experts has been challenged and a few, like Anne Casale, have risen to the occasion.

The Long Life Cookbook helps make healthy eating a joy with easy-to-prepare recipes that call for the kinds of ingredients that would make nutritionists smile with approval. The suggested menus will please all cooks concerned with keeping calorie intake reasonable, food preparation time minimal, and their budgets intact, without having to skimp on the enjoyment they get from eating food that's pleasing to the eye as well as the palate.

The baby boomers are now entering their fifth decade. They would do well to follow Anne Casale's recipes to help ensure that they too live a longer and healthier life.

Robert N. Butler, M.D.
May 28, 1987
New York City

THE ⋘
LONG LIFE
COOKBOOK

INTRODUCTION: COOKING AND EATING THE LONG LIFE WAY

≪≪≪

It's amazing what you can learn about people while walking up and down the aisles of a supermarket. One's taste, style of eating, and values are on public display to the well-trained eye. I have a terrible habit of looking into other people's shopping carts while marketing or at the checkout counter. When I see all those so-called convenience foods, the frozen dinners, the premixed, precooked, processed products, I have to restrain myself from pulling things out of carts. Instead, I shrug my shoulders, shake my head and think, "You poor souls, what are you doing to yourselves?" How I would love to take them by the hand and offer a little mini-course while walking through the supermarket. I would guide them up and down the aisles, introducing wholesome products and helping them to restructure old, unhealthy eating habits and discover enjoyable, healthy new ones.

My first lecture would be on reading labels. The majority of packages on supermarket shelves today provide nutritional information, and all have ingredients listed. A quick glance at those food labels reveals extraordinary amounts of fats, salt, and preservatives.

The tour would include brief visits to the dairy, meat, poultry, and seafood sections, where I would offer suggestions for making the best selections. The produce area would be scrutinized at length as we took in nature's bountiful array of fresh fruits, vegetables, and herbs. We would continue along the aisle offering an array of pastas and then move into the aisle filled with assorted flours and such grains as rice, bulgur, and barley. Our last stop would be the condiment aisle, overflowing with dried herbs, spices, oils, and vinegars. As the grand tour ended, we would return all the frozen dinners and premixed, precooked and processed products to the shelves and start shopping again . . . sensibly.

As I would guide those people through the supermarket, allow me to guide you through these pages. Let me share with you a practical, nutritional approach to food selection and preparation—a style I call "long life cooking."

The nutritional guidelines for *The Long Life Cookbook* are based on recommendations by the United States Department of Agriculture and the Department of Health and Human Services.* (See the section that follows, "Nutrition Guidelines", for further details.) While this book was specifically designed for individuals in the fifty-plus age group, its nutritional principles and philosophy apply to all adults who wish to eat sensibly.

In my quest for an appealing, healthful way of cooking, I've tried to be creative in my use of ingredients. Cholesterol-free olive and vegetable oils as well as unsalted margarine are used in limited quantities. In seasoning, salt has been reduced, eliminated, or replaced by such ingredients as fresh lemon juice, a dash of wine, herbs, and spices. Cream has been replaced with lighter enrichments of part-skim ricotta cheese and low-fat yogurt. Foods are sweetened naturally, not with artificial sweetners, but with small amounts of sugar and/or sweet vegetables and fruits. Long life cooking does not mean sacrificing the excitement and appeal of the foods you love. These recipes are both healthy *and* delicious. I believe that food is at its best when we guard its natural flavors. Each dish should have its own identity—one that is not camouflaged by heavy sauces and thickeners.

While most of the recipes in this book utilize foods that can be purchased in small quantities to serve two, many adapt themselves to cooking for one simply by halving the given amounts. Recipes can be easily increased if entertaining, and some (for instance soups, yeast breads, quick breads, and muffins) already have larger yields; many of these freeze well.

---

*United States Department of Agriculture and United States Department of Health and Human Services, "Dietary Guidelines for Americans," 2nd ed., and "The American Health Foundation Food Plan," rev. (Washington, D.C.: Government Printing Office, 1985).

The recipes have been designed in a simple step-by-step style for efficiency and ease. Ingredients are listed in the order in which they are to be used. All the recipes have been kitchen-tested and taste-tested to make sure that even an inexperienced cook can successfully complete them with the utmost confidence. With today's life-styles, no one wants to spend hours in the kitchen preparing meals. *The Long Life Cookbook* offers a wide range of delectable, imaginative recipes that can be prepared in a limited amount of time; in fact, many can be on your table in less than an hour.

The Long Life Cookbook is more than a collection of recipes. It is a modern, sensible, and satisfying approach to food with an emphasis on freshness and simplicity, dedicated to your good health.

Anne L. Casale

NUTRITION GUIDELINES

The fact that you have selected a cookbook with "long life" in the title indicates your interest in the connections between diet, aging, and health. If you are already fifty years old or more, you may be worried about or actually experiencing signs that could predict future health problems—signs such as elevations in your body weight, blood pressure, fasting blood sugar levels, or LDL cholesterol levels. (LDL is the "bad" blood cholesterol). If so, your concerns are justified, because these signs are associated with the development of degenerative conditions such as cardiovascular disease and diabetes. If you are in your twenties, thirties, or forties, you would be well advised to review and adjust your dietary habits now, because prevention is a lifelong process.

The news about the power of diet to protect against or reverse degenerative diseases is both good and bad. The bad news is that no one can give you an ironclad guarantee that proper diet can protect or restore your health. This is true for a number of reasons: each of us is biologically unique, the causes and progression of illness are complex, and nutrition information and theory is constantly changing. Today's "fact" has often become tomorrow's discarded theory. As an example, there are currently more questions than answers on the exact interactive roles of sodium, calcium, potassium, and magnesium in controlling blood pressure.

The good news is that many individuals have been successful in reversing conditions such as hypertension, elevated blood cholesterol, and abnormal blood sugar levels by some combination of diet, weight loss, exercise, abstinance from smoking, moderation in alcohol intake, and stress control. The United States government has enough faith in the current state of knowledge about nutrition and disease prevention to have released a second edition of the "Dietary Guidelines for Americans" in 1985. These guidelines contain general recommendations about the types of foods to cut down on and those to emphasize. The main points are as follows: 1) eat a variety of foods daily; 2) achieve and maintain a desirable weight; 3) avoid too much total fat, saturated fat, and cholesterol; 4) eat foods with adequate starch and fiber; 5) avoid too much sugar; 6) avoid too much sodium; 7) if you drink alcohol, do so in moderation.

You may find these guidelines a bit frustrating, because it is hard to know how much is "adequate" and how much is "too much." The answers depend on many personal characteristics, such as your gender, age, present health status, your family history, the prescriptions you take, and so on. If you are serious about taking charge of your health, your first move should be to have a complete physical examination. This book was not written for people who have been prescribed a strict diet such as one for diabetes. If your physical reveals the need for a therapeutic diet, ask the physician to refer you to a qualified nutritionist so that the two of you can work out a personal diet plan. For the rest of us, the painless and modest changes reflected in these recipes should suffice. What follows is a general discussion of the points in the government guidelines.

Obesity, Dietary Fat, Saturated Fat, and Cholesterol

For most adults, it is generally agreed that "too much" dietary fat means that more than 25 to 30 percent of one's total daily caloric intake is fats. Take the example of a fifty-five-year-old woman who is five feet four and weighs 125 pounds. Weight tables may say that she is within her desirable weight range, but this is true only if not more than one-quarter of her weight is body fat. Assuming that she is moderately active, she probably eats somewhere between 1300 and 1500 calories daily to maintain her weight. Unless she has increased her physical activities proportionately, she has found that each decade of adulthood brings about a 5 percent decrease in the amount of calories she can eat to keep her weight steady. Ideally, of the 1300 daily calories from carbohydrate, protein, and fat, only about 350 of them should come from fat. How does this translate into food? Each teaspoon of butter, margarine, or oil contains 45 fat calories; each ounce of lean meat contains 27 fat calories; each ounce of cheddar cheese contains 72 fat calories. If you do a little arithmetic, you can calculate that 350 calories of fat does not stretch very far!

The recipes in this cookbook are helpful because they suggest modest serving sizes of meats and poultry and they offer alternatives to fatty spreads for breads. If you find that the serving sizes for meats don't fill you up, do as the guidelines suggest and incorporate more low-fat, starchy foods to balance the meal (pasta, brown or white rice, bulgar, bread, and the like).

As for saturated fat and cholesterol, these need a bit of further explanation. Cholesterol is not found in meat products only. You may be surprised to learn that chicken and beef are nearly equal in cholesterol content. Why then do nutritionists suggest more skinless poultry and less beef? The answer is that their saturated fat contents differ. Saturated fat is found in both animal and vegetable products. Palm and coconut oils, as well as hydrogenated shortenings, are examples of highly saturated food fats. Together with dietary cholesterol, these fats are believed to increase many individuals' risk of cardiovascular disease. On the other hand, polyunsaturated vegetable fats (such as those found in corn and safflower oils), monounsaturated fats (such as those found in olive and nut oils), and fish fat (omega 3 fatty acids such as found in salmon, sardines, and other fatty fish) are currently believed to have the opposite effect on cardiovascular disease risk. What does this mean for our hypothetical fifty-five-year-old woman? If she has approximately 350 daily fat calories to play with, she'd be best off consuming about 250 (two-thirds) of these fat calories in vegetable oils and fatty fish meals. That leaves little or no room for extra helpings of meat. The "typical American" meal featuring a generous portion of meat does not fit comfortably into these recommendations. Drastic changes are probably not necessary for most of us, but as you use this book, consider serving some of the pasta dishes as main courses, and plan each week to have a few vegetarian meals based on legumes.

Starch, Fiber, and Sugar

What's the difference between consuming 250 carbohydrate calories from a glass of soda pop and eating a serving of brown rice? All carbohydrate foods eventually are broken down to glucose for the bloodstream, but there are some differences in the way different carbohydrate sources behave. First, it takes longer for your body to break down the starch in the rice to simple sugar. This puts less of an immediate strain on your insulin production system. In addition, the rice, unlike the pop, has additional nutrients such as B vitamins and minerals, and it is a good source of fiber.

We've all been hearing a lot lately about the possible protection that adequate dietary fiber can afford against certain types of cancers and gastrointestinal disorders. What you may not know is that there are different types of fibers in foods. Wheat bran, oats, and apples all contain important fiber, but they are not interchangable. Therefore, you can't rely on one food such as a bran cereal to provide all of your fiber needs for the day. It is recommended that you get your daily fiber from a variety of unrefined grain products and unprocessed fruits and vegetables daily. Four or more servings per day from these categories will probably be sufficient. As with most other things, too much of something good can turn out to be harmful. Overemphasis on fiber may interfere with your absorption of certain minerals. Moderation and balance are the key, and the recipes in this book reflect that philosophy. Reducing but not omitting the sugar from several dessert recipes is an example.

Sodium

Most of us know that table salt is really sodium chloride, but did you know that sodium is found in a variety of other forms in food? In general, fruits, grains, and most vegetables are naturally low in sodium. On the other hand, meats, dairy products, and canned foods tend to be high in sodium. The question of how much sodium is "too much" is the subject of much scientific debate of late. It is generally agreed that humans can survive nicely on a diet free of added table salt and highly processed foods such as corned beef, franks, and instant chocolate pudding. The amount of sodium found naturally in a variety of fresh foods is adequate to prevent most people from developing a sodium deficiency. Very low-salt diets do tend to taste dull, however. Do we all need to pass up the salt shaker? If current research on calcium, potassium, and magnesium in relationship to hypertension are consistent with preliminary studies, the answer is probably going to be that a moderate salt intake can be counter-balanced by adequate amounts of the latter three minerals. For the present, you should be following your prescribed sodium restriction if you have one. The rest of us should probably go light on the salt and avoid highly salted processed foods and fast foods. Again, the recipes in this book reflect this philosophy, suggesting a pinch of salt in many recipes if desired for taste, and emphasizing fresh ingredients whenever practical.

Alcohol

It has not been suggested that a modest alcohol intake for nonpregnant adults is harmful, but much current research has confirmed that excessive alcohol consumption can be dangerous indeed. The United States government defines "excessive" as more than one or two drinks (twelve ounces of beer, three ounces of wine, or one and a half ounces of distilled spirits equal a drink) daily. Alcohol in excess of this amount has been linked to unhealthy rises in blood pressure, increased risk of certain cancers, increased risk of malnutrition (particularly protein and vitamin deficiencies), escalation of osteoporotic bone changes, and liver damage. In addition, driving or operating machinery under the influence of alcohol greatly increases the risk of accident and injury. You needn't worry about the alcoholic beverages used as ingredients in some of these recipes, however. In cooking, the alcohol evaporates and you are left with only the flavor base. When you are decreasing the amount of salt in your recipes you will find that wine can provide a concentrated and pleasant flavor.

Calcium and the Risk of Osteoporosis

Although the United States dietary guidelines do not address the issue of calcium intake and the prevention of osteoporosis, we are daily bombarded by publicity about this condition. The research reports on the protective effects of long-term adequate calcium intake have been mixed, however, with the latest evidence suggesting that calcium is but one important dietary component and that diet is but one aspect of long-term prevention. Weight-bearing exercises, abstinance from smoking, and estrogen replacement therapy if and when needed are examples of interactive prevention measures that work along with dietary changes. As you use this book, remember to incorporate good calcium sources into your daily menus by choosing recipes that contain low-fat milk products and cheeses, as well as dark leafy green vegetables.

Conclusions

The objective of these few pages is to start you thinking about nutrition. If you are interested in learning more about nutrition and health promotion, your local dietetic association may be able to provide you with a recommended reading list. The most important point is that modest and realistic dietary changes may pay off in increased longevity or better health. As a nation we are already living longer; we must now begin to concentrate on living healthier. Diet can be one aspect of a personal health promotion campaign, and this book is a good place to begin planning your strategies. Good eating and good health!

Paula Fishman, Ed.D.

SAFETY TIPS FOR THE KITCHEN

The kitchen is the heart of the home. It is a special place where one works at a joyful task filled with pleasurable anticipation, a special place linked with feelings of warmth, safety, and security. It is easy to lose sight of the fact that the kitchen is also potentially the most dangerous place in one's home. Many accidental injuries occur in this room. Extra care around the kitchen can reduce risks and prevent hazards.

The following suggestions will help to avoid kitchen accidents.

- Never climb on chairs or tables to reach high places. Use a well-balanced step stool to avoid injury from a fall.
- Make sure all drawers and cabinet doors are closed so that you will not get clothing hooked on drawers or hit your head against higher cabinets.
- Buff waxed floors to make them less slippery or use a nonslip floor wax.
- Place a rubber-backed rug near the sink area or use rubber under-pads to anchor the rug in that area.
- Wipe up spilled liquid immediately.
- Sweep up broken glass immediately. Always pick up glass slivers with a dampened paper towel, never with your bare hands.
- Cook in a well-ventilated kitchen. Always keep your range hood or exhaust fan on while cooking.
- Use a heavy cutting board when slicing or chopping. A dampened dish cloth under the board will help to prevent sliding.
- Knives should be stored in a knife block or on a magnetic bar.
- Treat all cuts or scratches that break the skin with disinfectant. Store Band-Aids in a cabinet near your work area. (There is a type of Band-Aid marked "kitchen assortment" that I always have on hand.)

- Wear an apron when cooking and keep a pair of pot holders near the cooking area but away from stove flame.
- If you have a gas range that must be lit with a match, make sure both the broiler and oven doors are open when lighting the oven. Turn the gas on after striking the match, never before. Light immediately.
- Store matches in a fireproof container.
- Keep a box of bicarbonate of soda (baking soda) near the stove area to smother any burning fat, or use metal cover to smother. Small fire extinguishers designed for kitchens are available in major department and hardware stores.
- If you must leave the kitchen while baking or cooking, set your kitchen timer for the amount of time required for recipe.
- Always check the range and oven when finished cooking to make sure both are turned off.
- Avoid burns and scalds by turning pot and pan handles toward the back of the range.
- Whether they are hung from a rack or lined up on a shelf near the stove, store pots and pans above the waist, preferably at eye level.
- Do not overload wall sockets with electrical appliances.
- Never touch any electrical appliance when your hands are wet.
- Unplug all kitchen appliances when not in use.
- Never jerk cords out of outlets—grip the plug only.
- Follow the manufacturer's instructions carefully before using and storing any new kitchen appliance.

COOKS' TOOLS

An artist carefully selects his brushes, paints, and canvas, a carpenter his tools, nails, and lumber to perform his tasks. So must you, the cook, like any other artisan, have the right implements to perform your craft. Blunt knives and equipment of the wrong size, shape, or weight are the enemies of a fine cook, and too often spell the difference between success and failure in the kitchen. A kitchen filled with the trendy gadgets of the day is a coldly functional place, while one equipped with well-chosen tools that you are comfortable handling is a place where the act of preparing food will fill you with joy and satisfaction. It is more economical to put your money into sound, sturdy equipment of the finest quality. It cooks better, lasts longer, gives you reliable service, and never lets you down. Proper cooking equipment makes the work easier and should be a cook's most prized possession.

Topping my list of favorite kitchen appliances is the Cuisinart food processor. I consider this versatile machine a necessity, not a luxury, for anyone who enjoys cooking. I strongly urge you to purchase one if you don't already own one; you won't be sorry. I often refer to my food processor as my miracle worker in the kitchen because it cuts down the time it takes to do many tedious cooking chores. While I will admit that I do not use the machine if I only have one shallot to chop or a small amount of parsley to mince, I turn to it constantly for kneading bread doughs, making quick breads and muffins, puréeing soups, and slicing or chopping ingredients.

An ideal way to store and organize the utensils most commonly used in your kitchen is in a revolving utensil holder with compartments to accommodate tools of different sizes. I have found this versatile holder a good way to achieve a clean counter and still have my most often used implements—wooden spoons, spatulas, cooking forks, whisks, and the like at my fingertips. This type of receptacle

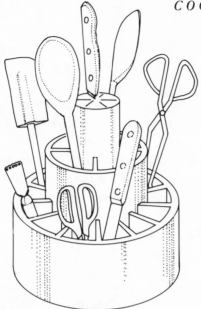

also helps maximize storage in kitchen drawers. Such units are available in most department stores. If you do not have room for a revolving holder, select a container such as a wide-mouthed ceramic vase or pitcher large enough to hold your most frequently used utensils.

To help you thread your way through the great variety of today's tools for cooks, the following discussion groups implements according to categories: pots and pans, knives, bakeware and baking accessories, mixing tools, measuring tools, straining tools, and special miscellaneous tools. Listed with each group are recommendations as to number needed, size, and material. For some utensils, practical information as to function is also supplied.

Equipped with the right tools, you, the artisan, can turn the craft of cooking from a chore into a creative experience.

Pots and Pans

As every good cook knows, a variety of pots and pans of differing materials and design are essential tools in the kitchen.

The most important thing to know when purchasing any new piece of cookware is how efficiently it cooks. You can't tell by looking at it, but you can get a good idea if you know what it is made of and how it is constructed. Check the weight or gauge. A light-gauge pot that heats rapidly is useful for boiling pasta or blanching vegetables. Such a pan, however, would be too thin for other kinds of cooking such as braising or sautéing. For this type of cooking a medium- to heavy-gauge metal, particularly at the base, is recommended.

Check the pan for balance. It should not tip when standing. The handle(s) should be heat-resistant and ovenproof. A ring or hole at the end of the handle is useful for hanging the pan on a rack. Try the lid (especially in saucepans) to see that it fits the pot properly. I do not recommend putting any pan in the dishwasher; they always take up too much room.

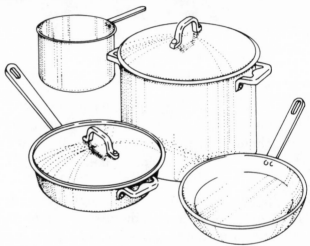

I always discourage anyone who asks me from buying a large set or starter set of matched pots and pans. While they may look pretty in your kitchen, some of the pots and pans may fit your needs while others will remain unused. This is a good point to consider especially when cooking for two. In the long run, you are better off choosing each pan individually. Buy each one in the material most suited to its function and in the size most suited to your kitchen. Also, be sure to read manufacturers' tags carefully for warranties.

If possible, pots and pans should be stored at eye level or at least above the waist, either hanging from a rack or lined up on a shelf near the stove. Keeping them in a special place will prevent them from getting scratched and chipped.

I strongly suggest that you go to a reliable department store or gourmet shop to search out the following types of cookware.

SAUCEPANS

- ½-quart capacity—no lid
- light to medium gauge
- stainless steel exterior and interior or anodized aluminum exterior with stainless steel interior

- 1½-quart, 2½-quart, 3½-quart, and 5-quart capacities, with tight-fitting lids
- medium to heavy gauge
- copper exterior with stainless interior or anodized aluminum exterior with stainless steel interior or copper sandwiched between exterior and interior layers of stainless steel

POT

- 5-quart capacity, with lid and two handles (for boiling pasta and blanching vegetables)
- light gauge
- stainless steel interior and exterior with aluminum core

SKILLETS

- 10- and 12-inch diameter, with covers
- heavy gauge
- copper exterior with stainless steel interior or anodized aluminum exterior with stainless steel interior or copper sand-

wiched between exterior and interior layers of stainless steel

SAUTÉ PAN

- 10-inch diameter, with cover and ovenproof handle
- heavy gauge
- copper exterior with stainless steel interior or anodized aluminum exterior with stainless steel interior or copper sandwiched between exterior and interior layers of stainless steel

DUTCH OVEN

- 3-quart capacity
- heavy gauge
- anodized aluminum exterior with stainless steel interior or cast iron coated with enamel

STOCK POT

- 10-quart capacity, with cover and two handles
- medium gauge
- stainless steel interior and exterior with aluminum core or heavy-duty aluminum

WOK

- 14-inch diameter, with cover
- spun steel (follow manufacturer's suggestions for seasoning before using)

- round bottom for gas range; flat bottom for electric or Corningware-type cooking surface

ROASTING PAN

- 10 by 13 by 3 inches deep with handles
- medium to heavy gauge
- stainless steel or aluminum

ROASTING RACK

- adjustable V-shape type, preferably nonstick, to fit roasting pan

Knives

A good sharp knife that is comfortable to hold is one of the most essential tools in the kitchen. Before selecting the right shape of knife for the particular tasks you have in mind, it is important to know what factors raise a kitchen knife into the top-quality class. There are three parts to a knife that should be considered: the blade, the handle, and the tang.

Two kinds of steel are used in knife blades, carbon steel and stainless steel. Either kind must be of high quality to take a sharp edge. Many professionals still believe that carbon steel holds the finest cutting edge. However, it rusts and stains easily. For today's cook, we have high-carbon stainless steel, sometimes called "no stain." This type of blade will never pit or rust. With regular sharpening this type of blade can be kept in good condition for many years.

Always judge a handle by how it feels and by the quality of its finish. Handles on the best knives will be of either high quality plastic (which I find most practical), plastic-impregnated wood, or close-grained hardwood.

A hard-bladed knife, such as a chef's (or sometimes called a cook's) knife should be balanced by the tang, which is the extension of the blade seated into the handle; it runs the full length of the handle.

Your skills at handling a knife should determine which size knives you use. A skilled cook can adapt a 10-inch wide-bladed chef's knife to almost any kitchen job. For most people, a better all-purpose knife is the 8-inch chef's knife; it is smaller and easier to manage.

All my knives are kept in a knife block on the counter close to my work area. A unit like this can make the difference between order and chaos in your kitchen. If your knives are constantly dull from banging around in a drawerful of kitchen utensils, storing them in a block will help keep the blades sharp and the most often used knives close at hand.

There are a few general rules for taking care of knives:

- Use a knife only on a wooden cutting surface and only for proper jobs.
- Wash and dry knives immediately after use.
- Never put any knives into a dishwasher.
- Store knives, separately, either in a knife block or on a magnetized knife rack to protect them and you from damage.

A knife must keep a sharp cutting edge for maximum efficiency. While you can keep a good edge by frequently using a sharpening steel, I strongly urge you to take your knives to a professional knife sharpener at least once a year. If you do not know of one, look in the buyers' guide of your telephone directory under locksmiths. Many of them do perform this service. Your local butcher may also be able to provide you with a source.

PARING KNIVES

- two: 3- to 3½-inch blade with sharp pointed ends (for light jobs—peeling, paring, and cutting small fruits and vegetables)

UTILITY KNIFE	• 5- to 7-inch blade with sharp pointed end (for heavier jobs—peeling, paring, and chopping large fruits and vegetables and trimming fat from meat and poultry)
CHEF'S KNIFE	• 8- or 10-inch blade (most used knife in the kitchen—for chopping, mincing, and dicing fruits, vegetables, meats, and fresh herbs)
CARVING KNIFE	• 9- or 10-inch narrow blade (for slicing meat, poultry, and fish)
SERRATED KNIVES	• two: 10-inch blade (for slicing yeast and quick breads)
	• 4½-inch narrow blade (for slicing tomatoes)
SHARPENING STEEL	• classic round hard-chromed steel—10- or 12-inch sharpening surface with either plastic or wooden handle

Bakeware and Baking Accessories

Baking requires its own special equipment and accessories. The shape of the baking pan you use depends entirely on what you are baking and what you want it to look like. For the best results, the pan must be the right size, and of the right material and weight, especially for batter or yeast breads. The following list includes necessary bakeware for recipes in this book.

BAKING DISHES

- three: 8 by 8 by 2 inches deep
- 9 by 13 by 2 inches deep
- Pyrex or ovenproof porcelain
- 2½-cup capacity, shallow
- oval or round
- ovenproof porcelain

CASSEROLES

- two: 1½-quart capacity, shallow with lid
- ovenproof porcelain or earthenware
- 2-quart capacity, deep with lid

CUSTARD CUPS

- two: 6-ounce capacity (only two are needed for recipes in this book but a set of 6 comes in handy)
- white ovenproof porcelain or earthenware

LOAF PANS

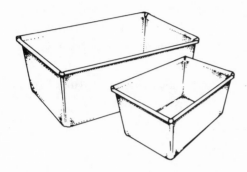

- 9 by 5 by 3½ inches deep
- heavy gauge tinned steel or heavy gauge aluminum (for large quick breads)

- two: 8½ by 4½ by 3 inches deep
- black baker's steel (for yeast breads)
- heavy gauge tinned steel or heavy gauge aluminum (for medium-sized quick breads)

- four: 5 by 2½ by 2½ inches deep
- heavy gauge tinned steel (for small yeast and quick breads)

MUFFIN PAN

- 8 section, each cup 2½ inches in diameter by 1 inch deep
- heavy gauge aluminum or heavy gauge tinned steel

BAKING SHEET

- 10 by 13½ inches
- heavy gauge aluminum

WIRE COOLING RACKS

- two: round 12- to 15-inch diameter
- tinned steel wire

CAKE TESTER

- stiff wire with bright-colored coated plastic handle, 6¾ inches long (easier to find with colored handle in bright red or green)

PASTRY BRUSH

- 3-inch flat natural bristles with wood handle

PASTRY BOARD

- 24- by 18- by ¾-inch with lip
- hardwood (for kneading dough)

ROLLING PIN

- ball-bearing with 12-inch roller length
- hardwood

SIFTER

- 5-cup triple screen
- aluminum or stainless steel

Mixing Tools
BOWLS

- six: 2- to 3-ounce capacity (handy for placing ingredients before cooking)
- porcelain or glass

- set of three mixing bowls in graduated sizes, ½-, 1- and 1½-quart capacities
- Pyrex or Melamine with rubber grip ring at base

- deep 2½-quart capacity (for bread rising)
- ceramic or porcelain

FORKS

- one set of two 12-inch wooden forks (for cooking and tossing pasta)

- two-pronged metal cooking fork

LADLE

- 4-ounce capacity
- stainless steel

SPATULAS

- 14-inch metal wok spatula with wooden handle (for stir-frying)

- three rubber spatulas in assorted sizes (for folding egg whites and for cleaning out bowls)

- 10- to 12-inch stiff plastic spatula (for scraping inside work bowl of food processor or blender)

- flexible spatula (for turning and lifting foods out of pans)
- stainless steel

- narrow-blade spatula (for spreading)
- stainless steel with wooden handle

TONGS

- narrow metal tongs 9¾ inches long, with handles (handy for turning meat or poultry in sautéing)

- pair of 16-inch metal tongs with gripping teeth (for grilling)

WOODEN SPOONS

- set of four: 8, 10, 12, and 16 inches long with thin handles

MIXERS

- electric mixer, preferably heavy duty type with beater, paddle, and dough hook attachments (only needed for recipes in this book if you do not have a food processor)

- portable hand mixer
- plastic with chrome steel beaters

WHISKS

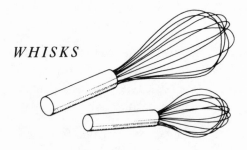

- Two: 8-inch stainless steel (for mixing salad dressings)
- 16-inch stainless steel (for sauces and beating egg whites)

Measuring Tools

MEASURING SPOONS

- two metal standard sets of ¼ teaspoon, ½ teaspoon, 1 teaspoon, and 1 tablespoon (for measuring both liquid and dry ingredients)

METAL MEASURING CUPS

- a graduated set of ¼ cup, ⅓ cup, ½ cup, and 1 cup (for measuring dry ingredients; second set comes in handy if you do a lot of baking)

GLASS MEASURING CUPS

- 1-cup size, 2-cup size, and 1-quart size, each with pouring lip (for measuring liquids)

KITCHEN SCALE

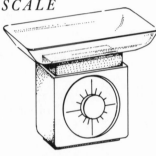

- spring-balance type with plastic tray that inverts for holding ingredients, and magnified dial on the front showing measurements in pounds and grams

MEAT THERMOMETER

- instant-read thermometer, 1-inch diameter dial (for meat, poultry, and testing liquid for proofing yeast in bread baking)
- stainless steel with glass face, nylon pocket sheath

PASTA MEASURE

- wood or plastic with graduated holes for different portion sizes

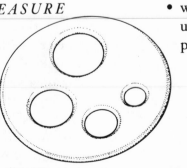

Straining Tools

CHEESECLOTH

- one package (for lining strainers)

COLANDER

- 3-quart capacity with handles (for draining pasta and cut vegetables)
- aluminum, stainless steel, or enamelware

SALAD SPINNER

- plastic (excellent for drying salad greens; also good for drying strawberries and blueberries)

SKIMMER

- 16-inch metal with fine mesh holes (for skimming broth)

STRAINERS

- set of three: 2½-inch diameter with fine mesh strainer (for dusting confectioner's sugar)
- 4½-inch diameter with fine mesh strainer (for draining ricotta, yogurt, and cut-up fruits)

- 8½-inch diameter with medium mesh strainer (for draining vegetables and straining broth)

SLOTTED SPATULA

- 14-inch with wooden handle and perforated stainless steel blade about 7¾ inches long by 3 inches wide (excellent for lifting fish slices from pan or from poaching liquid)

SLOTTED SPOON

- 11¾-inch stainless steel with perforated or slotted holes

Special Miscellaneous Tools

BASTER

- aluminum or stainless steel with rubber bulb

CHOPPING BOARD

- 12 by 16 by 2 inches thick
- hardwood, such as maple

CITRUS JUICER

- plastic or glass with strainer

COTTON STRING

- small ball for trussing

GRATER AND SHREDDER

- two: metal box grater with scallop edge and coarse, medium, and fine shredding grids
- stainless steel

	• small Mouli rotary (for grating small amounts of Parmesan cheese) • stainless steel
ICE CREAM SCOOP	• chrome-plated with stainless steel spring
ICE CUBE TRAYS	• two sets, for storing broth for sauces
KITCHEN SHEARS	• one pair that is sturdy and comfortable to handle, preferably with plastic handles (Joyce Chen's are my favorite)
KITCHEN TIMER	• round 90-minute timer • plastic or metal
MELON BALLER	• double melon-ball cutter, to cut balls of two different sizes • stainless steel with wood handle
METAL SKEWERS	• set of 8: 12 inches long with sharp pointed ends (only 4 are needed but extras come in handy for entertaining) • stainless steel
NUTMEG GRATER	• tin or stainless steel

PEPPER MILLS

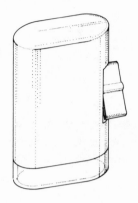

- two: one for black pepper-corns and one for white peppercorns

VEGETABLE BRUSH

- stiff fiber brush with wooden handle

VEGETABLE PEELER

- swivel-action peeler with carbon steel blade

ZESTER

- stainless steel blade with wooden or plastic handle, about 5½ inches long (to remove thin strips of lemon or orange peel)

<<<

GLOSSARY: INGREDIENTS

When it comes to ingredients, it is impossible to overstate the virtue of using the finest products possible. Their value is not measured in cost but in excellence of taste, quality, and freshness.

ARROWROOT

Arrowroot, obtained by drying and grinding the rootstalks of a tropical plant of the same name, is used as a thickening agent. Arrowroot gives a clearer, more transparent sauce than other thickening agents such as cornstarch or flour, and leaves no floury aftertaste. Dissolve arrowroot in a little cold water, broth, or wine. Remove pan from heat before adding the arrowroot mixture to any sauce or gravy. Cook sauce, stirring constantly, over medium heat, until slightly thickened.

BREAD CRUMBS, DRY AND FRESH

Dry. Arrange slices of bread in a single layer on a cookie sheet. Preheat oven to 250 degrees and toast bread until crisp and golden, about 30 minutes. Break into 1-inch chunks and whirl in food processor fitted with metal blade until finely ground. Place crumbs in fine mesh strainer and sift into larger bowl. Discard any large crumbs or whirl again in food processor. Place in jars and keep in cool, dry place until needed. Store in the refrigerator during summer months.

Fresh. Cut up fresh or day-old bread, including crust, or tear it gently with fingers. Place in food processor fitted with metal blade. Run machine until bread is reduced to coarse crumb consistency.

CAPERS

These are the flower buds from a low, trailing, thorny shrub that thrives in the hot, dry Mediterranean climate. After harvesting, the unopened buds are dried in the open air, then pickled in casks of salted vinegar or dry-cured in coarse salt. Capers should always be thoroughly rinsed and drained before being added to any dish or sauce. For recipes in this book, I suggest you buy the tiny variety called "nonpareil," which are pickled in salted vinegar. Experts say this variety has more flavor than the larger buds. Spoon capers out of jar with a small spoon and place in a small strainer set over a cup. Pour strained vinegar from cup back into jar. (Jar can be refrigerated indefinitely without fear of spoilage if capers are covered with vinegar.) Then rinse the measured capers thoroughly under running water, and drain.

EGGS

Sizes are specified with each recipe. If they are to be separated, use eggs taken directly from refrigerator. A cold egg breaks cleanly and the yolk is less likely to rupture than one at room temperature. It is critical that no egg yolk find its way into the whites, for even a trace of yolk will prevent them from reaching full volume when beaten. If part of the yolk should fall into the white, use the shell to scoop it out. If beaten egg whites are used in desserts, these recipes specify that cream of tartar be added to stabilize them.

FLOUR

Recipes in this book call for different varieties of flour. Read labels and recipes carefully. Spoon the flour lightly into the measuring cup; do not shake the cup or pack or press the flour. Level lightly with the back of a knife. (Bread flour may not be available in some parts of the country.)

Unbleached All-Purpose Flour. This type of flour is made from a blend of high-gluten hard wheat and low-gluten soft wheat. It is suitable for baking a complete range of products including cakes, biscuits, muffins, and quick breads. If bread flour is unavailable, this type of flour is also recommended for yeast breads. Unbleached flour should be stored in an airtight container at room temperature and should be used within six months of purchase.

Bread Flour. This type of flour is milled from hard wheat, which has a high gluten content. The high-gluten protein in bread flour gives risen breads a light, fluffy texture. Bread flour should be stored in an airtight container at room temperature and should be used within six months of purchase.

Whole Wheat Flour. The entire kernel of whole wheat flour, also called graham flour, is milled from hard wheat, which has a high content of germ and bran. Place in an airtight container and store in the refrigerator. (The natural germ in the flour may turn rancid if stored at room temperature.) Before using it in any recipe, the amount needed should be allowed to come to room temperature.

Wondra Flour. For coating, I recommend Gold Medal Wondra, an instant, all-purpose flour that pours like salt. It will give a much lighter coating for sautéing.

LEMONS

An indispensable flavoring in many of my dishes. Try to pick smooth-skinned lemons; they have more juice. The juice can be substituted for vinegar in salad dressing. Use only freshly squeezed juice, never the reconstituted type, which leaves a bitter aftertaste. Make sure you scrub the lemon's outer skin well to remove any coating before using the rind in any dish.

OILS

Olive Oil. Purchase only imported olive oil. The important phrase to look for on a bottle of olive oil is "100% Pure Cold Pressed." This type of olive oil has been purified and has extra virgin oil added to it. For cooking, I prefer an olive oil from Tuscany, such as Bertolli or Berio. For salads or plain boiled vegetables, I use only extra virgin olive oil. The highest quality extra virgin oils are made entirely by hand and use only the finest olives, which are picked by hand and pressed in a manually operated cold-stone press. The resulting oil is then filtered through cheesecloth. This is the primary reason for the oil's high cost. Once you have sampled it, you will never forget its fruity taste. My personal favorites are Raineri from Liguria and Badia a Coltibuono from Tuscany. Olive oil does not have to be kept in the refrigerator, but it should be kept sealed and stored in a cool, dark place.

Vegetable Oil and Cooking Sprays. Only small amounts of vegetable oil are used for recipes in this book, primarily for stir-frying. I prefer Mazola corn oil for this type of cooking. For greasing pans, use Mazola No-Stick Corn Oil Cooking Spray, or Pam.

THE ONION FAMILY

The strong-flavored members of the onion family, including chives, garlic, leeks, red onion, scallions, shallots, and yellow onion are used as seasonings. They offer a variety of interesting tastes of different intensities. While many can be used interchangeably, each type has a particular use and all share a starring role in the kitchen.

Chives. Thin, dark green, tubular chive leaves are the mildest flavoring in the onion family. They add wonderful seasoning to salads and baked potatoes, and may also be used as an attractive garnish.

Garlic. Buy bulbs that are tightly closed, with unwrinkled skins of white, pink to purple, or white with purple streaks. Store in a cool, dark place. For easy peeling, place a clove under the broad side of a chef's knife. Thump the blade to split the garlic's clinging skin; it will then slip off easily. It is better to chop or mince garlic with a knife than to mash through a press.

Leeks. Buy leeks with crisp, green, unwithered tops and clean, white bottoms. Leeks should be straight and cylindrical. If the ends are very bulbous, the leeks will probably be tough and woody. To clean, trim roots and a portion of the fibrous leaf tops. Cut the stalks in half lengthwise and wash thoroughly under running water, holding the layers apart, until no sand remains.

Red Onion. This type of onion is also called Spanish onion. It is relatively mild and sweeter tasting than the yellow onion. Red onions can be used for the same purpose as yellow onion in cooking, or eaten raw in salads. Store in a cool, dry place.

Scallions. Select those with crisp, green, unwithered tops and clean, white bottoms. Try to pick scallions with large, bulbous ends. Trim roots and any brown or limp tops. Wash thoroughly and blot dry with paper towel. Wrap in paper towel and store in sealed plastic bag in refrigerator. Use within four or five days.

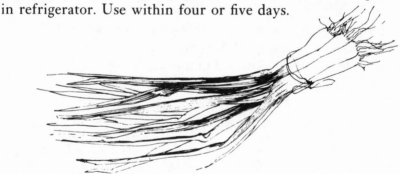

Shallots. These slender, pear-shaped bulbs are about the size of walnuts and are more perishable than onions. They should be stored in a cool, dark place. The shallot's flavor is more delicate than onion and it's more easily digestible. To use, divide the cloves. Cut off tops and tails of the shallots. Peel with a small paring knife, pulling away the first layer of flesh with the skin that is usually firmly attached to it.

Yellow Onion. Yellow onions are considered to be the most pungent of all the globe onions. Look for ones with no trace of moisture at the base or the neck and with no growth of light greenery at the top—a sign that they have begun to sprout. Select smaller globe onions rather than the larger specimens; once cut, they do not keep well. Store in a cool, dark place.

MARGARINE

Substituting margarine for butter won't help your waistline, but it may help your heart. Butter is an animal fat, rich in saturated fat, which tends to increase the level of cholesterol in the blood. Vegetable oils such as safflower, corn, or soybean are polyunsaturated fats, which tend to lower the level of blood cholesterol. Most margarines contain a greater portion of vegetable oil and thus less saturated fat. When buying margarine, check the nutrition information panel on the package and choose a margarine with more polyunsaturated fat than saturated fat.

PARMESAN CHEESE

This rich, nutty, flavorful cheese is essential to many pasta dishes in this book. Parmesan cheese should be grated just before using so that flavor is at its best. The production of imported Parmesan cheese labeled Parmigiano Reggiano is very strictly controlled. Ask to see the wheel and make sure it is stamped "Reggiano." To store, wrap in a thin layer of dampened cheesecloth, then in plastic wrap. Place in a plastic bag and seal tightly. Store in refrigerator. It must be stored in this manner because it dries out much more quickly than other cheeses. When freshly cut and moist, Parmesan is also an excellent table cheese with grapes or sliced Bosc pears.

PART-SKIM RICOTTA CHEESE

A soft, moist, snow-white cheese made from part-skim milk and whole milk, ricotta is very perishable. Always check the expiration date before purchasing. Some brands of part-skim ricotta cheese tend to be a little watery. If there is a thin layer of liquid on top of the cheese, drain it before using. Line a fine mesh strainer with a double thickness of dampened cheesecloth. Spoon ricotta into lined strainer set over a bowl. Place, uncovered, in refrigerator to drain thoroughly for at least three hours.

When ricotta is whipped in a blender or food processor, it has the dairy-rich flavor and smooth creamy texture of thick whipped cream. To make whipped ricotta, empty a 15-ounce container of fresh, part-skim ricotta into blender or food processor fitted with metal blade. Process until the graininess disappears and ricotta is the consistency of thick whipped cream: about 30 seconds. Stop machine once and scrape down inside blender or work bowl with plastic spatula. Spoon cheese back into container in which it was purchased and store in refrigerator.

Whipped ricotta is so versatile that I always have some on hand in the refrigerator. Its smooth texture blends well with dishes ranging from pasta to desserts. For breakfast, whipped ricotta is excellent spread thinly on toasted muffins or whole wheat bread. A delightful addition to ricotta-covered toast is a layer of sliced fresh fruit or a little cinnamon-sugar. One of my favorite breakfasts is bite-size shredded wheat drizzled with a little orange blossom honey and topped with 1 heaping tablespoon whipped ricotta. It reminds me of the Italian pastry *sfogliatelle.* For a quick dessert, spoon 1 tablespoon whipped ricotta sweetened with 2 teaspoons of your favorite liqueur (Grand Marnier is my favorite) per serving over cut fresh fruit.

Whipped ricotta may be used for any recipe in this book using ricotta.

SALT

You hear it all the time: Americans eat too much salt. The most obvious way to reduce your intake of salt is to leave the shaker in the cabinet and not on the table. You can also cut down on salt by not adding any to cooking water for vegetables or pasta, and by never salting your food before tasting it. Most recipes will specify an amount of salt to use if desired, or to taste. In some instances, I definitely feel that a little salt is needed, especially in yeast breads. You will also find many recipes that do not have any salt listed in their ingredients because they have been adequately seasoned with herbs, spices, lemon juice, or vinegar.

VINEGAR

Recipes call for either red or white wine vinegar. Use a good imported brand of vinegar for best results, especially in salads. The brands I use are Badia a Coltibuono and Sasso for red vinegar and Sasso for white vinegar. For raspberry vinegar, I recommend Silver Palate brand. These vinegars are available in better supermarkets and gourmet shops.

LOW-FAT YOGURT

Plain low-fat yogurt is a culture made from pasteurized milk, skim milk, and nonfat milk solids. Always check the expiration date on the container before purchasing. Many of the lowfat yogurts tend to be watery and should be drained thoroughly before using. Line a fine mesh strainer with a double thickness of dampened cheesecloth. Spoon a 16-ounce container of yogurt into the lined strainer set over a bowl. Place, uncovered, in refrigerator to drain for at least three hours. Yogurt will exude as much as ½ cup of liquid; discard liquid. After draining, yogurt will have the consistency of lightly whipped heavy cream. Spoon back into container in which it was purchased and store in refrigerator until needed. It can be used as a spread on toast, as a topping for baked potatoes, or just mixed with cut fresh fruit for a simple dessert. I also use yogurt for yeast breads, quick breads, salad dressings, and in other dessert recipes.

HERBS

One of the joys of the summer months is to look out my kitchen window at my herb garden. My daughters, Joanne and Amy, plant my herb garden every year as a gift for Mother's Day. Use fresh herbs whenever possible. Many supermarkets now carry fresh herbs year-round. If fresh herbs are not available, use the dried variety for many recipes. I provide both fresh and dry measurements. A general rule of thumb: One tablespoon of minced or chopped fresh herbs is equivalent to one teaspoon crumbled dried. When buying dried herbs, always look for those that are green rather than pale or powdered; the latter usually have less flavor. Buy herbs in glass jars so that you can see the color and judge the freshness. Store jars away from sunlight and heat. For full flavor, rub the herb between your palms.

Basil. The most common basil of the more than a hundred different varieties available worldwide is sweet basil. These whole, bright green leaves are deliciously aromatic. This herb is best when the fresh leaf is available. (Many super-markets now stock fresh basil year-round.) Pluck off the tender leaves just before you use them, so they won't bruise or go limp. Wash in cold water, drain well, and blot dry between two layers of paper towel. Basil marries perfectly with tomato, whether in salads or sauces. It also has a great affinity with sautéed egg-plant or zucchini and is an indispensable flavor-ing for Basil-Ricotta Pesto Sauce. I often use this fresh herb in place of lettuce in a sandwich. Try it just once, and you'll be hooked!

Bay Leaf. Fresh or dried, use bay leaf sparingly, for it has a strong flavor. If purchasing dry, always buy whole leaf, never crumbled or powdered. Look for leaves that are still tinged with green; if they are more than a year old, they will have lost their flavor as well as their color. Used sparingly, bay leaf adds a wonderful, subtle flavoring to roast pork, beef soup, and stews.

Dill. The pungent flavor of this herb is excellent either fresh or dried. If purchasing dried, I prefer the type labled "dillweed," the dried fronds rather than dill seed. Use either fresh or dried for soups, salads, salad dressings, poultry, and especially fish. It also adds won-derful zest to either baked or boiled white potatoes.

Fennel. This whole seed has a licorice taste and should be crushed before being added to any dish. To crush fennel seeds use a mortar and pestle. Alternatively, place fennel seeds in a mound on cutting board and give them a good thump with the broad side of a chef's knife to crush partially; then finely chop with knife. Fennel is excellent when sprinkled on top of broiled fish, roast pork, or cooked peas that are dressed with a little olive oil.

Marjoram. Use this strong, sweet, sagelike herb sparingly. Either fresh or dried marjoram adds distinct flavor in marinades for fish or poultry.

Mint. There are many varieties of this herb. Besides peppermint and spearmint, there are also pineapple, apple, and orange mints that can be used in fruit salads or as a garnish in cold summer drinks. Use peppermint or spearmint for the recipes in this book. Mint, which may be used fresh or dried, is very easy to grow and dry. Collect the leaves on a hot, sunny day, preferably just before flowering time. Wipe them with a damp cloth and dry on paper towel for a couple of days. Mint is a wonderful flavoring with roast lamb, broiled fish, or in salad dressings.

Oregano. Always use oregano sparingly because of the herb's strong, spicy flavoring, which is sharper than marjoram. Try to buy whole bunches of the dried plant; they hold their flavor longer in storage. The best quality comes from Italy, Greece, and Mexico. Oregano is an indispensable flavoring for marinara sauce, and marvelous on a tomato salad simply dressed with extra virgin olive oil, a pinch of sugar, and freshly milled black pepper.

Parsley. Parsley is a refreshing and versatile herb. It can be used with almost any meat, fowl, fish, or vegetable; finely minced, it will dress up any dish. The flat leaf variety known as Italian parsley is more pungent in taste than the curly leaf. Use curly leaf for garnishing; use Italian parsley for flavor. Stems can be wrapped in bundles, frozen,

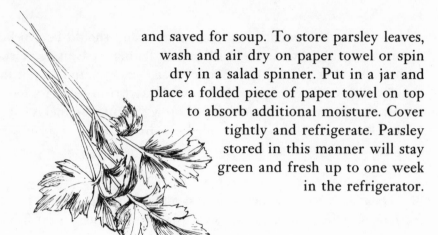

and saved for soup. To store parsley leaves, wash and air dry on paper towel or spin dry in a salad spinner. Put in a jar and place a folded piece of paper towel on top to absorb additional moisture. Cover tightly and refrigerate. Parsley stored in this manner will stay green and fresh up to one week in the refrigerator.

Rosemary. Rosemary's powerful flavor is traditionally used with lamb, but it is equally good with chicken. The spiky dried leaves retain their flavor well.

Sage. Sage has velvety, grayish green leaves with a slightly musky taste. This herb must be used sparingly, especially fresh sage, a hardy perennial very easy to grow in a sunny garden. Fresh or dried, sage adds zesty flavor to chicken or pork.

Savory. A robust and very aromatic herb that tastes similar to thyme. There are two varieties of this herb: Summer savory is an annual with a mild, sweet taste; winter savory is a perennial species with a more robust flavor. Both summer and winter savory have a pleasant, piquant quality especially suited to poultry.

Tarragon. This herb has a slight hint of anise. Fresh tarragon, available through the summer months, harmonizes wonderfully with chicken and adds great flavor to zucchini and carrots. You might also want to try some snipped in your tossed green salad.

Thyme. A tiny-leaved herb with a warm, earthy smell, thyme is a hardy plant, easy to grow. Leaf thyme or common thyme is used for the recipes in this book. To dry, just hang in bunches in a warm, dry place, then rub the leaves off and store in a jar. If it is available, use lemon thyme, which has a faint citrus tang and is excellent on broiled chicken, lamb, or fish.

SPICES

Purchase all your in glass jars and store away from sunlight and heat.

Allspice. Allspice tastes like a blend of cinnamon and nutmeg, but is actually a single spice ground from the under-ripe berry of a tropical evergreen tree. The ground variety is recommended for all recipes in this book.

Cinnamon. Both whole stick cinnamon and good imported ground cinnamon should be kept on hand. The whole stick can be ground with a mortar and pestle.

Ginger. Ginger comes from the root of the ginger plant. For all recipes in this book, the ground powdered variety is used.

Nutmeg. Select whole nutmegs and grate with a small grater whenever needed. You will find their flavor much better than the powdered variety.

Pepper. Pepper, both black and white, is probably the most widely used of all spices. The whole peppercorns are the dried berries of the tropical pepper vine. The black come from under-ripe berries that have been dried and cured, the white from dried, ripe berries whose dark outer shell has been removed. The two varieties of black peppercorns I use are Tellicherry, which comes from India, and Java, which is imported from the East Indies. Best when freshly ground, both black and white pepper enhance all savory dishes. White pepper is used in light-colored sauces, some salad dressings, and mayonnaise.

‹‹‹

SOUPS

Unsalted Beef Broth   49

Unsalted Chicken Broth   51

Asparagus Soup   52

Broccoli Soup   53

Cauliflower Soup with Parsley   55

Chicken Soup with Herbs   56

Chilled Cucumber Soup   57

Cold Melon Soup   58

Leftover Soup   59

Lentil and Brown Rice Soup   60

Minestrone Soup   62

Raw Mushroom Soup   64

Pumpkin Apple Soup   65

Grated Potato Soup   66

Chilled Tomato Mint Soup   67

Vegetable Barley Soup   68

Julienned Vegetable Soup   69

My love for soup comes from my childhood. During the Depression years, soup was a staple in our home. My mother served it almost daily for lunch, especially during the winter months, and at least once a week for the main meal year round.

I can remember being sent to the butcher shop to purchase meat for soup. At that time, beef hind shank or boneless chuck cost twelve cents a pound. The butcher would always ask, "Is your mother making soup today?" and throw in extra bones when I nodded yes.

Whenever I teach soup classes, my students ask, "Can I use boullion cubes or canned broth?" Well, you can probably guess that my answer is "Homemade only," and for good reason. Bouillon cubes contain too much salt and no meat; canned broths are also too salty and greasy for my taste. What I want is the good, full-bodied character that comes only from broth you prepare at home. I do not add any salt to broths because the amount of salt that seems barely sufficient to season a full pot may be far too much when the liquid has reduced by the end of cooking. In using a salt-free broth, I can control the amount added (if any at all) to the finished soup.

Broths are easy to make and will keep in the freezer for months. Rich broths are also the foundation for sauces, braised dishes, and stews. Do not be disturbed by the long simmering time that it takes to make broths. I usually choose to make my supply when I will be home all day to keep an eye on things. There is no need to watch the pot as long as there is sufficient liquid covering the ingredients. During the first forty-five minutes of cooking, I check the broth frequently, adjusting the heat, if necessary, to prevent the broth from boiling too vigorously. I place a sixteen-inch wooden spoon across one side of the stock pot and tilt the lid on the spoon to partially cover the pan. This will prevent steam from building up and overheating the broth. Once the broth has settled to a slow simmer, I know it will tend itself, leaving me free to do other chores around the house.

‹‹‹

SUGGESTIONS FOR MAKING
AND STORING BROTHS

- *Bring broth to a very slow boil over low heat without stirring. It will take forty-five minutes to one hour to come to a slow boil, and during that time the fat and albuminious, grayish scum will rise to the surface of the pot.*

- *Grayish scum must be skimmed from broth several times; this insures that the finished product will be clear.*

- *Garlic should be added to broth unpeeled. Peeled garlic will fall apart as it cooks, and tends to make broth cloudy.*

- *Simmering broth slowly over low heat brings out its full flavor. To extract even more flavor, allow the broth to rest for at least two hours before straining.*

- *Always strain the broth through a fine mesh strainer lined with a double thickness of dampened cheesecloth. Dampening the cloth will prevent it from sliding around in strainer, and a damp cloth also strains out more of the fat than a dry cloth. (If you don't have cheesecloth, you can substitute a dampened piece of muslin or thin linen tea towel.)*

- *If using broth within one week, transfer cooled broth to wide-mouth jars and store in refrigerator. (Storing in a wide-mouth jar will make it easier to spoon off and discard any solidified surface fat later.) For freezing, transfer broth to one and one-half-pint plastic containers, leaving one and one-half inches of headspace to allow for expansion. Storing in this type and size container will simplify removal when ready to use. Run the bottom of the container under a little warm water and frozen broth will pop right out into a saucepan. You can easily scrape off any frozen surface fat with a small paring knife before defrosting. After defrosting, you will have approximately two cups of broth per container.*

- *Freeze some broth in ice cube trays for sauces, braised dishes, and stews. To do this, transfer two and one-half cups broth to a 1-quart glass measure or small pitcher. Carefully pour into the sections of a plastic ice cube tray. Freeze overnight. If you have difficulty removing frozen cubes (especially beef broth cubes), run the bottom of the tray briefly under warm water before popping. Using a small paring knife, scrape any frozen, solidified fat from cubes, then transfer them to a plastic bag, seal tightly, and place in freezer. Broth can be kept frozen up to four months. I recommend using Rubbermaid plastic ice cube trays for freezing broth cubes. This type tray has sixteen sections and each section holds 2 tablespoons. If a recipe calls for a quarter cup of broth, all you need do is remove two frozen cubes from the plastic bag, defrost, and add to ingredients.*

Soup is so versatile! It can be a delicate first course of julienned vegetable or chilled cucumber to sharpen the appetite, or a satisfying, hearty one-course meal of lentil and brown rice or minestrone to serve during the crisp, cold days of fall and winter.

There is one thing that all soups have in common: Friends and family find them irresistible.

‹‹‹

Unsalted Beef Broth

Initial browning in the oven will caramelize the vegetables and intensify the flavor of the meat juices. This broth is the essential foundation for many of the soups in this book, and may also be used to add richness and body to sauces, braised dishes, and stews. The meat from stock may be reserved for sandwiches; remove any fat or sinew and slice meat thin. It is delicious served on whole wheat toast thinly spread with horseradish and mustard and topped off with slices of red onion.

YIELDS 2 ½ QUARTS

2 medium-sized yellow onions (12 ounces), peeled, halved, and cut into 1-inch wedges

4 medium-sized carrots (10 ounces), trimmed, scrubbed, and cut into 2-inch pieces

3 large celery ribs (6 ounces), trimmed, scrubbed, and cut into 2-inch pieces

2 medium-sized parsnips (6 ounces), trimmed, scrubbed, and cut into 2-inch pieces

2½ pounds beef hind shank, cut into 3 crosscuts, or boneless chuck roast, cut into 3 pieces

1½ pounds beef bones

1 cup water

1 teaspoon whole black peppercorns

3 large cloves garlic, unpeeled

1 large bay leaf

2 sprigs fresh thyme or ½ teaspoon dried thyme

10 parsley stems or sprigs

3½ quarts cold water, approximately

1 cup canned, whole, peeled tomatoes, coarsely chopped, juice included

1. Adjust rack to center of oven and preheat to 475 degrees.
2. Place onions, carrots, celery, and parsnips in an even layer in a deep 14-inch ovenproof skillet or small roasting pan. Arrange meat pieces on top of vegetables and put bones between pieces of meat.

Place pan in preheated oven. Roast the meat and bones until well browned on both sides, turning once, about 30 minutes on each side. Transfer meat and bones to a 10-quart stock pot, leaving vegetables in the pan.

3. Add 1 cup water to skillet or roasting pan. Bring to a boil over high heat, scraping any fragments of meat and vegetables that cling to bottom and sides of pan with wooden spoon. Transfer vegetable mixture to stock pot. Add peppercorns, garlic, bay leaf, thyme, and parsley.

4. Add 3½ quarts of cold water to stock pot (or enough water to cover meat and vegetable mixture by 2 inches). Bring to a boil very slowly, partially covered, over medium-low heat. It will take approximately 45 minutes to bring the broth to a boil.

5. Using a skimmer or small strainer, remove all the grayish scum as it collects on the surface while the water comes to a boil. Repeat skimming 3 or 4 times until there is no scum visible. Turn heat down to low and simmer, partially covered, for 3½ hours. Add chopped tomatoes and cook for an additional 30 minutes. (The addition of chopped tomatoes during the last 30 minutes of cooking time will give the broth a beautiful amber color.) Turn heat off, cover pot, and let broth rest for at least 2 hours before straining.

6. Using a pair of tongs, transfer meat to a platter and reserve for sandwiches. Remove bones and discard. Strain broth through a fine mesh strainer lined with a double thickness of dampened cheesecloth into another pot. Squeeze cheesecloth after straining broth, to extract as much liquid as possible. Discard remaining solids. Cool broth to room temperature and pour into jars with tight-fitting lids. Broth may be kept in refrigerator for 1 week, or it may be frozen in plastic containers and ice cube trays for up to 4 months. (See page 47 for storing method.) When ready to use, discard solidified fat from surface.

⫷

Unsalted Chicken Broth

This rich golden broth is not only fundamental for many soups in this book but equally essential to enhance the flavorings of numerous sauces and braised dishes.

YIELDS 2 ½ QUARTS

3 ½ pounds chicken parts such as necks, backs, wings, thoroughly washed in cold water

3 ½ quarts cold water, approximately

1 medium-sized yellow onion (6 ounces), peeled and halved

3 large celery ribs with leaves (6 ounces), trimmed, scrubbed, and cut into 2-inch pieces

2 medium-sized carrots (5 ounces), trimmed, scrubbed, and cut into 2-inch pieces

2 medium-sized parsnips (6 ounces), trimmed, scrubbed, and cut into 2-inch pieces

10 parsley stems or sprigs

3 large cloves garlic, unpeeled

½ teaspoon whole black peppercorns

1. Place chicken parts in a 10-quart stock pot. Add 3 ½ quarts of cold water to stock pot (or enough water to cover chicken parts by 3 inches). Slowly bring to a boil, partially covered, over low heat. Using skimmer or small strainer, remove all the grayish scum as it collects on the surface while the water comes to a boil. Repeat skimming 2 or 3 times until there is no more scum on the surface, and only a little white froth left floating on top. Add remaining ingredients and continue simmering, partially covered, over low heat for 2 hours. Turn off heat, cover pot, and let broth rest for at least 2 hours before straining.

2. Strain broth through a fine mesh strainer lined with a double thickness of dampened cheesecloth into another pot. Squeeze cheesecloth, after straining broth, to extract as much liquid as possible. Discard the solids. Cool broth to room temperature and pour into jars with tight-fitting lids. Broth may be kept in refriger-

ator for 1 week, or it may be frozen in plastic containers and ice cube trays for up to 4 months. (See page 47 for storing method.) When ready to use, discard solidified fat from surface.

Asparagus Soup

A very refreshing first course in early spring when asparagus are abundant.

YIELDS 2½ CUPS
SERVES 2

1 pound asparagus (about 12 large spears)	⅛ teaspoon salt, if desired
2 teaspoons unsalted margarine	⅛ teaspoon freshly milled black pepper
½ cup thinly sliced scallions	
2 cups unsalted chicken broth, preferably homemade (page 51)	

1. Wash asparagus several times in cold water to get rid of sand. Using a sharp knife, cut off tough part at base of spear. With a vegetable peeler, peel spears up from the base of each, leaving tips intact. Cut off tips and reserve. Slice each stalk in half lengthwise and then cut crosswise into ½-inch pieces.
2. In a 2½-quart saucepan, melt margarine over low heat. Add scallions and sauté, stirring frequently, until slightly softened, about 3 minutes. Add asparagus stalks and broth. Turn heat to high and bring to a boil. As soon as soup reaches a boil, turn heat down to low and simmer, covered, until stalks are extremely soft, about 30 minutes (test by pressing a piece against side of pan with a fork).
3. While soup is simmering, cook asparagus tips in 1½ cups boiling water until crisp tender when tested with the tip of a knife, about 3 minutes. Drain in strainer and reserve.

4. Ladle half of the soup into a blender or food processor fitted with metal blade. Run machine nonstop until you have a smooth purée. Transfer soup to a clean pot; purée remaining soup. Season with salt and pepper.
5. When ready to serve, reheat, covered, over low heat. Place asparagus tips in soup bowls, ladle hot soup into bowls, and serve immediately.

Broccoli Soup

A fresh-tasting soup, lovely as a first course, satisfying as the mainstay of a luncheon, and very simple to make with the aid of a food processor. Vegetables, cut into 1-inch chunks, can be chopped in the processor fitted with metal blade.

YIELDS 1 ½ QUARTS
SERVES 4

1 medium-sized bunch broccoli (about 1¼ pounds)
1 quart unsalted chicken broth, preferably homemade (page 51)
1 large leek (6 ounces), trimmed, split in half, thoroughly washed, and finely chopped
1 large celery rib (2 ounces), strings removed, finely chopped

1 large carrot (4 ounces), peeled and finely chopped
1 tablespoon arrowroot or cornstarch
¼ cup cold water
¼ teaspoon salt, if desired
¼ teaspoon freshly milled black pepper

1. Remove broccoli florets, including approximately ½ inch of stem. Cut or break florets into ½-inch pieces. Wash in cold water, drain, and set aside. Remove and discard the coarse leaves from stems and

cut off about ½ inch of tough lower part of stalks. Wash thoroughly and peel stalks with vegetable peeler. Chop fine.

2. Place chicken broth, chopped broccoli stems, leek, celery, and carrot in a 5-quart saucepan. Turn heat to high and bring to a boil. As soon as soup reaches a boil, turn heat down to low and simmer, covered, until vegetables are cooked, about 20 minutes. Add broccoli florets and continue cooking, covered, for an additional 10 minutes.

3. In a small cup, dissolve arrowroot or cornstarch in cold water. Stir into soup and cook over low heat, stirring constantly, until thickened, about 5 minutes. Remove from heat and let soup rest for 1 hour so that the flavors meld together.

4. Ladle half of the soup into a blender or food processor fitted with metal blade. Run machine nonstop until you have a smooth purée. Transfer soup to a clean pot; purée remaining soup. Season with salt and pepper.

5. When ready to serve, reheat, covered, over low heat, stirring once or twice with wooden spoon. Ladle into individual bowls and serve immediately.

N O T E : Soup freezes very well and can be kept frozen up to two months.

Cauliflower Soup with Parsley

The crisp tender texture of the cauliflower florets is a perfect contrast to this velvety smooth puréed soup. A delicious first course, or it can be served for lunch with Whole Wheat Cinnamon Muffins (page 330).

YIELDS 1 ½ QUARTS
SERVES 4

1 large head cauliflower (about 1¾ pounds)
1 tablespoon unsalted margarine
1 medium-sized yellow onion (6 ounces), finely chopped
2 large celery ribs (4 ounces), strings removed, finely chopped
2 tablespoons flour

1 quart unsalted chicken broth, preferably homemade (page 51), heated
¼ teaspoon freshly grated nutmeg
¼ teaspoon salt, if desired
¼ teaspoon freshly milled white pepper
¼ cup minced Italian parsley leaves, well packed

1. Remove cauliflower florets, including about ¼ inch of stem. Cut or break florets into ½-inch pieces. Wash thoroughly in lukewarm water and drain in colander. Cook cauliflower in 1 quart boiling water until barely tender (test by tasting), about 6 minutes. Drain well in colander and refresh briefly under cold water. Transfer 1 cup florets to a small bowl and reserve.
2. In a 5-quart saucepan, melt margarine over low heat. Add onion and celery; sauté, stirring frequently, until vegetables are slightly softened, about 3 minutes.
3. Using a whisk, stir in flour and ¼ cup of the heated broth. Cook, whisking constantly, until vegetable mixture is smooth, about 1 minute. Slowly whisk in remaining heated broth (whisking broth in slowly will prevent any lumps from forming). Add florets, turn heat to high, and bring to a boil. Turn heat to low, cover pot, and simmer, stirring occasionally, for 30 minutes. Remove from heat and let soup cool to almost room temperature.

4. Ladle half of the soup into a blender or food processor fitted with metal blade. Run machine nonstop until you have a smooth purée. Transfer soup to a clean pot; purée remaining soup.
5. Add reserved florets to puréed soup. Add nutmeg; season with salt and pepper.
6. When ready to serve, reheat, covered, over low heat, stirring once or twice with wooden spoon. Remove from heat and stir in parsley. Ladle into individual bowls and serve immediately.

Chicken Soup with Herbs

An excellent soup to make when you have any leftover chicken.

YIELDS 1 QUART
SERVES 4

1 tablespoon olive oil
¼ cup finely chopped yellow onion
¼ cup finely chopped carrot
¼ cup finely chopped celery, strings removed
1 small zucchini (4 ounces) washed, trimmed, and thinly sliced
2½ cups unsalted chicken broth, preferably homemade (page 51)
1 cup cooked chicken, skinned, boned, and cut into ½-inch dice

1 teaspoon fresh lemon juice
2 teaspoons snipped fresh chives or thinly sliced scallions (green part only)
1 scant teaspoon minced fresh tarragon or ¼ teaspoon crumbled dried tarragon
2 teaspoons minced Italian parsley leaves
¼ teaspoon salt, if desired
¼ teaspoon freshly milled black pepper

1. In a 2½-quart saucepan, heat olive oil over medium-low heat. Add onion, carrot, and celery; cover pan and cook, stirring occasionally, until soft, about 10 minutes. Add zucchini and cook, partially

covered, until barely crisp tender, about 1 minute. Add broth and chicken and simmer, partially covered, for 10 minutes. Stir in lemon juice, chives or scallions, tarragon, and parsley. Season with salt and pepper. Ladle into bowls and serve immediately.

Chilled Cucumber Soup

A particular favorite of mine during the summer months. This soup must be prepared and chilled at least 4 hours or overnight before serving to allow the flavors to blend.

YIELDS 3 CUPS
SERVES 2

2 cucumbers (about 1 ¼ pounds)
¼ cup thinly sliced scallions
1 ½ cups unsalted chicken broth, preferably homemade (page 51)
1 teaspoon fresh lemon juice

½ teaspoon minced fresh dill or ⅛ teaspoon crumbled dried dillweed
¼ cup low-fat yogurt
⅛ teaspoon salt, if desired
⅛ teaspoon freshly milled white pepper

1. Slice one cucumber in half, wrap exposed end with plastic wrap, and reserve in refrigerator. Peel, halve lengthwise, seed, and coarsely chop remaining 1 ½ cucumbers. (You can cut cucumbers into 1-inch pieces and chop them in a food processor fitted with metal blade.)

2. Combine cucumbers, scallions, and broth in a 1 ½-quart saucepan. Bring to a boil, covered, over high heat. Turn heat to low and simmer, covered, stirring once or twice, for 30 minutes. Remove from heat and let cool to room temperature.

3. Ladle half of the soup into a blender or food processor fitted with metal blade. Run machine nonstop until you have a smooth purée. Transfer soup to a bowl and purée remaining soup. Stir in lemon juice and dill. Cover with plastic wrap and refrigerate for at least 4 hours or overnight.
4. One hour before serving, peel, halve lengthwise, seed, and finely dice reserved cucumber; set aside.
5. When ready to serve, stir yogurt into chilled soup with whisk or fork until completely blended. Season with salt and pepper. Place half of the diced cucumber in each soup bowl, ladle soup over, and serve immediately.

Cold Melon Soup

Brilliant orange color, a pleasure to look at, with a flavor that is totally refreshing. This light soup starts a warm weather meal in the right direction.

YIELDS 2 CUPS
SERVES 2

¼ cup fresh orange juice, strained
1 tablespoon fresh lime juice, strained
¼ cup dry white wine
1 tablespoon honey, preferably orange blossom

⅛ teaspoon salt, if desired
1½ cups extremely ripe diced cantaloupe (cut into 1-inch dice)
2 sprigs fresh mint leaves (optional garnish)

1. Place orange juice, lime juice, white wine, honey, and salt in a 1-cup glass measure. Stir with a fork until honey is dissolved and mixture is completely blended.
2. Put diced melon in food processor fitted with metal blade. Run machine until melon is finely chopped. With machine running,

pour juice mixture through feed tube until mixture is a smooth
purée, about 1 minute. Stop machine once and scrape down inside
of work bowl with plastic spatula. Transfer soup to a 1½-pint jar.
Chill in refrigerator for at least 3 hours, shaking jar once or twice
to keep mixture blended.
3. When ready to serve, shake jar once again and pour cold soup into
wine glasses, garnish with a sprig of mint, and serve.

VARIATION: You may substitute 1½ cups extremely ripe diced
honeydew for the cantaloupe.

Leftover Soup

*This soup is made quite often in my household after a dinner party or at the
end of the week when I have a collection of leftovers. I prefer a thick soup using
a ratio of 1 cup broth to 1½ cups cooked vegetables. If you like a lighter soup,
use 1 cup broth to 1 cup vegetables.*

YIELDS 2½ CUPS
SERVES 2

1½ cups cooked vegetables
such as carrots, peas,
potatoes, green beans,
broccoli and the like

1 cup unsalted chicken or
beef broth, preferably
homemade (page 51 or
page 49)
2 teaspoons minced Italian
parsley leaves

1. Place vegetables and broth in a blender or food processor fitted
with metal blade. Process until you have a smooth purée. Transfer
soup to a 1½-quart saucepan.
2. Cook soup, covered, over low heat, stirring once or twice, for 20
minutes. Remove from heat and stir in parsley. Ladle into individual bowls and serve immediately.

Lentil and Brown Rice Soup

A lusty one-dish meal! A great soup to serve family or friends for an informal Sunday night supper. All that is needed as an accompaniment is a lovely mixed green salad and some crisp rolls. If you have a food processor, you can have this soup assembled in 5 minutes. Cut leeks, parsnips, and carrots into 1-inch chunks before processing them, separately, with the metal blade. Garlic can also be chopped in the food processor by turning the machine on first and dropping clove through the feed tube to mince.

YIELDS 2 QUARTS
SERVES 6 — MAIN COURSE

1 cup dried lentils
2 cups unsalted beef broth, preferably homemade (page 49)
2 cups water
½ cup parboiled brown rice (Uncle Ben's) picked over to remove any dark brown grains
One 16-ounce can whole peeled tomatoes, coarsely chopped, juice included (can be chopped in food processor fitted with metal blade)
1 large leek (6 ounces), trimmed, split in half, thoroughly washed, and finely chopped

1 teaspoon minced garlic
1 medium-sized parsnip (3 ounces), trimmed, peeled, and finely chopped
2 medium-sized carrots (5 ounces), trimmed, peeled, and finely chopped
1 tablespoon minced fresh basil or 1 teaspoon crumbled dried basil
2 large bay leaves
¼ teaspoon salt, if desired
½ teaspoon freshly milled black pepper

1. Spread lentils in a single layer on a flat plate and discard any bits of foreign matter. Put lentils in a strainer and rinse with cold water.

2. In a 5-quart saucepan, combine broth and water. (If using frozen beef broth, take directly from freezer, scrape off any solidified surface fat with a small knife, and put the frozen block in the saucepan. Defrost with the water over low heat.)

3. Add lentils, rice, tomatoes, leek, garlic, parsnip, carrots, basil, and bay leaves to pan. Bring soup to a boil, uncovered, stirring once or twice, over high heat. As soon as soup reaches a boil, turn heat to low, cover pan, and simmer, stirring frequently, until lentils and rice are cooked (test by tasting), about 45 to 55 minutes. Remove from heat and season with salt and pepper. Let soup rest for 2 hours before serving so that all the flavors meld together.

4. When ready to serve, remove bay leaves and reheat, covered, over low heat. Ladle into individual bowls and serve immediately.

N O T E : Soup freezes very well and can be kept frozen up to 2 months. If soup is extremely thick after defrosting, add about ¼ cup water to each pint before reheating.

Minestrone Soup

Today, everyone seeks out hearty, robust soups, especially tasty with homemade bread in the winter months. Whenever it snows, friends and family usually call me because they always know bread is rising and this good old-fashioned soup is simmering away on my back burner. All of the vegetables can be prepared with the aid of a food processor. Cut onions, carrots, and celery into 1-inch chunks before processing, separately, with metal blade.

YIELDS 2 QUARTS
SERVES 6 — MAIN COURSE

1 small head cabbage (8 ounces), preferably savoy

2 tablespoons olive oil

1 medium-sized yellow onion (6 ounces), finely chopped

One 16-ounce can whole peeled tomatoes, coarsely chopped, juice included (can be chopped in food processor fitted with metal blade)

1 teaspoon sugar

1 tablespoon minced fresh basil or 1 teaspoon crumbled dried basil

2 medium-sized carrots (5 ounces), peeled and finely chopped

3 large celery ribs (6 ounces), strings removed, finely chopped

1 quart plus 1½ cups water

¼ cup converted long-grain white rice (Uncle Ben's), picked over to remove any dark grains

One 10½-ounce can red kidney beans, rinsed and well drained (1 cup)

¼ teaspoon salt, if desired

½ teaspoon freshly milled black pepper

Freshly grated Parmesan cheese (1 tablespoon per serving)

1. Discard any bruised outer leaves from cabbage. Wash cabbage and blot dry with paper towel. Quarter cabbage and remove center core. Shred each quarter on the large holes of a grater or in food processor fitted with shredding disc. Set aside.

2. In a 5-quart saucepan, heat olive oil over medium-low heat. Add onion and sauté until soft but not brown, about 4 minutes. Add tomatoes, sugar, and basil. Cook sauce, partially covered, stirring frequently, until slightly thickened, about 10 minutes. Add cabbage, carrots, and celery. Cook, partially covered, stirring frequently, just until vegetables are slightly softened, about 8 minutes. Stir in water and bring to a boil, uncovered, over high heat. As soon as soup reaches a boil, turn heat to low, cover pot, and simmer, stirring frequently, until vegetables are cooked, about 45 minutes.

3. Stir in rice, cover pot, and cook undisturbed over low heat for 15 minutes. Stir in beans; cook, covered, for an additional 5 minutes. Remove pot from heat and season with salt and pepper. Let soup rest for 2 hours before serving so that all the flavors meld together.

4. When ready to serve, reheat over low heat. Ladle into individual bowls and sprinkle with freshly grated Parmesan cheese.

N O T E : Soup freezes very well and can be kept frozen up to 2 months. If soup is extremely thick after defrosting, add about ¼ cup water to each pint before reheating.

Raw Mushroom Soup

The tender raw mushrooms in the heated beef broth add a refreshing, crisp touch to this excellent first course.

YIELDS 3 CUPS
SERVES 2

2 cups unsalted beef broth, preferably homemade (page 49)
4 medium-sized mushrooms (2 ounces) wiped, trimmed, and sliced paper-thin to make ¾ cup

1 tablespoon thinly sliced scallions
1 teaspoon minced Italian parsley leaves
⅛ teaspoon salt, if desired
⅛ teaspoon freshly milled black pepper

1. In a 1½-quart saucepan, bring broth to a boil, covered, over high heat. Stir in mushrooms and cook, uncovered, until heated, about 30 seconds. Add scallions and parsley; remove from heat. Season with salt and pepper. Ladle into individual bowls and serve immediately.

⋘

Pumpkin Apple Soup

Easy to make for a delightful first course in late fall to reflect the season's golden hues. I also love this soup for lunch during the fall and winter months. For an unusual lunch, try serving this full-bodied soup with Cranberry Nut Bread (page 317).

YIELDS 1 QUART
SERVES 4

2 teaspoons unsalted
   margarine
¼ cup finely chopped
   yellow onion
¼ cup finely chopped
   celery, strings removed
¼ cup finely chopped carrot,
   peeled before chopping
1 medium-sized tart green
   apple (5 ounces), Granny
   Smith or greening,
   peeled, halved, cored, and
   cut into ½-inch cubes

One 16-ounce can Libby's
   natural pumpkin
2 cups unsalted chicken
   broth, preferably
   homemade (page 51)
¼ teaspoon freshly grated
   nutmeg
¼ teaspoon salt, if desired
¼ teaspoon freshly milled
   black pepper

1. In a 3½-quart saucepan, melt margarine over low heat. Add onion, celery, and carrot; sauté, stirring frequently until vegetables are slightly softened, about 3 minutes. Stir in apple, pumpkin, and broth. Turn heat to high and bring to a boil. As soon as soup reaches a boil, turn down to low and simmer, partially covered, until apple is soft, about 15 minutes. Remove from heat and let soup cool to almost room temperature.
2. Ladle half of the soup into blender or food processor fitted with metal blade. Run machine nonstop until you have a creamy purée. Transfer soup to a clean pot and purée remaining soup. Add nutmeg and season with salt and pepper.
3. When ready to serve, reheat, covered, over low heat stirring once

or twice with wooden spoon. Ladle into individual bowls and serve immediately.

N O T E : Soup freezes very well and can be kept frozen up to 2 months. If soup is extremely thick after defrosting, add 2 tablespoons water to each pint before reheating.

Grated Potato Soup

Select boiling potatoes for this textured soup. Baking potatoes (Idaho or russet) tend to be mealy and will break down more rapidly than the waxy boiling type. This recipe is an adaptation of one that was developed by my twin sister Louisa, a fabulous soup-maker.

YIELDS 1 QUART
SERVES 4

2 cups unsalted beef broth, preferably homemade (page 49)

2 cups water

3 medium-sized white potatoes (1 pound), peeled and coarsely grated (can be grated in food processor fitted with shredding disk)

2 large celery ribs (4 ounces), strings removed, finely chopped

1 medium-sized yellow onion (6 ounces) peeled and finely chopped

1 large bay leaf

¼ teaspoon salt, if desired

¼ teaspoon freshly milled white pepper

1 tablespoon minced Italian parsley leaves

1. In a 5-quart saucepan, combine broth and water; bring to a boil, covered, over high heat. Add potatoes, celery, onion, and bay leaf. Turn heat to low and simmer, covered, stirring frequently to pre-

vent potatoes from sticking to bottom of pan, until potatoes are cooked, about 25 to 30 minutes. (Test by pressing a few shreds against the inside of saucepan with a wooden spoon.) Season with salt and pepper. Remove from heat and let soup rest for 1 hour so that all the flavors meld together.

2. When ready to serve, remove bay leaf; reheat, covered, stirring frequently over low heat. Stir in parsley, ladle into individual bowls and serve immediately.

Chilled Tomato Mint Soup

A refreshing starter for those hot summer days.

YIELDS 2 CUPS
SERVES 2

1½ cups low-fat yogurt
1½ cups tomato juice, preferably low-sodium
1 tablespoon fresh lime juice, strained
2 drops Tabasco sauce

1½ teaspoons minced fresh mint or ½ teaspoon crumbled dried mint
2 tablespoons minced fresh chives
1 teaspoon low-fat yogurt (garnish)
2 fresh mint leaves (garnish)

1. In a deep bowl, whip yogurt with a wire whisk until smooth. Add tomato juice, ½ cup at a time, and whisk until blended. Add remaining ingredients and stir with whisk to combine. Transfer to jar and refrigerate until well chilled, about 2 hours.

2. To serve, pour into bowls and garnish each serving with ½ teaspoon yogurt and 1 mint leaf in center. (For an unusual presentation, serve in stemmed goblets, omitting yogurt garnish.)

Vegetable Barley Soup

Nothing is more satisfying than this flavorful soup to start a meal on crisp, chilly evenings. For a luncheon, try serving steaming bowls of it with Corn-meal and Wheat Muffins (page 326), fresh from the oven.

Y I E L D S 1 Q U A R T
S E R V E S 4

1 quart unsalted beef broth, preferably homemade (page 49)

2½ tablespoons pearl barley

½ cup diced carrots (¼-inch dice), peeled before dicing

½ cup diced celery (¼-inch dice), strings removed before dicing

¼ pound green beans, trimmed, washed and cut into 1-inch lengths

One 8¾-ounce can whole-kernel corn, thoroughly rinsed and drained (1 cup)

¼ teaspoon salt, if desired

⅓ teaspoon freshly milled black pepper

1. In a 5-quart saucepan, bring beef broth to a boil, covered, over medium-low heat. Turn heat to low, add barley, cover pan and simmer until tender, about 45 minutes. Add carrots, celery, and green beans. Simmer, covered, until beans are cooked, about 20 minutes (test by tasting). Add corn and simmer, covered, for an additional 5 minutes. Season with salt and pepper. Remove from heat and let soup rest for 1 hour so that all the flavors meld together.
2. Reheat, covered, over low heat when ready to serve.

Julienned Vegetable Soup

The raw julienned vegetables add a touch of crispness, a splash of color, and delicate flavoring to this Japanese-style soup.

YIELDS 3 CUPS
SERVES 2

2 cups unsalted chicken broth, preferably homemade (page 51)

¼ cup finely grated carrots, peeled before grating

3 small tender romaine lettuce leaves (1 ounce), washed, drained, and sliced crosswise into ¼-inch julienne strips

1 teaspoon snipped fresh chives

6 snow peas (1 ounce), washed, trimmed, strings removed, and sliced lengthwise into ¼-inch julienne strips

1 teaspoon minced Italian parsley leaves

⅛ teaspoon salt, if desired

⅛ teaspoon freshly milled black pepper

1. In a 1½-quart saucepan, bring broth to a boil, covered, over high heat. Add snow peas, carrots, and romaine and stir to combine. Cook, uncovered, until vegetables are heated, about 30 seconds. Add chives and parsley; remove from heat. Season with salt and pepper. Ladle into individual bowls and serve immediately.

PASTA AND SAUCES

<<<

TOMATO-BASED SAUCES

Tomato Basil Sauce   75

Spaghetti with Tomato Basil Sauce   76

Linguine with Marinara Sauce   77

Fusilli with Uncooked Tomato Sauce and Ricotta   78

Green Noodles with Tomato and Mushroom
Sauce   80

Spaghettini with Tomato and Chicken Sauce   81

VEGETABLE AND HERB SAUCES

Spaghettini with Creamy Artichoke Heart Sauce   82

Vermicelli with Asparagus   84

Small Shells with Beans and Sage   85

Linguine with Broccoli   86

Green Noodles with Carrots and Parsnips   88

Spaghettini with Parsley-Ricotta Pesto   89

Spaghettini with Basil-Ricotta Pesto   90

Spaghettini with Spinach-Ricotta Pesto   90

So many dishes run their course—soar in popularity and then disappear. Not so with pasta. Americans have adopted this Italian staple, making it their own. It is easy to prepare and inexpensive. When it comes to creating a tasty topping for your favorite pasta, just about anything goes, from tomatoes, vegetables, and legumes to seafood. Pasta offers infinite possibilities of combinations for creating gastronomic delight.

I grew up in an Italian home where pasta was served at least three times a week, on Sunday, Tuesday, and Thursday evenings. I still remember trips to the local Italian grocer where pasta was sold loose in bins lined with a dark blue tissuelike paper. The first packaged pasta I can recall seeing on the grocer's shelf was La Rosa. On the side of each box was a premium coupon. It was my job to cut off the coupons, which were saved until we accumulated enough to send for free gifts such as a colander or a large pasta pot. They even ran a baby constest, which my cousin Lorraine won. While I haven't seen La Rosa pasta in years, I do see Lorraine regularly, and she is as beautiful now as she was when she won the contest.

Whenever possible, purchase the imported Italian varieties of pasta made from semolina flour. Semolina flour is made from hard, durum wheat, which produces a pasta higher in fiber and contains the complex carbohydrates, protein, vitamins, and minerals essential to a well balanced diet. Imported pasta also holds up better in cooking.

There isn't one sauce in the following pages that will take longer than thirty minutes to prepare. Many, in fact, will take much less time. Several can be readied while the pasta water comes to a boil. Many sauce and pasta combinations are hearty enough to constitute one-dish meals, especially when accompanied by crusty bread and a salad.

Note that I tend to favor the thinner types of pastas. Four ounces will serve two people. To measure four ounces, divide one pound of long pasta (such as spaghetti, vermicelli, or linguine) into four portions. If you cannot judge the correct amount, you can use a calibrated pasta measure, available in many department stores and gourmet shops.

‹‹‹‹

PREPARING PERFECT PASTA

You'll need a large enough pot (at least 5 quarts) so that the pasta can swim freely; otherwise it will stick together.

For each four ounces of pasta, bring three quarts of water, covered, to a rolling boil. Add pasta and stir with a wooden fork. Cover pot briefly just until the steam starts to escape around the rim of pot, bringing the water back to a rolling boil. (Watch carefully so that the water doesn't boil over the rim of pot.) Place a twelve-inch wooden fork off to one side of the pot and place the lid tilted on top to partially cover pan while cooking pasta. (Tilting the lid at this angle allows the steam to escape while the pasta is boiling, and the fork is handy for frequent stirring.)

Stir the pasta frequently with the wooden fork to separate the pieces. (Don't leave the pot once the pasta has been added to the boiling water.) The cooking time will vary with the size and shape. Pasta will take anywhere from five to twenty minutes of boiling. The only way to tell whether it is done is to lift a piece from the water with a wooden fork and bite into it. The pasta should be cooked "al dente," which means it should be slightly resistant to the bite. Begin testing after four minutes of cooking time. Keep testing every few minutes until pasta is al dente. The moment the pasta is done, drain quickly in a large colander, shaking vigorously to remove excess liquid.

Transfer to a bowl and immediately toss the amount of sauce recommended in each recipe with the pasta. Since pasta cools very rapidly, the sauce should be ready to use the instant the pasta is drained. Sauce should be used sparingly. It should coat the pasta pieces evenly and thoroughly, but should never be so abundant that the pasta drowns or swims in it. The pasta should be drained, sauced, and served within moments of the time it leaves the pot.

TOMATO-BASED SAUCES
⫷⫷⫷

Tomato Basil Sauce

A savory sauce alive with the flavor of basil, equally delectable mixed with cooked white rice or spaghetti. This recipe provides an ample amount for freezing (see Note) and is frequently referred to throughout this book.

YIELDS 3 ½ CUPS

One 35-ounce can Italian plum
   tomatoes
1 ½ tablespoons olive oil
  ½ cup finely chopped
   yellow onion
  2 large cloves garlic, peeled
   and split in half

½ teaspoon sugar
1 ½ tablespoons minced fresh
   basil or 1 ½ teaspoons
   crumbled dried basil
¼ teaspoon salt, if desired
½ teaspoon freshly milled
   black pepper

1. Place tomatoes in a strainer set over a bowl to drain thoroughly; reserve juice. Gently squeeze each tomato in strainer to get rid of most of the seeds; discard seeds. Cut each tomato into 1-inch pieces and place in blender or food processor fitted with metal blade. (Cutting tomatoes before processing will insure an even chop.) Process until tomatoes are finely chopped, about 15 seconds. Stir tomatoes into reserved juice and set aside.
2. In a 10-inch sauté pan, heat olive oil over medium heat. Add onion and turn heat to low. Cook, partially covered, stirring frequently, until soft but not brown, about 5 minutes. (The slow sautéing of the onion creates a mild, sweet taste to complement the tomatoes). Add garlic and continue cooking, partially covered, stirring frequently until soft but not brown, about 3 minutes. Stir in tomatoes and sugar. Increase heat to high. Bring sauce to a boil, stirring constantly. As soon as sauce reaches a boil, turn heat to low. Simmer, partially covered, stirring frequently until slightly thickened,

about 30 minutes. Stir in basil and season with salt and pepper. Remove pan from heat, cover pan and let sauce rest for at least 1 hour before serving or storing so that all the flavors meld together. Remove garlic after sauce has rested for 1 hour.

NOTE: To freeze, spoon 4 tablespoons (¼ cup) sauce into each ½-cup plastic container. Storing in this size container will simplify removal when ready to use. If you do not have small containers, you can freeze sauce in a plastic ice cube tray. Spoon 2 tablespoons sauce into each section. Freeze overnight in tray. Next day, pop out the frozen cubes and transfer them to a plastic bag, seal tightly, and place in freezer. Sauce can be kept frozen up to 3 months. If sauce is extremely thick after defrosting, stir 1 tablespoon water into each ¼ cup before reheating.

Spaghetti with Tomato Basil Sauce

I like serving this tomato sauce with spaghetti, but it blends well with any type of thin pasta (spaghettini, linguine or vermicelli). During the summer months when fresh basil is available, sprinkle 2 teaspoons snipped fresh basil (instead of parsley) over pasta as a garnish.

SERVES 2

1½ cups Tomato Basil Sauce (page 75)
4 ounces spaghetti
2 teaspoons minced Italian parsley leaves (garnish)

2 tablespoons freshly grated Parmesan cheese (for serving)

1. Place tomato sauce in small saucepan and reheat over low heat while cooking pasta.
2. Cook pasta in 3 quarts boiling water just until al dente. Drain pasta

in colander and transfer to a bowl. Toss ¾ of the sauce with pasta. Spoon remaining sauce on top and garnish with minced parsley. Serve with Parmesan cheese.

Linguine with Marinara Sauce

Anyone who adores garlic and hot pepper will just love this sauce. Adding the oregano after the sauce has finished cooking will give perfect flavoring and prevent a bitter aftertaste. Do not serve any cheese with this sauce; it would mask the flavors of garlic, tomato, and oregano.

SERVES 2

1 tablespoon olive oil
1½ teaspoons minced garlic
One 16-ounce can whole
    peeled tomatoes, coarsely
    chopped, juice included
    (can be chopped in food
    processor fitted with
    metal blade)

¼ teaspoon sugar
⅛ teaspoon dried hot
    pepper flakes
1 tablespoon minced fresh
    oregano or 1 teaspoon
    crumbled dried oregano
⅛ teaspoon salt
4 ounces linguine

1. In a 10-inch skillet, heat olive oil over medium-high heat. Remove pan from heat, add garlic, and tilt pan to a 45-degree angle. With a wooden spoon, push all the garlic to one spot and sauté until lightly golden (sautéing garlic in this manner will prevent it from burning).
2. Return pan to burner and turn heat to high. Stir in the tomatoes, sugar, and pepper flakes. Immediately cover with lid to prevent tomatoes from splattering. Bring sauce to a boil. Turn heat to low and cook, partially covered, stirring frequently, until sauce is slightly thickened, about 15 minutes. Remove from heat, stir in oregano, and season with salt.

3. Cook pasta in 3 quarts boiling water until al dente. Drain pasta in colander and transfer to a bowl. Mix ¾ of the sauce with pasta and spoon remaining sauce on top; serve immediately.

Fusilli with Uncooked Tomato Sauce and Ricotta

A refreshing dish to make during the summer months when fresh basil and fully ripened tomatoes are available. This can be served hot or at room temperature. Green Bean and Zucchini Salad (page 254) would be a perfect choice to complete the meal.

SERVES 2

1 pound ripe tomatoes (4 large plum or 3 medium round)

2 teaspoons olive oil

1 large clove garlic, peeled and thinly sliced

1 tablespoon minced fresh basil or 1 teaspoon crumbled dried basil

1 tablespoon minced Italian parsley leaves

⅛ teaspoon salt, if desired

⅛ teaspoon freshly milled black pepper

1½ cups fusilli

⅓ cup part-skim ricotta cheese, or whipped part-skim ricotta cheese (page 37)

2 tablespoons freshly grated Parmesan cheese (for serving)

1. Plump fresh tomatoes in 3 quarts boiling water for 1 minute. Rinse under cold water, core tomatoes, and peel skins with a small paring knife. If using plum tomatoes, cut in half lengthwise. If using round tomatoes, cut in half crosswise. Gently squeeze each half and discard most of the seeds. Cut tomatoes into ½-inch cubes and place in strainer set over bowl; reserve juice.

2. In a 10-inch skillet, heat olive oil over low heat. Add garlic and sauté until lightly golden, pressing the garlic flat in pan with wooden spoon. With a slotted spoon, remove garlic and discard. (If you are a garlic lover, leave it in the pan.) Add cubed tomatoes to pan and immediately cover with a lid so that tomatoes will not splatter. Uncover pan, turn heat up to medium-high and cook, stirring constantly, just until tomatoes are incorporated into the olive oil, about 30 seconds. Stir in basil and parsley. Season with salt and pepper; remove from heat.
3. Cook pasta spirals in 3 quarts boiling water just until al dente.
4. While pasta is cooking, whisk ricotta in a small bowl with 2 table-spoons of the reserved tomato juice until smooth and creamy. (If using whipped ricotta, just stir in juice to blend.)
5. Drain cooked pasta in a colander and transfer to bowl. Spoon ricotta mixture and ¾ of the tomato sauce over pasta and toss well. Spoon remaining sauce on top and serve with Parmesan cheese.

NOTE: If serving at room temperature, reserve remaining ¼ of sauce for topping. Cover dish with plastic wrap and leave at room temperature until needed, but no more than 2 hours. When ready to serve, toss pasta once again. If pasta seems a little dry, add 2 table-spoons of reserved juice and toss again. Spoon reserved sauce on top just before serving.

Green Noodles with Tomato and Mushroom Sauce

A colorful, appetizing presentation. If spinach noodles are unavailable, you can substitute spaghetti or linguine—not as colorful but just as tasty.

SERVES 2

2 teaspoons olive oil
2 tablespoons finely chopped shallots
One 16-ounce can peeled whole tomatoes, coarsely chopped, juice included (can be chopped in food processor fitted with metal blade)
¼ teaspoon sugar
1½ teaspoons minced fresh basil or ½ teaspoon crumbled dried basil

¼ pound medium-sized mushrooms, wiped, trimmed, and thinly sliced
⅛ teaspoon salt, if desired
⅛ teaspoon freshly milled black pepper
4 ounces green noodles [box variety]
2 tablespoons freshly grated Parmesan cheese (for serving)

1. In a 10-inch sauté pan, heat olive oil over medium-high heat. Add shallots and sauté, stirring constantly until lightly golden, about 1 minute. Add tomatoes, sugar, and basil. Turn heat to medium and cook, uncovered, stirring frequently, until sauce is slightly thickened, about 10 minutes. Turn heat to high, add mushrooms, and cook, stirring constantly, until they are tender when tested with the tip of a knife, about 2 to 3 minutes. Season with salt and pepper; remove from heat.
2. Cook noodles in 3 quarts boiling water just until al dente. Drain noodles in a colander, transfer to bowl, and quickly toss with ¾ of the sauce. Spoon remaining sauce on top; serve with Parmesan cheese.

⫷⫷⫷

Spaghettini with Tomato and Chicken Sauce

Tomatoes blended with succulent chicken breasts seasoned with the distinct flavor of sage makes this sauce truly elegant. All you need is a lovely mixed green salad to accompany this very satisfying entrée.

SERVES 2

2 teaspoons olive oil
1 whole (10 ounces) boneless, skinless chicken breast, split in half, fat removed, washed, and blotted dry with paper towel
½ cup dry vermouth
¼ cup finely chopped yellow onion
¼ cup finely chopped carrot
One 16-ounce can whole peeled tomatoes, coarsely chopped, juice included (can be chopped in food processor fitted with metal blade)
1½ teaspoons minced fresh sage or ½ teaspoon crumbled dried sage
⅛ teaspoon dried hot red pepper flakes
⅛ teaspoon salt, if desired
1½ teaspoons minced Italian parsley leaves
4 ounces spaghettini
2 tablespoons freshly grated Parmesan cheese (for serving)

1. In a 10-inch sauté pan, heat olive oil over medium-high heat. Add chicken and sear on both sides until lightly golden; transfer to a small plate. (If chicken starts to stick to pan while searing, gently loosen with a wide metal spatula.) Add vermouth to pan, turn heat to high, and cook, stirring constantly, scraping bottom of pan to loosen any fragments that might be stuck. Continue cooking until vermouth is reduced by half, about 1 minute. Turn heat to low, stir in onion and carrot, and cook, stirring constantly, until soft but not brown, about 4 minutes. Add tomatoes, sage, and pepper flakes. Return chicken and any accumulated juices on plate to pan. Cook sauce over low heat, partially covered, stirring and spooning

sauce over chicken frequently to keep chicken moist, until slightly thickened, about 20 minutes. Season with salt; remove from heat. Cover pan and let sauce cool to room temperature so that all the flavors meld together.

2. Remove chicken from sauce. Slice breast in half crosswise and then slice lengthwise into ¼-inch strips. Return chicken to sauce and mix well. When ready to serve, reheat sauce, covered, over low heat. Remove from heat and stir in minced parsley.

3. Cook pasta in 3 quarts boiling water until al dente. Drain pasta in a colander and transfer to bowl and quickly toss with ¾ of the sauce. Spoon remaining sauce on top; serve with Parmesan cheese.

VEGETABLE AND HERB SAUCES
«←

Spaghettini with Creamy Artichoke Heart Sauce

The delectable flavor of artichoke hearts combined with whipped ricotta adds a smooth creamy texture to this northern Italian pasta sauce.

SERVES 2

One 9-ounce package frozen artichoke hearts
2 teaspoons unsalted margarine
¼ cup thinly sliced scallions
½ teaspoon minced garlic

¼ cup unsalted chicken broth, preferably homemade (page 51)
¼ cup whipped part-skim ricotta cheese (page 37)
⅛ teaspoon salt, if desired

⅛ teaspoon freshly milled
white pepper
4 ounces spaghettini
2 teaspoons minced Italian
parsley leaves (garnish)

2 tablespoons freshly grated
Parmesan cheese (for
serving)

1. Rinse frozen artichokes under warm water and very carefully
separate. Cut each artichoke heart into ½-inch wedges and place
in a strainer to drain (artichokes will be easier to slice if partially
frozen). Set aside.
2. In a 10-inch skillet, melt margarine over low heat. Add scallions
and garlic. Cook, stirring constantly until scallions are barely tender, about 1 minute. Add artichoke wedges and cook, partially
covered, stirring once or twice, until tender when tested with a
fork, about 4 minutes. Stir in chicken broth and cook, covered, for
an additional minute. Stir in whipped ricotta and continue to cook,
uncovered, on low heat, stirring constantly, until mixture is
creamy, about 1 minute. Season with salt and pepper; remove from
heat.
3. Cook pasta in 3 quarts boiling water just until al dente. Drain pasta
in colander and transfer to a bowl. Toss ¾ of the sauce with pasta.
Spoon remaining sauce on top and garnish with minced parsley.
Serve with Parmesan cheese.

⋘

Vermicelli with Asparagus

This pasta dish is made quite frequently in my household during early spring when asparagus is abundant at the market. To ensure even cooking, select asparagus of the same size.

SERVES 2

1 pound medium-sized
asparagus (about 16 spears)
1 tablespoon olive oil
1 large clove garlic, peeled
and thinly sliced
¼ cup unsalted chicken broth,
preferably homemade (page
51) (see Note)

⅛ teaspoon salt, if desired
⅛ teaspoon freshly milled
black pepper
4 ounces vermicelli
2 tablespoons freshly grated
Parmesan cheese (for
serving)

1. Wash asparagus several times in cold water to get rid of sand. Using a sharp knife, cut off woody ends at base of spear. With a vegetable peeler, peel stalks from the base of the spear up, leaving tips intact. Slice stalks diagonally into 2-inch lengths; reserve tips.
2. In a 10-inch skillet, heat oil over medium heat. Add garlic, turn heat to low, and sauté until lightly golden, pressing the garlic flat in the pan with the back of a wooden spoon. With a slotted spoon, remove garlic and reserve. (If you are not a garlic lover, discard.) Place sliced asparagus stalks in pan and simmer, covered, stirring once or twice, until barely tender when tested with the tip of a knife, about 3 minutes. Add asparagus tips and continue cooking, covered, until barely tender when tested. Raise heat to high and continue cooking, uncovered, stirring constantly until asparagus are a light golden color. Stir in broth and season with salt and pepper; remove from heat.
3. Cook pasta in 3 quarts of boiling water until al dente. Drain pasta in a colander, transfer to bowl and quickly toss with sautéed garlic and half of the asparagus mixture. Spoon remaining asparagus mixture on top and serve with Parmesan cheese.

NOTE: If you do not have chicken broth, remove ¼ cup of the pasta water before draining and substitute it for broth.

Small Shells with Beans and Sage

This is one of the Depression dishes that was served weekly during the winter months when I was a child. I, too, make this savory Tuscan dish quite often as a main course, accompanied with a Lettuce and Carrot Salad (page 257).

SERVES 2

1 tablespoon olive oil
½ cup finely chopped yellow onion
1 cup unsalted chicken broth, preferably homemade (page 51)
1½ teaspoons minced fresh sage or ½ teaspoon crumbled dried sage
One 10½-ounce can white cannellini beans, rinsed and well drained (1 cup)

⅛ teaspoon salt, if desired
⅛ teaspoon freshly milled black pepper
1 cup small pasta shells
2 teaspoons minced Italian parsley leaves
Freshly milled black pepper (for serving)

1. In a heavy 3½-quart saucepan, heat olive oil over low heat. Add onion and cook, covered, stirring once or twice until soft but not brown, about 6 minutes. Add chicken broth and sage. Turn heat to high and bring to a boil. Add beans, turn heat to low, and cook, covered, for 2 minutes. Season with salt and pepper; remove from heat.
2. Cook pasta in 3 quarts boiling water until al dente. Drain in colander, transfer to saucepan containing bean mixture and mix with

a wooden spoon. Cover pan and let rest for 5 minutes before serving. (Allowing this dish to rest before serving enhances the flavor by letting the pasta absorb most of the broth.)
3. Stir in parsley, ladle into individual bowls, and serve with freshly milled black pepper.

Linguine with Broccoli

This pasta dish for all of you broccoli lovers is alive with the pungent flavor of garlic and the tantalizing tinge of hot pepper.

SERVES 2

1 small bunch fresh broccoli (10 ounces)	⅛ teaspoon salt, if desired
1 tablespoon olive oil	4 ounces linguine
1½ teaspoons minced garlic	2 tablespoons freshly grated
⅛ teaspoon dried hot pepper flakes	Parmesan cheese (for serving)

1. Remove florets from broccoli, leaving about ½ inch of the stems. Cut or break florets into 1-inch pieces. Wash in cold water, drain and set aside. Remove and discard the large coarse leaves from stems and cut off about ½ inch of tough lower part of stalk. Wash stalks thoroughly and peel with a vegetable peeler. Cut stalks in half lengthwise. (If stalks are more than 1 inch in diameter, cut into quarters.) Cut halved or quartered stalks into 1-inch pieces.
2. Bring 3 quarts of water to a boil. Add broccoli stalks and cook until tender when tested with a fork, about 6 minutes. Add florets and continue cooking until tender when tested with fork, about 3 minutes. With a skimmer or slotted spoon, transfer broccoli to a colander and set aside to drain thoroughly. Reserve liquid for cooking pasta.

3. In a 10-inch skillet, heat olive oil over medium-high heat. Remove pan from heat, add garlic, and tilt pan to a 45-degree angle. Using a wooden spoon, push all the minced garlic to one spot and sauté until lightly golden. (Sautéing garlic in this manner will prevent it from burning.) Turn heat to medium and stir in pepper flakes. Add broccoli and cook, stirring constantly, until heated and well combined with garlic mixture, about 1 minute. Season with salt and remove from heat.
4. Return water in which broccoli was cooked to a boil. Break pasta in half, add to pot, and cook until al dente. (Breaking pasta in half before cooking will make it easier to toss with the broccoli mixture.) Before draining pasta, remove about ¼ cup pasta water and set aside. Drain pasta in colander and transfer to a bowl. Add ¾ of the broccoli mixture and toss well. Add about 3 tablespoons of pasta water; toss quickly to loosen. Spoon remaining broccoli mixture on top and serve with Parmesan cheese.

Green Noodles with Carrots and Parsnips

A very light dish with a beautiful contrast in color, making a stimulating presentation. Select carrots and parsnips that are the same size to ensure even cooking.

SERVES 2

2 medium-sized carrots (5 ounces), washed, trimmed, and lightly peeled with a vegetable peeler

2 medium-sized parsnips (6 ounces), washed, trimmed, and lightly peeled with a vegetable peeler

2 teaspoons unsalted margarine

⅓ cup thinly sliced scallions

1½ teaspoons minced fresh dill or ½ teaspoon crumbled dried dillweed

2 teaspoons minced Italian parsley leaves

⅛ teaspoon salt, if desired

⅛ teaspoon freshly milled black pepper

4 ounces green noodles (box variety)

2 tablespoons freshly grated Parmesan cheese (for serving)

1. Cook carrots and parsnips in 3 quarts of boiling water until barely tender when tested with a fork (cooking time may vary depending on size; carrots will cook faster). With a skimmer or slotted spoon, transfer vegetables to a colander and thoroughly drain. Reserve liquid for cooking pasta. When vegetables are cool enough to handle, blot dry with paper towel. Slice vegetables into 2- by ¼-inch julienne strips.

2. In a 10-inch skillet, melt margarine over medium heat. Add scallions and cook, partially covered, stirring constantly until tender, about 2 minutes. Add carrots and parsnips; cook, partially covered, stirring frequently until tender when pierced with tip of a knife,

about 2 minutes. Stir in dill and parsley. Season with salt and pepper; remove from heat.

3. Return water in which vegetables were cooked to a boil. Add noodles and cook until al dente. Before draining pasta, remove about ¼ cup pasta water and set aside. Drain cooked noodles in a colander and transfer to a bowl. Add ¾ of the vegetable mixture and toss well. Add about 3 tablespoons of pasta water; toss quickly to loosen. Spoon remaining vegetable mixture on top; serve with Parmesan cheese.

Spaghettini with Parsley-Ricotta Pesto

This Ligurian favorite can be whipped up with the aid of a food processor in a matter of seconds while the pasta is cooking. See variations at bottom of recipe.

SERVES 2

¼ cup well packed Italian parsley leaves

½ cup part-skim ricotta cheese, or whipped part-skim ricotta cheese (page 37)

2 teaspoons olive oil

⅛ teaspoon salt, if desired

¼ teaspoon freshly milled black pepper

1 medium shallot (1 ounce), peeled and quartered

4 ounces spaghettini

2 tablespoons freshly grated Parmesan cheese (for serving)

1. Place parsley, ricotta, olive oil, salt, and pepper in food processor fitted with metal blade. Turn machine on and drop quartered shallot, one piece at a time, through the feed tube. Stop machine once or twice and scrape down inside work bowl with plastic spatula. Run machine until parsley and shallot are finely minced and mixture is a smooth creamy consistency, about 1 minute.

2. Bring 3 quarts of water to a boil. Break pasta in half, add to pot, and cook until al dente. (Breaking pasta in half before cooking will make it easier to toss with the pesto sauce.) Before draining pasta, remove about ¼ cup pasta water and set aside. Drain pasta in colander, transfer to a bowl, and quickly toss with half of the pesto sauce and 2 tablespoons of pasta water; toss quickly to loosen. Add remaining pesto sauce and toss once again. Serve with Parmesan cheese.

VARIATIONS

Basil-Ricotta Pesto

Follow procedure for parsley-ricotta pesto, substituting ¼ cup well packed basil leaves for the parsley and 1 small clove garlic, peeled and split in half, for the shallot. Use same food processor technique of dropping garlic through feed tube with machine running to mince.

Spinach-Ricotta Pesto

Follow procedure for parsley-ricotta pesto, substituting 3 ounces (1 cup packed) fresh spinach leaves, thoroughly washed and drained for the parsley and ¼ cup thinly sliced scallions for the shallot. Place scallions in food processor with pesto ingredients.

‹‹‹‹‹‹‹

Shells with Peas and Herbs

Allowing this dish to rest for five minutes before serving adds to the flavor by letting the pasta absorb most of the broth and providing time for the peas to search for shells to fill.

SERVES 2

2 teaspoons olive oil
⅓ cup finely chopped celery, strings removed
½ cup finely chopped yellow onion
5 ounces (1 cup) tiny frozen peas, defrosted
1 cup unsalted chicken broth, preferably homemade (page 51)
1½ teaspoons minced fresh basil or ½ teaspoon crumbled dried basil

1½ teaspoons minced fresh mint or ½ teaspoon crumbled dried mint
⅛ teaspoon salt, if desired
⅛ teaspoon freshly milled black pepper
1¼ cups medium-sized pasta shells
2 teaspoons minced Italian parsley leaves

1. In a heavy 2½-quart saucepan, heat olive oil over low heat. Add celery and onion; cook, covered, stirring once or twice until soft but not brown, about 8 minutes. Add peas and chicken broth. Cover pan and simmer over low heat just until peas are tender, about 5 minutes. Stir in basil and mint. Season with salt and pepper; remove from heat.
2. Cook pasta in 3 quarts boiling water until al dente. Drain in a colander, transfer to saucepan containing pea mixture, and mix with wooden spoon. Cover pan and let rest for 5 minutes before serving. Stir in minced parsley, ladle into individual bowls, and serve immediately.

NOTE: Vegetable mixture can be prepared up to 3 hours before serving. Reheat, covered, over low heat while cooking pasta.

Linguine with Zucchini and Ricotta

For those days when you're just too busy to cook, here's a simple yet satisfying one-dish meal. All you need add is a salad of some sliced tomatoes drizzled with two teaspoons extra virgin oil, sprinkled with a pinch of salt and freshly milled black pepper, and topped off with a tablespoon of minced Italian parsley leaves—dinner is on the table in a matter of minutes.

SERVES 2

2 medium-sized zucchini (12 ounces total weight)
1 tablespoon olive oil
½ cup thinly sliced red onion
1½ teaspoons minced fresh basil or ½ teaspoon crumbled dried basil
⅓ cup part-skim ricotta cheese, or whipped part-skim ricotta (page 37)

⅛ teaspoon salt, if desired
⅛ teaspoon freshly milled black pepper
4 ounces linguine
2 tablespoons freshly grated Parmesan cheese (for serving)

1. Scrub zucchini and blot dry with paper towel. Trim ends and cut zucchini into 2-inch lengths. Slice each piece in half lengthwise and slice into ¼-inch julienne strips.
2. In a 10-inch skillet, heat olive oil over medium heat. Add onion and cook, partially covered, stirring frequently with wooden spoon until soft and very lightly golden, about 3 minutes. Add zucchini and cook, partially covered, stirring frequently until tender, about 3 minutes. Stir in basil and ricotta; cook, uncovered, stirring constantly until mixture is creamy, about 30 seconds. Season with salt and pepper; remove from heat.
3. Cook pasta in 3 quarts boiling water until al dente. Before draining pasta, remove about ¼ cup pasta water and set aside. Drain pasta in colander and transfer to a bowl. Spoon half of the zucchini

mixture over pasta and toss well. Add about 3 tablespoons of pasta water; toss quickly to loosen. Spoon remaining zucchini mixture on top; serve with Parmesan cheese.

PASTA SALADS
⋘

Pasta Salad with Chicken and Broccoli

An inspiring entrée to make when you have leftover chicken. All that is needed to complete this meal is a lovely Red Onion and Tomato Salad (page 259).

SERVES 2

1½ cups broccoli florets, including ½ inch of stems, washed and broken or cut into ½-inch pieces
3 tablespoons low-fat yogurt
1½ tablespoons mayonnaise, preferably homemade (page 263)
1½ teaspoons snipped fresh dill or ½ teaspoon crumbled dried dillweed
¼ teaspoon Dijon mustard

½ teaspoon apple cider vinegar
¼ teaspoon sugar
⅛ teaspoon salt, if desired
⅛ teaspoon freshly milled white pepper
1½ cups fusilli
1½ cups cooked chicken, skinned, boned, and cut into ½-inch dice
2 tablespoons snipped fresh chives

1. Bring 3 quarts of water to a boil. Add broccoli florets and cook until tender when tested with a fork, about 3 minutes. With a

skimmer, transfer florets to a colander, refresh under cold water, drain well, blot dry with paper towel, and set aside. Reserve liquid for cooking pasta.

2. Place yogurt, mayonnaise, dill, mustard, vinegar, sugar, salt, and pepper in a small bowl. Beat dressing with a fork or small whisk to combine.

3. Return water in which broccoli was cooked to a boil. Cook pasta spirals until al dente. Drain pasta in colander and transfer to a bowl.

4. Toss hot pasta with dressing. Add chicken and chives and toss once again. Let pasta salad cool to room temperature, about 30 minutes. (Stir frequently to hasten cooling.)

5. Add broccoli, toss lightly once again, and serve. (Adding broccoli to cooled pasta will ensure a bright green color.)

NOTE: The entire salad may be made up to 2 hours before serving. Cover with plastic wrap and leave at room temperature. When ready to serve, lightly toss salad once again.

Pasta Salad with Green Beans and Pimientos

A perfect do-ahead summer pasta salad, which can be prepared up to 3 hours before serving. This salad can also be a main course for lunch.

SERVES 2

¼ pound green beans, washed, trimmed, and sliced diagonally into 1-inch pieces to make about ¾ cup

2 teaspoons imported white wine vinegar
¼ teaspoon Dijon mustard
1½ teaspoons minced fresh basil or ½ teaspoon crumbled dried basil

¼ teaspoon sugar
⅛ teaspoon salt, if desired
⅛ teaspoon freshly milled
   black pepper
1 tablespoon olive oil
1½ cups fusilli

One 4-ounce jar whole
   pimientos, rinsed, blotted
   dry with paper towel,
   and sliced into 1- by
   ¼-inch strips
2 tablespoons thinly sliced
   scallions

1. Bring 3 quarts of water to a boil. Add green beans and cook until tender when tested with a fork, about 5 minutes. With a skimmer, transfer beans to a colander, refresh under cold water, drain well, blot dry with paper towel, and set aside. Reserve liquid for cooking pasta.
2. Place vinegar, mustard, basil, sugar, salt, and pepper in a small bowl. Beat with a fork or small whisk to combine. Add oil, a little at a time, and beat dressing vigorously with a fork or whisk to incorporate; set aside.
3. Return water in which beans were cooked to a boil. Cook pasta spirals until al dente. Drain pasta in colander and transfer to a bowl.
4. Whisk dressing once again and toss with hot pasta. Add pimientos and scallions; toss once again. Let pasta salad cool to room temperature, about 30 minutes. (Stir frequently to hasten cooling.)
5. Add green beans, toss once again and serve. (Adding green beans to cooled pasta will ensure a bright green color.)

N O T E : Entire salad can be made up to 3 hours before serving. Cover with plastic wrap and leave at room temperature. When ready to serve, lightly toss salad once again.

⫷⫷⫷

SEAFOOD SAUCES

«<

Linguine with Scallops and Parsley Sauce

Linguine paired with scallops and parsley is not only mouthwatering for seafood lovers but spectacular in presentation as well.

SERVES 2

½ pound sea scallops
1 tablespoon unsalted margarine
¼ cup minced Italian parsley leaves
1 tablespoon minced shallots
½ cup dry vermouth
⅛ teaspoon freshly grated nutmeg

⅛ teaspoon salt, if desired
⅛ teaspoon freshly milled black pepper
4 ounces linguine
2 tablespoons Parmesan cheese (for serving)

1. Wash scallops several times in cold water to remove sand. Place in a strainer and blot dry with paper towel. Cut scallops horizontally into ¼-inch slices.
2. In a 10-inch skillet, melt margarine over medium heat. Add 2 tablespoons parsley and the shallots. Cook, stirring frequently until shallots are soft but not brown, about 2 minutes. Turn heat to medium-high, add vermouth, and cook, stirring constantly until reduced by one-third, about 30 seconds.
3. Turn heat down to medium, add scallops, and cook, stirring constantly, just until they turn opaque, about 2 minutes. Stir in remaining 2 tablespoons parsley, nutmeg, salt, and pepper; mix well and remove from heat.

4. Cook pasta in 3 quarts boiling water just until al dente. Drain pasta in colander and transfer to a bowl. Toss ¾ of the scallop mixture with pasta. Spoon remaining scallop mixture on top and serve with Parmesan cheese.

Spaghettini with Shrimp and Lemon Sauce

This piquant sauce is ready in minutes, and guaranteed to please.

SERVES 2

½ pound medium-sized
   shrimp (about 12)
1 tablespoon olive oil
1 teaspoon minced garlic
2 tablespoons fresh lemon
   juice, strained
1 teaspoon finely grated
   lemon rind

1 tablespoon minced Italian
   parsley leaves
⅛ teaspoon salt, if desired
⅛ teaspoon freshly milled
   black pepper
4 ounces spaghettini

1. Shell and devein shrimp (for directions, see page 205). Wash thoroughly in cold water, blot dry with paper towel, and set aside.
2. In a 10-inch skillet, heat olive oil over medium-high heat. Remove pan from heat, add garlic, and tilt pan to a 45-degree angle. With a wooden spoon, push all the minced garlic to one spot and sauté until very lightly golden. (Sautéing garlic in this manner will prevent it from burning.) Add shrimp and cook, stirring constantly, just until shrimp turn pink, about 2 to 3 minutes. Add lemon juice and cook, stirring constantly until incorporated, about

15 seconds. Stir in lemon rind and parsley. Season with salt and pepper; remove from heat.

3. Cook pasta in 3 quarts boiling water until al dente. Drain pasta in colander and transfer to a bowl. Add ¾ of the shrimp mixture and toss well. Spoon remaining shrimp mixture on top and serve immediately.

Vermicelli with Tomato-Tuna Sauce

The addition of small nonpareil capers gives this pasta dish its intriguing flavoring. For this hearty entrée, all you need as an accompaniment is a lovely Cucumber and Radish Salad (page 251), or Lettuce and Carrot Salad (page 257).

SERVES 2

One 16-ounce can whole
    peeled tomatoes
One 6½-ounce can
    water-packed solid white
    albacore tuna
2 teaspoons olive oil
½ cup finely chopped
    yellow onion
1½ teaspoons minced fresh
    basil or ½ teaspoon
    crumbled dried basil

¼ teaspoon sugar
2 teaspoons nonpareil
    capers, thoroughly rinsed
    and drained
¼ teaspoon freshly milled
    black pepper
1 tablespoon minced
    parsley
4 ounces vermicelli

1. Place tomatoes in a strainer set over a bowl and drain thoroughly; reserve juice. Coarsely chop tomatoes (they can be chopped in food processor fitted with metal blade). You should have 1¼ cups after chopping; set aside.

2. Place tuna in strainer and rinse thoroughly under cold water. Drain well and break into bite-sized pieces; set aside.
3. In a heavy 2½-quart saucepan, heat olive oil over medium heat. Add onion, turn heat to low and cook, covered, until onion is soft but not brown, about 5 minutes. Add chopped tomatoes, 3 tablespoons of the reserved juice, basil, and sugar. Bring sauce to a boil over high heat. Turn heat down to medium and cook sauce, covered, stirring once or twice, until thickened, about 10 minutes. Add tuna and capers and cook, covered, stirring once or twice, for an additional 5 minutes. Season with pepper and remove from heat. Stir parsley into sauce just before tossing with pasta.
4. Cook pasta in 3 quarts boiling water until al dente. Drain pasta in colander, transfer to bowl and quickly toss with ¾ of the sauce. Spoon remaining sauce on top and serve immediately.

N O T E : Sauce may be prepared up to 3 hours before serving. Reheat, covered, over low heat while pasta is cooking.

⫷⫷⫷

RICE, BULGUR, AND BARLEY

When I go to the supermarkets it always amazes me to note the popularity of the many precooked and premixed varieties of grains, especially rice. To me these varieties are for those people who would rather eat fast than eat well. Almost all of the premixed varieties are too salty for my taste. My trial testing experience has also proved that there is little if any time saved in their preparation compared to the recipes in this chapter.

Among all the grains, rice (white or brown) is arguably the most versatile of foods. Whether it be served plain, made into an elegant pilaf, or served cold as a salad, rice teams well with any poultry, meat, or seafood dish. Rice is by no means the only grain that offers a tempting range of presentations. For something just a little different as a side dish, you may want to try *Bulgur Pilaf* (page 115) or *Barley and Mushroom Casserole* (page 117). Both pair extremely well with many of the dishes with which you would team rice.

For all the recipes calling for white rice in this chapter, I have found Uncle Ben's converted rice to be the best. Parboiled or "converted" rice should not be confused with precooked rice. It is not an "instant rice." This type of rice is treated in a special steam and pressure process before milling. The grains remain firmer during cooking and are less likely to become sticky. When cooked, each grain is separate, with a smooth, clean appearance. Parboiled rice also gives a greater yield after cooking than regular milled rice.

For all the brown rice recipes, again I have found that Uncle Ben's parboiled brown rice cooks just perfectly. If you live near a health food store, you may want to try either the medium- or long-grain brown rice available there. The cooking time may vary just slightly from that of Uncle Ben's. Brown rice takes considerably longer to cook than white rice because when it is milled, only the outer hull and a small portion of the bran layer are removed, while white rice has both the outer hull and all the bran layers removed. Because of the increased cooking time, brown rice requires more liquid. When cooked, brown rice has a nutlike taste and a pleasantly crunchy texture. Because of the bran layer, brown rice has a shorter shelf life than white rice, and should be stored in the *refrigerator if kept for an extended period of time. This is my favorite type of rice. It is reasonable in price and excellent in taste.*

Bulgur or cracked wheat is the staple grain of eastern Mediterranean countries and it is delicious! Bulgur is simply unbleached cracked wheat berries with the nutty flavor of whole-grained bread. Look for it in the supermarkets next to the rice, dried beans, or sometimes in the breakfast cereal section. It is also available in health food stores and specialty shops, where it is sold in bulk. Buy the unrefined brand, because the nutrients are mostly in the dark husk.

Pearl barley, sometimes called soup barley, is the whole kernel of barley groats, processed by a polishing method so that it is mild and tender when cooked. Pearl barley is ground in a revolving drum until the hull and germ are removed from the grains. In this process the grains are reduced to small balls called pearls. In addition to the two recipes in this chapter, you may want to try one of my favorite winter soups, Vegetable Barley Soup (page 68).

The recipes that follow have been designed to add variety to your menus and high fiber to your diets.

⋘

White Rice

This simple method of simmering converted long-grain white rice in a measured amount of water will produce moist, fluffy grains. Once you have mastered this technique of cooking perfect rice, you will no longer need a recipe.

SERVES 2

½ cup converted long-grain white rice (Uncle Ben's), picked over to remove any dark grains

1 ¼ cups cold water
⅛ teaspoon salt, if desired

1. Place rice in a heavy 2 ½-quart saucepan. Pour cold water over rice. Add salt and stir rice with a fork to distribute evenly in water.
2. Bring to a rolling boil, uncovered, over high heat. Cover pan with a tight-fitting lid, turn heat to low, and simmer undisturbed for 20 minutes.
3. Remove pan from heat and let rice rest, covered, for 10 to 12 minutes before serving. (During the resting period, the grains will absorb any moisture left in pan.)
4. Remove cover and fluff rice with two forks before serving.

⫷⫷⫷

Herb Rice

Adding the fresh herbs after the rice is cooked will guarantee a delicate flavor. I recommend you make this dish only if and when fresh herbs are available.

SERVES 2

2 teaspoons olive oil
¼ cup thinly sliced scallions
¼ cup finely chopped celery, strings removed
½ cup converted long grain white rice [Uncle Ben's], picked over to remove any dark grains
1⅓ cups unsalted chicken broth, preferably homemade (page 51)

1½ teaspoons minced fresh basil
1½ teaspoons minced fresh mint
1 tablespoon minced Italian parsley leaves
⅛ teaspoon salt, if desired
⅛ teaspoon freshly milled white pepper

1. In a heavy 2½-quart saucepan, heat oil over low heat. Add scallions and celery and cook, covered, stirring frequently with a wooden spoon until slightly softened but not brown, about 3 minutes. Add rice and stir until opaque and well coated with vegetable mixture. Add broth, turn heat to high, and bring to a boil, uncovered, stirring once or twice. Cover pan with a tight-fitting lid, turn heat to low, and simmer undisturbed for 25 minutes. At this point, the liquid should be completely absorbed into the cooked rice. If it isn't, cover pan and continue to cook for an additional minute or two.

2. Remove pan from heat and stir in basil, mint, and parsley. Season with salt and pepper. Cover pan and let rice rest for 5 minutes before serving so that all the flavors meld together. Transfer to bowl and serve immediately.

⋘

Lemony Rice

Lemony rice is a good accompaniment to any of the main-dish fish or seafood recipes in this book.

SERVES 2

White Rice (page 104),
prepared through Step 2
2 teaspoons unsalted
margarine, softened
½ teaspoon finely grated
lemon rind

2 teaspoons fresh lemon
juice, strained
⅛ teaspoon freshly milled
white pepper
2 teaspoons snipped fresh
chives

1. As soon as rice is cooked, stir in margarine, lemon rind, lemon juice, and pepper. Cover pan and let rice mixture rest for 10 minutes so that all the flavors meld together.
2. Remove cover and fluff rice mixture with two forks. Stir in snipped chives, transfer to bowl, and serve immediately.

Rice with Peas

I love the flavor of rice, peas, and mint. See variation at the end of this recipe using zucchini, which is equally good.

SERVES 2

White Rice (page 104),
prepared through Step 2
2 teaspoons olive oil
1 tablespoon minced
shallots
½ cup tiny frozen peas,
defrosted and well
drained

⅛ teaspoon freshly ground
white pepper
1½ teaspoons minced fresh
mint or ½ teaspoon
crumbled dried mint

1. While rice is cooking, heat oil in a 1½-quart saucepan over medium heat. Sauté shallots, stirring constantly until lightly golden, about 2 minutes. Stir in peas and cook, covered, stirring once or twice until barely tender, about 2 minutes. Remove from heat and set aside.
2. As soon as rice is cooked, stir pea mixture into rice. Season with pepper and stir in mint. Cover pan and let rice mixture rest for 10 minutes so that all the flavors meld together.
3. Transfer to bowl and serve immediately.

VARIATION

Rice with Zucchini

Substitute 1 medium-sized zucchini (6 ounces) for the peas. Scrub zucchini, trim ends, slice lengthwise and then crosswise into ½-inch lengths. Follow same procedure but cook zucchini 3 minutes.

⋘

Rice with Tomato Sauce

A very simple dish to make when you have the tomato basil sauce on hand.
It is an excellent accompaniment to Turkey Cutlets with Mushrooms and
Tarragon (page 190) or Oven-fried Fillet of Sole (page 212).

SERVES 2

White Rice (page 104),
prepared through Step 2
⅓ cup Tomato Basil Sauce
(page 75), at room
temperature
⅛ teaspoon freshly milled
black pepper

2 tablespoons freshly grated
Parmesan cheese
1 tablespoon minced Italian
parsley leaves

As soon as rice is cooked, stir in sauce, pepper, Parmesan cheese, and
parsley. Cover pan and let rice mixture rest for 10 minutes so that
all the flavors meld together. Transfer to bowl and serve immediately.

Rice Salad

This salad is perfumed with the sweet aromatic scent of basil and parsley. A good accompaniment to any of the main-dish fish recipes in this book.

SERVES 2

White Rice (page 104), prepared through Step 2

1 medium-sized zucchini (6 ounces)

1 tablespoon minced red onion

1 ½ teaspoons minced fresh basil or ½ teaspoon crumbled dried basil

1 tablespoon minced Italian parsley leaves

1 ½ teaspoons imported white wine vinegar

½ teaspoon freshly milled white pepper

1 tablespoon olive oil, preferably extra virgin

1. While rice is cooking, scrub zucchini under cold running water until the skin feels clean and smooth. Trim both ends. Cook zucchini, uncovered, in 1 ½ cups boiling water until barely tender when tested with the tip of a knife, about 3 minutes. Transfer to a strainer and refresh under cold water. Blot dry with paper towel and cool to room temperature. Slice into 2-inch lengths. Slice each piece in half lengthwise and slice into ¼-inch julienne strips; set aside.
2. As soon as rice is cooked, transfer it to a strainer and refresh under cold water to hasten cooling. Place strainer over a bowl and thoroughly blot rice dry with paper towel.
3. Transfer rice to serving bowl and add zucchini, onion, basil, and parsley; thoroughly mix with two forks.
4. Place vinegar and pepper in a small bowl. Add oil a little at a time and stir with a fork or small whisk to combine. Pour dressing over salad and thoroughly mix with two forks. Cover bowl with plastic wrap and refrigerate salad for at least 3 hours before serving. (Salad may be prepared up to 5 hours before serving.) Return to room temperature 30 minutes before serving.
5. Lightly toss salad once again and serve.

Brown Rice

Simmered, parboiled brown rice should be cooked in the size pan and exact amount of water recommended. If you follow this procedure, the rice will cook evenly and no liquid need be drained off after the rice has rested. Brown rice takes longer to cook than white but is well worth the time for its delightful nutlike flavor and crunchy texture.

SERVES 2

½ cup parboiled brown rice [Uncle Ben's], picked over to remove any dark brown grains

1½ cups cold water
⅛ teaspoon salt, if desired

1. Place rice in a heavy 2½-quart saucepan. Pour cold water over rice. Add salt and stir rice with a fork to distribute evenly in water.
2. Bring to a rolling boil, uncovered, over high heat. Cover pan with a tight-fitting lid, turn heat down to low, and simmer, undisturbed, for 50 minutes.
3. Remove pan from heat and let rice rest, covered, for 10 minutes before serving. (As the rice rests, the grains will absorb any additional moisture left in pan.)
4. Remove cover and fluff rice with two forks before serving.

⋘

Brown Rice with Carrots and Tarragon

Sweet-tasting carrots mixed with aromatic tarragon combine with the crunchy texture of simmered brown rice to create the intriguing flavor of this unusual side dish.

SERVES 2

Brown Rice (page 110), prepared through Step 2
2 medium-sized carrots (3 ounces), trimmed, peeled, and cut into ¼-inch dice, to make ½ cup
2 teaspoons unsalted margarine, softened

1½ teaspoons minced fresh tarragon or ½ teaspoon crumbled dried tarragon
⅛ teaspoon freshly milled black pepper
2 teaspoons minced Italian parsley leaves (garnish)

1. While rice is cooking, cook carrots in 2 cups boiling water until tender, about 4 minutes. Transfer to strainer and drain thoroughly. Set aside.
2. As soon as rice is cooked, stir margarine, carrot, tarragon, and pepper into hot rice. Cover pan and let rice mixture rest, covered, for 10 minutes so that all the flavors meld together.
3. Transfer to serving bowl and garnish with minced parsley. Serve immediately.

Brown Rice Pilaf

The tasty combination of onion, celery, and beef broth brings out the full flavor of this rice pilaf.

SERVES 2

2 teaspoons olive oil
¼ cup finely chopped yellow onion
¼ cup finely chopped celery, strings removed
½ cup parboiled brown rice [Uncle Ben's], picked over to remove any dark brown grains

1 cup unsalted beef broth, preferably homemade (page 49)
⅔ cup water
⅛ teaspoon salt, if desired
⅛ teaspoon freshly milled black pepper
1 tablespoon minced Italian parsley leaves (garnish)

1. In a heavy 2½-quart saucepan, heat oil over low heat. Add onion and celery; cook, covered, stirring frequently until slightly softened but not brown, about 4 minutes. Add rice and stir until opaque and well coated with the vegetable mixture. Add broth and water, turn heat to high, and bring to a boil, uncovered, stirring once or twice. Cover pan with a tight-fitting lid, turn heat low, and simmer undisturbed for 50 minutes. At this point the rice should be tender and all the liquid completely absorbed. Test by tasting a few grains. If rice is still chewy, cover pan and continue cooking over low heat for an additional 2 to 3 minutes. Season with salt and pepper; remove from heat. Cover pan and let rice rest for 10 minutes before serving so that all the flavors meld together.
2. Transfer rice to serving bowl, garnish with parsley, and serve immediately.

Brown Rice with Red Kidney Beans

A good hearty winter side dish, and a delicious partner to Oven-fried Beef and Spinach Patties (page 124) or Turkey Cutlets with Mushrooms and Tarragon (page 190).

SERVES 2

Brown Rice (page 110),
prepared through Step 2
2 teaspoons olive oil
¼ cup finely chopped red
onion
½ cup canned red kidney
beans, rinsed and
thoroughly drained

1½ teaspoons minced fresh
savory or ½ teaspoon
crumbled dried savory
⅛ teaspoon freshly milled
black pepper

1. While rice is cooking, heat oil in a 1½-quart saucepan over medium heat. Sauté red onion, stirring constantly, until lightly golden, about 3 minutes. Add beans and savory, turn heat to low, and cook, stirring once or twice, just until beans are heated, about 1 minute. Remove from heat, cover pan, and set aside.
2. As soon as rice is cooked, stir bean mixture into rice. Season with pepper. Cover pan and let rice mixture rest for 10 minutes so that all the flavors meld together.

⫷⫷

Fruity Brown Rice Salad

Easy on the budget, easy to make, and an excellent accompaniment to Yummy Pork Chops (page 145).

SERVES 2

Brown Rice (page 110),
prepared through Step 2
2 tablespoons dark seedless
raisins
1 small Golden Delicious
apple (4 ounces), peeled,
halved, cored, and cut into
¼-inch dice to make ¾
cup
¼ cup low-fat yogurt

1 tablespoon honey,
preferably orange blossom
⅛ teaspoon freshly ground
nutmeg
2 teaspoons fresh lemon
juice, strained
2 large lettuce leaves
(garnish)

1. As soon as rice is cooked, stir raisins into hot rice. Cover pan and let rice rest, covered, until raisins are plumped, about 10 minutes. Transfer mixture to strainer set over a bowl and cool to room temperature. (Stir frequently with fork to hasten cooling.) Thoroughly squeeze out any excess moisture with your hands.
2. Place rice mixture in a bowl, add apple, and stir to combine.
3. Place yogurt, honey, nutmeg, and lemon juice in a small bowl. Stir dressing with a fork or small whisk to combine. Add dressing to salad and mix thoroughly with a fork. Cover bowl with plastic wrap and refrigerate salad for at least 2 hours before serving. (Salad may be prepared up to 4 hours before serving.)
4. When ready to serve, arrange lettuce leaves on two salad plates. Lightly toss salad with fork once again, spoon onto lettuce leaves, and serve immediately.

⫷⫷⫷

Bulgur Pilaf

I was introduced to bulgur pilaf by a friend who lived in Lebanon. When cooked, the bulgur has the chewy nutlike flavor of good whole-grained bread. I like serving it with grilled lamb chops and frequently use it as a substitute for rice.

SERVES 2

2 teaspoons unsalted margarine

1½ tablespoons minced shallots

2 tablespoons minced celery, strings removed

½ cup bulgur

1½ cups unsalted chicken broth, preferably homemade (page 51)

⅛ teaspoon salt, if desired

⅛ teaspoon freshly milled black pepper

1 tablespoon minced Italian parsley leaves

1. In a heavy 2½-quart saucepan, melt margarine over low heat. Add shallots and celery. Cook, covered, stirring frequently with a wooden spoon until slightly softened but not brown, about 2 minutes. Add bulgur and stir until the grains are well coated with the vegetable mixture. Add broth, turn heat to high, and bring to a boil, uncovered, stirring once or twice. Cover pan with a tight-fitting lid, turn heat to low, and simmer, undisturbed, until the broth is completely absorbed into the grain, about 20 minutes. Season with salt and pepper. Remove from heat and let pilaf rest for 5 minutes before serving.
2. Stir in parsley, transfer to bowl, and serve immediately.

Tabbouleh

This unusual Lebanese salad is a distinctive, delicious combination of bulgur, red onion, mint, and lots of parsley, in a tangy lemony dressing. The texture is pleasantly chewy because the grains are soaked in hot water rather than cooked. I make this salad quite often in the summer months when fresh mint is available. It is an excellent accompaniment to any of the grilled meat dishes or broiled fish dishes in this book.

SERVES 2

½ cup bulgur
2 cups boiling water
2 tablespoons finely chopped red onion
¼ cup minced Italian parsley leaves
1 tablespoon minced fresh mint
1 tablespoon fresh lemon juice, strained

⅛ teaspoon salt, if desired
⅛ teaspoon freshly milled black pepper
1 tablespoon olive oil, preferably extra virgin
1 small tomato (4 ounces), halved, cored, seeded, and cut into ¼-inch dice
4 small romaine lettuce leaves (garnish)

1. Place bulgur in a deep ovenproof bowl. Pour boiling water over and let bulgur soak for 1 hour. Transfer to a fine mesh strainer and drain thoroughly. Place strainer over a bowl and thoroughly squeeze out excess moisture with your hands.
2. Transfer bulgur to a bowl. Add red onion, parsley, and fresh mint. Mix thoroughly with fork to combine.
3. Place lemon juice, salt, and pepper in a small bowl. Stir with a fork or small whisk to combine. Add oil, a little at a time, and beat with fork or whisk to combine. Spoon dressing over salad and mix thoroughly with fork. Cover with plastic wrap and refrigerate for at least 3 hours before serving. (Salad may be prepared up to 5 hours before serving.) Remove from refrigerator 30 minutes before serving.
4. Lightly toss salad with two forks. Add tomatoes and toss once

again. (Adding the tomatoes just before serving will prevent the salad from getting soggy.)

5. Arrange two romaine leaves on each salad plate. Spoon salad onto romaine and serve.

⬰

Barley and Mushroom Casserole

If you are a lover of barley mushroom soup, you will like this casserole just as well. I often serve this dish as an accompaniment to Broiled Rock Cornish Game Hen (page 186) or Chicken Breast with Piquant Vinegar Sauce (page 171).

SERVES 2

1 tablespoon unsalted margarine
2 tablespoons minced shallots
1/4 pound medium-sized mushrooms, wiped, trimmed, and thinly sliced
1/3 cup pearl barley

1/8 teaspoon salt, if desired
1/8 teaspoon freshly milled black pepper
1 1/4 cups unsalted beef broth, heated, preferably homemade (page 49)
2 teaspoons minced Italian parsley leaves (garnish)

1. Adjust rack to center of oven and preheat to 350 degrees. Lightly grease bottom and sides of a shallow 1-quart ovenproof casserole; set aside.

2. In a 10-inch skillet, heat margarine over medium heat. Add shallots and sauté, stirring frequently with a wooden spoon until lightly golden, about 2 minutes. Add mushrooms and sauté, stirring constantly, just until they begin to exude their juices, about 1 minute. Add barley and stir until opaque and well coated with mushroom mixture, about 30 seconds. Season with salt and pepper. Spoon

barley mixture into greased casserole and spread evenly with the back of a spoon. Pour heated broth over barley mixture.

3. Cover casserole and cook in preheated oven until barley is tender and all the liquid is completely absorbed, about 45 to 50 minutes. Garnish with minced parsley and serve immediately.

Barley Pilaf with Raisins

A spicy way to prepare barley and a wonderful side dish with Pork Tenderloin with Apples and Prunes (page 146) or Poached Chicken with Apricot Sauce (page 176).

SERVES 2

2 teaspoons olive oil
¼ cup finely chopped yellow onion
⅓ cup pearl barley
1 small bay leaf
⅛ teaspoon ground cinnamon

1⅓ cups water
⅛ teaspoon salt, if desired
⅛ teaspoon freshly milled black pepper
2 tablespoons dark seedless raisins

1. In a heavy 2½-quart saucepan, heat oil over medium heat. Add onion and sauté, stirring frequently with a wooden spoon until lightly golden, about 5 minutes. Add barley and stir until opaque and well coated with onion mixture. Add bay leaf, cinnamon, and water. Turn heat to high and bring to a boil, stirring once or twice with wooden spoon. Cover pan, turn heat to low, and simmer undisturbed for 35 minutes. At this point barley should be tender and all the liquid completely absorbed. Test by tasting a few

grains. If barley is still chewy, cover pan and continue cooking over low heat until tender, about 3 to 5 minutes more.

2. Remove pan from heat and season with salt and pepper. With a fork, stir in raisins. Cover pan and let pilaf rest until raisins are plumped, about 5 minutes. Remove bay leaf, transfer to serving bowl, and serve immediately.

⋘

MEATS

BEEF

Oven-fried Beef and Spinach Patties   124

Stir-fried Beef with Broccoli and Sesame Seeds   125

Stir-fried Beef with Snow Peas and Green Pepper   127

Grilled Filet Mignon   129

Stuffed Beef Rolls with Wine Sauce   130

VEAL

Grilled Veal Chops   133

Veal Chops with Carrots and Onion   134

Veal Scallops with Mushrooms   135

Veal Piccata   136

Veal Cutlets with Parmesan Topping   137

Sweet and Sour Veal Chops   138

Veal Stew   140

PORK

Oven-fried Pork Chops   141

Grilled Pork Chops with Rosemary   142

The following sections offer step-by-step instructions for the different methods of cooking beef, veal, pork, and lamb: broiling, grilling, braising, roasting, sautéing, and stir-frying.

Since nutritionists recommend that we all reduce our intake of meats, especially red meats, it is increasingly important to become more conscientious consumers. The cuts recommended for these recipes are the choicest, leanest cuts of meat. Judgment and guidance are often needed to make the best selections.

Most butchers will give you friendly advice at no extra charge. If you can deal with a butcher personally, either in his own shop or in the specialty section of a supermarket, he will assist you by carefully choosing, cutting, and trimming the meat. If, however, you must shop at a supermarket where a butcher is unavailable for consultation, here are a few pointers:

- Check expiration dates on all packaged meats. Packaged meat should look silky, not wet.
- Where there are bones, they should be sawn smoothly, not chopped jaggedly.
- Select meat that is neatly trimmed, particularly chops and steaks, with most of the excess fat removed.
- Always unwrap meat as soon as you get home and store in the coldest part of the refrigerator loosely wrapped in foil so that a little air can circulate around.
- Always use fresh meat within 1 to 2 days of purchase.
- If freezing meat, remove all excess fat before wrapping for the freezer. For freezing, wrap meat in plastic wrap first and then in heavy-duty foil or extra-thick moisture- and vapor-proof freezer bags. If using freezer bags, make sure that all of the air is expelled before sealing them so that the meat will not develop freezer burn. Always defrost frozen meat in the refrigerator.

BEEF

《《←

Oven-fried Beef and Spinach Patties

These meat patties have great flavor and are a cinch to make with the aid of a food processor.

SERVES 2

½ cup tightly packed spinach leaves (2 ounces), thoroughly washed, blotted dry with paper towel, and snipped into 1-inch pieces

¼ cup wheat germ

1 tablespoon freshly grated Parmesan cheese

1 ½ teaspoons snipped fresh basil leaves or ½ teaspoon crumbled dried basil

⅛ teaspoon salt, if desired

⅛ teaspoon freshly milled black pepper

1 medium-sized shallot (1 ounce), peeled and quartered

½ large egg (beat 1 large egg lightly and use half, about 2 tablespoons)

8 ounces very lean ground round or sirloin steak

¼ cup Tomato Basil Sauce (page 75)

1 teaspoon minced Italian parsley leaves (optional garnish)

1. Adjust oven rack to top shelf of oven and preheat to 400 degrees. Lightly grease a shallow baking pan; set aside.
2. Place spinach leaves, wheat germ, Parmesan cheese, basil, salt, and pepper in food processor fitted with metal blade. Turn machine on and drop quartered shallot, one piece at a time, through the feed tube. Stop machine once and scrape down inside work bowl with plastic spatula. Run machine until spinach and shallot are finely minced, about 30 seconds. Add egg and run machine for 5 seconds

to combine. Transfer mixture to a bowl. Add meat and mix well with your hands. In same bowl, divide meat mixture into 4 portions. Roll them with the palms of your hands and shape into 4 patties, each about 2½ inches in diameter and 1 inch thick.

3. Place patties in prepared pan and cook in preheated oven until underside is lightly golden, about 10 to 12 minutes. Turn patties with a broad metal spatula and continue cooking until second side is golden, about 7 to 9 minutes.

4. Transfer patties to serving platter. Heat sauce over low heat and spoon 1 tablespoon over each patty. Garnish with minced parsley and serve immediately.

Stir-fried Beef with Broccoli and Sesame Seeds

While you will only need 6 ounces of flank steak for this recipe, you may want to purchase a whole flank steak weighing approximately 1 pound. Trim all the fat and gristle from the meat. Hold the knife at a 45-degree angle and slice meat in half crosswise (at this angle you will be slicing against the grain). Use half for this recipe and freeze remaining half for another stir-fry dish. The garlic and hot pepper flakes add zestful flavoring to this one-dish meal, which should be accompanied with cooked white rice.

S E R V E S 2

6 ounces flank steak, well trimmed of fat and gristle

Holding knife at a 45-degree angle, slice the meat crosswise into long strips about ¼ inch thick (you will be slicing against the grain). Cut slices in half crosswise and then lengthwise into ¼-inch strips.

Marinade

1 teaspoon sugar
2 teaspoons low-sodium light
   soy sauce (Kikkoman Lite)

1 tablespoon dry sherry
2 teaspoons cornstarch
2 teaspoons water

1. Place all of the marinade ingredients in a shallow bowl. Stir marinade with a fork until cornstarch is dissolved and mixture is smooth.
2. Add beef strips and toss well to coat each piece. Marinate beef at room temperature for 15 to 20 minutes, or as long as it takes you to prepare broccoli.

To Assemble and Cook

1 small bunch broccoli (10
   ounces)
1 tablespoon vegetable oil,
   preferably corn oil
1 teaspoon minced garlic
⅛ teaspoon red pepper flakes

½ cup unsalted beef broth,
   preferably homemade
   (page 49)
1 teaspoon cornstarch
1 tablespoon water
1 tablespoon unhulled sesame
   seeds

1. Remove florets from broccoli, leaving about ½ inch of stems. Cut or break florets into 1-inch pieces. Wash in cold water, drain, and thoroughly blot dry with paper towel; put in a bowl. Remove and discard the large coarse leaves from stems and cut off about ½ inch of tough lower part of stalk. Wash thoroughly and peel stalks with a vegetable peeler. Cut stalks diagonally into ¼-inch slices and put in bowl with florets. (If stalks are more than 1 inch in diameter, slice in half lengthwise before slicing diagonally.)
2. Heat wok or heavy 12-inch skillet over high heat for 1 minute. When a drop of water sizzles immediately on contact with pan, slowly pour in 2 teaspoons oil and swirl pan to coat surface. Turn heat down to medium-high. Add beef strips and toss lightly with long metal spatula. Cook, stirring and lightly tossing constantly to separate strips just until meat is a pale pink, about 1 to 1½ minutes. Transfer with spatula to a platter.

3. Add remaining teaspoon oil and swirl pan once again to coat. Turn heat to medium-high and add garlic and pepper flakes. Stir-fry just until garlic starts to sizzle, about 3 seconds. Add broccoli and stir-fry for 30 seconds. Stir in broth, cover pan, turn heat to high, and cook just until broccoli is barely tender, about 1 minute.
4. In a small bowl, combine cornstarch with water and stir until cornstarch is dissolved.
5. Return beef to pan, turn heat down to medium-high, and stir to combine. Pour cornstarch mixture into pan and continue stirring until the sauce thickens and glaze coats the beef and broccoli. Sprinkle sesame seeds in pan and toss with spatula to combine. Transfer to platter and serve immediately.

Stir-fried Beef with Snow Peas and Green Pepper

For this simple stir-fry, the first step is to marinate the meat for approximately 20 minutes or as long as it takes you to prepare the vegetables. For an attractive presentation, arrange thinly sliced tomatoes in an outer border on platter and fill center with the beef and vegetables. To complete this meal, serve cooked white rice.

SERVES 2

6 ounces flank steak, well trimmed of fat and gristle

Holding knife at a 45-degree angle, slice the meat crosswise into long strips about ¼ inch thick (you will be slicing against the grain). Cut slices in half crosswise and then lengthwise into ¼-inch strips.

Marinade

2 teaspoons cornstarch
1 teaspoon sugar

2 teaspoons low-sodium light
   soy sauce (Kikkoman Lite)
2 tablespoons water

1. Place all of the marinade ingredients in a shallow bowl. Stir marinade with a fork until cornstarch is dissolved and mixture is smooth.
2. Add beef strips and toss well to coat each piece. Marinate beef at room temperature for 15 to 20 minutes.

To Assemble and Cook

1 tablespoon vegetable oil,
   preferably corn oil
2 scallions, washed, trimmed,
   cut lengthwise, and sliced
   diagonally into 1-inch
   pieces to make ½ cup
½ teaspoon minced garlic
18 small snow peas (about 3
   ounces), washed, trimmed,
   strings removed

1 medium-sized green pepper
   (5 ounces), washed, halved,
   cored, seeded, and sliced
   lengthwise into ⅛-inch
   strips
½ cup unsalted beef broth,
   preferably homemade (page
   49)
1 teaspoon cornstarch
1 tablespoon water

1. Heat wok or heavy 12-inch skillet over high heat for 1 minute. When a drop of water sizzles immediately on contact with pan, slowly pour in 2 teaspoons oil and swirl pan to coat surface. Turn heat down to medium. Add beef strips and toss lightly with a long metal spatula. Cook, stirring and lightly tossing constantly, to separate the strips just until meat is pale pink, about 1 to 1½ minutes. Transfer with spatula to platter.
2. Add remaining teaspoon of oil and swirl pan once again to coat. Turn heat to medium-high, add scallions and garlic, and stir-fry for 30 seconds. Add snow peas and green pepper; stir-fry for another 30 seconds. Stir in broth, turn heat to high, and continue to stir-fry just until peppers are barely tender, about 1 minute.
3. In a small bowl, combine cornstarch with water and stir until cornstarch is completely dissolved.

4. Return beef to pan and stir over high heat to combine. Pour cornstarch mixture into pan and continue to stir-fry until glaze coats the beef and vegetables, about 30 seconds. Transfer to platter and serve immediately, or serve with a border of sliced tomatoes.

Grilled Filet Mignon

This section of the whole tenderloin is also called tournedos of beef. After trimming all the fat, make sure you remove the thin blue gray membrane around the steak's outside edge before cooking. Always give the raw meat time to reach room temperature so that it will cook evenly. These steaks are best when served medium rare or medium.

S E R V E S 2

2 slices filet mignon (12 ounces total weight), each 1 inch thick, well trimmed of fat and any attached membrane
1 large clove garlic, peeled and split in half

1 teaspoon olive oil, approximately
¼ teaspoon freshly milled black pepper
8 curly parsley sprigs (optional garnish)

1. Preheat charcoal grill until coals have turned a gray ashy color, or preheat gas or electric grill according to manufacturer's suggested time.
2. Using a piece of paper towel, thoroughly blot dry both surfaces of steaks. Place steaks on a flat plate and sprinkle a few drops of oil on the surface of meat and thoroughly spread across surface with your fingertips. Turn steaks over and repeat on other surface. (Rubbing a little oil into both surfaces will prevent steaks from sticking when placed on heated grill, and will help brown the meat as well.)

3. Place steaks on grill about 4 inches from the heat source. Sear the steaks 1 minute on each side, turning meat with long-handled tongs. Approximate cooking time after searing is 2 minutes on each side for medium rare and 3 minutes on each side for medium. Red droplets appearing on the steak's seared upper surface while the second side is still cooking indicate the meat is medium rare. Pink juices mean the steak is medium.
4. Transfer to platter and sprinkle both surfaces of steak with freshly milled black pepper. Garnish with parsley sprigs and serve immediately.

Stuffed Beef Rolls with Wine Sauce

A good hearty winter dish, especially when served with a border of brown rice and Parsleyed Baby Carrots (page 229). There will be ample sauce for spooning over rice as well as beef rolls.

SERVES 2

One 12-ounce slice top round steak about ½ inch thick

Trim all the fat from outside edges of meat. Cut steak in half crosswise. Place slices between sheets of waxed paper and pound each slice with a flat mallet or the broad side of a chef's knife; each slice should be slightly less than ¼ inch thick when finished. Make sure you pound the edges well so that when you roll and tuck the ends in they will stay in place and none of the filling will come out in cooking. Arrange meat slices on a work surface with ends facing you. In this way you will be rolling with the grain, and cooked beef rolls will be easier to slice.

Filling

¼ cup unsalted beef broth, preferably homemade (page 49)

¼ pound mushrooms, wiped, trimmed, and finely chopped (can be chopped in food processor fitted with metal blade)

¼ cup well packed fresh bread crumbs

1½ teaspoons minced fresh basil or ½ teaspoon crumbled dried basil

1 tablespoon freshly grated Parmesan cheese

⅛ teaspoon freshly milled black pepper

1. In a 10-inch skillet, bring beef broth to a boil over high heat. Add mushrooms and cook, stirring frequently, until they have exuded all their juices and there is no liquid left in pan, about 2 minutes. Remove from heat and stir in breadcrumbs, basil, cheese, and pepper.
2. Spread filling over beef slices, leaving a ¼-inch border of meat on all 4 sides. Starting from the end of steak, roll up like a jelly roll into a cylinder and tuck ends in. Tie each roll with kitchen twine at 1-inch intervals; tie lengthwise once. Do not tie too tightly or the twine will cut into the meat during cooking.

To Cook

2 tablespoons Wondra flour

⅛ teaspoon freshly milled black pepper

2 teaspoons olive oil

½ cup dry red wine

½ cup unsalted beef broth, preferably homemade (page 49)

2 medium-sized bay leaves

1. Adjust oven rack to center of oven and preheat to 350 degrees.
2. Combine flour and pepper in a shallow bowl. Dredge rolls in seasoned flour and shake off excess (dredge just before searing or beef rolls will become gummy).
3. In a 10-inch skillet, heat oil over medium-high heat. Sear beef rolls on all sides until lightly browned. (If rolls start to stick while searing, loosen with a metal spatula.) Transfer rolls to a shallow 1-quart ovenproof casserole.

4. Add wine to skillet and turn heat to high, scraping any fragments that cling to bottom of pan with wooden spoon; cook until wine is reduced to half, about 1 minute. Add beef broth and cook sauce for 2 minutes, stirring once or twice.

5. Pour sauce over beef rolls and add bay leaves to casserole. Bake, covered, in preheated oven, turning rolls and basting frequently until meat is tender when pierced with the tip of a knife, about 45 minutes. Transfer rolls to plate, cover with foil, and let rest for 10 minutes before slicing.

6. Remove bay leaves, transfer sauce to a small saucepan, and keep warm over low heat.

7. Snip the twine from beef rolls and cut rolls at a 20-degree angle into 1-inch slices. Arrange slices in a slightly overlapping pattern on platter. Spoon a little sauce over the meat and serve remaining sauce separately.

⋘

VEAL

⫷

Grilled Veal Chops

Rubbing a little garlic on the chops before grilling adds just the right taste to this dish, which is dressed with a little pepper and lime juice as soon as the meat is taken off the grill.

S E R V E S 2

2 rib veal chops, each ½ inch thick (1 pound total weight), well trimmed of fat
1 large clove garlic, peeled and split in half

1 teaspoon olive oil
¼ teaspoon freshly milled black pepper
2 tablespoons fresh lime juice

1. Place veal chops on a flat plate. Rub split garlic over both surfaces of chops. With your fingers, rub ½ teaspoon oil onto both surfaces of each chop. (Rubbing a little oil on surface of chops will prevent them from sticking when placed on heated grill.)
2. Preheat charcoal grill until coals have turned a gray ashy color. Preheat gas or electric grill according to manufacturer's suggested time.
3. Place chops on grill 4 inches from heat source. Sear the chops 1 minute on each side, turning meat with long-handled tongs. Continue cooking chops 2 more minutes on each side. To test for doneness, insert the tip of a small knife into the thickest part near the bone. If the juices run clear, with no traces of pink, the chops are done. If not, continue cooking for an additional 2 minutes. Test for doneness once again.
4. Transfer to platter and sprinkle both sides of chops with pepper. Spoon lime juice over chops and serve immediately.

Veal Chops with Carrots and Onion

Cooking the chops smothered with carrots and onion will keep them extremely moist and juicy.

SERVES 2

2 tablespoons Wondra flour
¼ teaspoon freshly milled black pepper
2 rib veal chops, each ½-inch thick (1 pound total weight), well trimmed of fat
2 teaspoons olive oil
½ cup finely diced carrots
½ cup minced yellow onion

1 teaspoon grated lemon rind
1½ tablespoons fresh lemon juice
1½ teaspoons minced fresh thyme or ½ teaspoon crumbled dried thyme
2 to 4 tablespoons water
2 teaspoons minced Italian parsley leaves (garnish)

1. In a wide, shallow bowl, combine flour and pepper. Dredge chops in seasoned flour and shake off excess. (Dredge just before browning or flour coating will become gummy.)
2. In a 10-inch skillet, heat oil over medium-high heat. Sauté the chops, turning once, until lightly golden on both sides, about 1½ minutes on each side. Transfer to plate.
3. Turn heat down to medium, add carrots and onion, and sauté, stirring constantly, scraping any fragments that cling to bottom of pan with a wooden spoon. Cook until carrots are barely tender, about 2 minutes. Stir in lemon rind, juice, and thyme. Return chops to pan and spoon all of the vegetable mixture on top. Spoon 2 tablespoons water around chops. Cover pan, turn heat to low, and cook until chops are tender when tested with the tip of a knife, about 8 minutes. Check liquid in pan after 4 minutes of cooking. If liquid has evaporated, spoon remaining 2 tablespoons water around chops.

4. Transfer chops to serving plate, spoon vegetable mixture over top, and garnish with minced parsley.

Veal Scallops with Mushrooms

Rice with Peas (page 107) would be a delicious accompaniment to this succulent entrée.

SERVES 2

4 veal scallops, each ¼ inch thick (8 ounces total weight)
2 tablespoons Wondra flour
¼ teaspoon freshly milled black pepper
1 tablespoon olive oil
1 tablespoon minced shallots

½ cup dry white wine
¼ pound medium-sized mushrooms, trimmed, wiped, and thinly sliced
2 teaspoons minced Italian parsley leaves
⅛ teaspoon salt, if desired

1. Cut veal scallops crosswise into 2-inch widths.
2. In a shallow bowl, combine flour and pepper. Lightly dredge each piece of veal in seasoned flour and shake off excess. (Dredge just before sautéing or the flour coating will become gummy.)
3. In a 10-inch skillet, heat oil over medium-high heat. Sauté veal, turning once, until lightly golden on both sides, about 1 minute on each side. Remove veal and set aside.
4. Add shallots to pan and sauté over medium heat until lightly golden, scraping any fragments that cling to bottom of pan with a wooden spoon, about 30 seconds. Add wine and turn heat to high. Cook, stirring constantly until wine is reduced to half, about 1 minute.
5. Add mushrooms, turn heat down to medium-high, and cook, stirring constantly until barely tender when tested with a fork, about

20 seconds. Return veal to pan and cook, spooning pan juices and mushrooms over veal, for an additional 30 seconds. Stir in parsley and season with salt; remove from heat.

6. Transfer veal to platter, spoon mushroom mixture over veal, and serve immediately.

Veal Piccata

This specialty is fast and simple to prepare. Vermouth and lemon juice provide its piquant flavoring.

SERVES 2

4 veal scallops, each ¼ inch thick (8 ounces total weight)
2 tablespoons Wondra flour
¼ teaspoon freshly milled black pepper
1 tablespoon olive oil
1 large clove garlic, thinly sliced
¼ cup dry vermouth
2 tablespoons fresh lemon juice
1 teaspoon grated lemon rind
1 tablespoon minced Italian parsley leaves
⅛ teaspoon salt, if desired

1. Cut veal scallops crosswise into 2-inch widths.
2. In a shallow bowl, combine flour and pepper. Lightly dredge each piece of veal in seasoned flour and shake off excess. (Dredge just before sautéing or the flour coating will become gummy.)
3. In a 10-inch skillet, heat oil over medium-high heat. Add garlic and sauté until lightly golden. Using a slotted spoon, remove garlic and discard.
4. Sauté veal, turning once, until lightly golden on both sides, about 1½ minutes on each side. Remove veal and set aside.
5. Add vermouth, turn heat to high, and cook, scraping any fragments that cling to bottom of pan with wooden spoon, until

vermouth is reduced by half, about 30 seconds. Stir in lemon juice. Return veal to pan and cook, spooning pan juices over veal, for an additional 30 seconds.

6. Remove pan from heat; stir in lemon rind and parsley. Season with salt. Transfer veal to platter, spoon pan juices over veal and serve immediately.

N O T E : You may substitute one whole, boneless, skinless chicken breast (10 ounces) for the veal. Remove fillets from under breast and leave whole. Slice breast in half lengthwise and lightly pound between pieces of waxed paper. Slice each halved breast lengthwise into 3 even pieces.

Veal Cutlets with Parmesan Topping

Sprinkling the cutlets with Parmesan cheese after they are cooked adds a flavor bonus to the crusty coating.

S E R V E S 2

2 tablespoons Wondra flour	2 veal cutlets, each ¼ inch
⅛ teaspoon freshly milled	thick (about 6 ounces total
black pepper	weight)
1 large egg	1 tablespoon olive oil
1½ teaspoons cold water	4 teaspoons freshly grated
½ cup fine dry bread crumbs	Parmesan cheese
2 teaspoons minced Italian	½ lemon, sliced into 4
parsley leaves	wedges (garnish)

1. In a shallow bowl, combine flour and pepper. In another bowl, beat egg and cold water with a fork. On a flat plate, combine bread crumbs and parsley. Dredge cutlets in seasoned flour, dip in beaten egg, and then thoroughly coat with bread crumb mixture. Refrig-

erate cutlets in a single layer on plate lined with waxed paper for at least 1 hour (chilling prevents coating from coming off during sautéing).

2. In a 10-inch skillet, heat oil over medium-high heat. Sauté the cutlets until lightly golden on both sides, about 1½ minutes on each side. As soon as second side is golden, sprinkle 2 teaspoons Parmesan cheese over each cutlet. Partially cover pan and cook until cheese melts, about 20 seconds.

3. Transfer to platter and serve with lemon wedges.

Sweet and Sour Veal Chops

The sweet taste of yellow or red bell pepper complements the vinegar, adding a piquant touch to the veal.

SERVES 2

2 tablespoons Wondra flour
⅛ teaspoon freshly milled black pepper
2 loin veal chops, ½ inch thick and well trimmed of fat (1 pound total weight)
1 tablespoon olive oil
1 large yellow or red bell pepper (8 ounces), washed, dried, halved, cored, seeded, and sliced lengthwise into ¼-inch strips

½ cup thinly sliced red onion
2 tablespoons imported white wine vinegar
2 teaspoons water
½ teaspoon sugar
⅛ teaspoon salt, if desired

1. In a shallow bowl, combine flour and pepper. Dredge chops in seasoned flour and shake off excess. (Dredge just before browning or flour coating will become gummy.)

2. In a 10-inch skillet, heat oil over medium-high heat. Sauté the chops, turning once, until lightly golden on both sides, about 1½ minutes on each side. Transfer to plate.
3. Turn heat down to medium; add pepper and onion slices. Sauté, stirring constantly with wooden spoon, scraping any fragments that cling to bottom of pan. Cook until peppers are crisp tender when tested with fork, about 3 minutes. Remove pan from heat. Return chops to pan and arrange vegetables over top.
4. In a small bowl, combine vinegar, water, and sugar. Stir mixture together until the sugar is completely dissolved (this is best done with your index finger so that you can feel when sugar is dissolved). Spoon vinegar mixture over top of vegetables.
5. Cover pan and return it to low heat. Simmer, basting frequently with pan juices, until chops are extremely tender when tested with the tip of a knife, about 10 minutes. Season with salt and additional pepper if needed.
6. Arrange chops on platter with a border of vegetables; serve immediately.

Veal Stew

This stew can be prepared up to 3 hours before serving and reheated over very low heat. Serve cooked white or brown rice or boiled potatoes to round out this hearty one-dish meal.

SERVES 2

1 tablespoon olive oil
8 ounces boned shoulder of veal, well trimmed of fat and cut into 1½-inch cubes
½ cup thinly sliced yellow onion
1 large carrot (5 ounces), trimmed, peeled, and sliced diagonally into 1-inch pieces
½ cup coarsely chopped canned tomatoes, juice included

1½ teaspoons minced fresh sage or ½ teaspoon crumbled dried sage
1 large bay leaf
¼ pound green beans, washed, trimmed, and sliced diagonally into 1-inch lengths
1 teaspoon grated lemon rind
⅛ teaspoon salt, if desired
⅛ teaspoon freshly milled black pepper

1. In a 3-quart dutch oven, heat oil over medium heat. Add veal and sauté, stirring frequently until lightly golden. Remove with a slotted spoon. Add onion and carrot; sauté, stirring constantly, scraping any fragments that cling to bottom of pan with wooden spoon.
2. Add tomatoes, sage, and bay leaf. Return meat to pan and bring to a boil, uncovered, over high heat, stirring constantly. Turn heat to low and cook, partially covered, stirring frequently until meat is extremely tender when pierced with the tip of a knife, about 45 minutes. (Watch cooking liquid; if it starts to evaporate, add about 2 tablespoons hot water.) Add green beans and cook, covered, stirring frequently until barely tender, about 15 minutes. Stir in lemon rind; season with salt and pepper.

3. When ready to serve, remove bay leaf, transfer stew to platter, and serve immediately.

PORK

Oven-fried Pork Chops

The savory bread crumb coating seals the chops so that they are juicy and tender when served.

SERVES 2

1½ teaspoons olive oil, approximately
½ cup fine dry bread crumbs
1 tablespoon minced Italian parsley leaves
1 teaspoon crushed fennel seeds (see Note)

4 boneless center cut pork chops, each about ¼ inch thick (12 ounces total weight), well trimmed of fat

1. Place olive oil in a shallow bowl. On a flat plate, combine bread crumbs, parsley, and crushed fennel seeds. Hold one end of each pork chop with your fingertips over bowl of olive oil and lightly brush both surfaces with oil. Firmly dredge pork chop in bread crumb mixture to coat both sides thoroughly; repeat with remaining pork chops. Refrigerate chops in a single layer on a platter lined with waxed paper for at least 1 hour (chilling prevents coating from coming off during cooking).
2. Adjust rack to top shelf of oven and preheat to 375 degrees. Lightly grease bottom of a shallow 9- by 13- by 2-inch baking pan.
3. Place pork chops in prepared pan and cook in preheated oven until

underside is lightly golden and slightly crispy, about 15 minutes (check by lifting with a broad metal spatula). Carefully turn chops with metal spatula and continue cooking until second side is slightly golden and crispy, about 15 minutes. Transfer to platter and serve immediately.

NOTE: Crush fennel seeds with a mortar and pestle, or place them in a mound on a cutting board, give them a good thump with the broad side of a chef's knife to partially crush, and then finely chop with a knife.

Grilled Pork Chops with Rosemary

Use only fresh rosemary for this grilled pork recipe. If rosemary is unavailable, you may substitute 8 whole sage leaves or 1 tablespoon minced fresh thyme. The strong taste of the rosemary mellows as it cooks, delicately flavoring the meat. The chops can also be broiled in a preheated oven 4 inches from the heat source.

SERVES 2

4 loin pork chops, each ½ inch thick (1 pound total weight), well trimmed of fat

2 teaspoons olive oil

1 tablespoon minced fresh rosemary

⅛ teaspoon freshly milled black pepper

8 curly parsley sprigs (optional garnish)

1. Place pork chops on a flat plate. With your fingers, rub ½ teaspoon olive oil on both surfaces of each chop. (Rubbing a little oil on surface of chops will prevent them from sticking when placed on heated grill.) With fingertips, press minced rosemary into both surfaces of chops. Let the chops stand at room temperature for 1 hour to allow the rosemary flavor to penetrate each chop.

2. Preheat charcoal grill until coals have turned a gray ashy color. Preheat gas or electric grill according to manufacturer's suggested time.

3. Place chops on grill about 4 inches from heat source. Sear the chops 1 minute on each side, turning meat with long-handled tongs. Cook chops for an additional 3 minutes on each side. To test for doneness, insert the tip of a small knife into the thickest part near the bone. If the juices run clear, with no traces of pink, the chops are done. If not, continue cooking for an additional 2 minutes. Test for doneness once again.

4. Transfer to platter, season with pepper, garnish with parsley, and serve immediately.

Stuffed Pork Chops

The savory blending of fruit, sage, and white wine gives this dish its full-bodied flavor. This recipe is an adaptation of one developed by my daughter Joanne—a gifted artist and mother of my two grandsons, John Paul and Colin Edward.

SERVES 3

2 rib pork chops, each 1 inch thick (1 pound total weight)

1 tablespoon minced shallots

2 tablespoons seedless dark raisins, plumped in hot water, thoroughly drained, and finely chopped

2 tablespoons applesauce

1½ teaspoons minced fresh sage or ½ teaspoon crumbled dried sage

⅛ teaspoon freshly ground nutmeg

¼ cup fresh bread crumbs

⅛ teaspoon salt, if desired

⅛ teaspoon freshly milled black pepper

2 teaspoons olive oil

½ cup dry white wine

1. With a small paring knife, trim excess fat from chops. To make pockets in pork for stuffing, cut a lateral slit down the center and the full length of each chop right to the bone (or have this done by the butcher). Place chops on a flat surface and open the pockets.
2. In a small bowl, combine shallots, raisins, applesauce, sage, nutmeg, bread crumbs, salt, and pepper. Divide stuffing in half.
3. Stuff each chop, bringing flaps together to enclose stuffing. Fasten the edges with 2 toothpicks.
4. In a 10-inch skillet, heat oil over medium heat. Add pork chops and brown lightly on both sides. Remove chops to a plate and pour off all the drippings. Add ¼ cup wine and turn heat to high, scraping any fragments that cling to pan with wooden spoon; remove pan from heat.
5. Return chops to pan and add remaining wine. Cover pan and cook chops over low heat, basting every 10 minutes with pan juices until chops are tender when pierced with the tip of a knife, about 35 minutes. If pan juices seem to be evaporating during cooking, add 2 teaspoons water.
6. Transfer chops to serving platter, remove toothpicks, and pour pan juices over each chop. Serve immediately.

N O T E : The pork chops may be cooked up to 2 hours before serving; keep covered after cooking and baste frequently with pan juices. When ready to serve, reheat over low heat for 10 minutes; check pan juices and add a little more white wine if needed.

‹‹‹‐

Yummy Pork Chops

The onion, lemon, brown sugar, and ketchup form a mahogany glaze for these succulent chops. This happens to be one of my husband John's favorite pork dishes, especially when served with either Applesauce Raisin Loaf (page 311), or Cranberry Nut Bread (page 317).

SERVES 2

2 teaspoons olive oil
4 rib pork chops, each ½ inch thick (1 pound total weight), well trimmed of fat
1 small yellow onion (5 ounces), peeled and sliced into paper-thin rounds

1 small lemon, washed, dried, ends removed, and sliced into 8 thin rounds
2 teaspoons ketchup
4 teaspoons dark brown sugar
3 to 4 tablespoons water

1. In a 10-inch skillet, heat oil over medium-high heat. Lightly brown chops on both sides, about 1 minute on each side; transfer to a platter. Remove skillet from heat, discard any pan drippings, and wipe pan out with paper towel.
2. In same skillet, arrange pork chops in a single layer. Arrange onion slices over chops in an overlapping pattern. Place 2 slices of lemon on top of each chop, spoon ½ teaspoon of ketchup over each chop, and sprinkle 1 teaspoon dark brown sugar over each. Add 3 table-spoons water to bottom of pan.
3. Cover pan and cook chops over low heat until cooking liquid forms a glaze, about 15 minutes. Continue cooking, covered, basting fre-quently, until chops are extremely tender when pierced with the tip of a knife, about 15 minutes. If glaze gets extremely thick while basting, stir in remaining tablespoon of water.
4. Transfer chops to a platter with a spatula and spoon glaze from bottom of pan over each. Serve immediately.

Pork Tenderloin with Apples and Prunes

Although this is a hearty winter dish, I strongly suggest that you try it in late summer when fresh Italian purple prune plums are in season. Substitute 4 plums (4 ounces), halved, pitted, and quartered, for the prunes. Bulgur Pilaf (page 115) would be an excellent accompaniment.

SERVES 2

2 tablespoons Wondra flour
¼ teaspoon freshly milled black pepper
One 8-ounce pork tenderloin, well trimmed of fat and any connecting membrane
2 teaspoons olive oil
¼ to ⅓ cup dry vermouth
1 large shallot (2 ounces) peeled and thinly sliced to make ¼ cup

1 medium-sized tart apple (6 ounces), such as Granny Smith or greening, peeled, halved, cored, seeded, and cut into ½-inch slices
4 large prunes, pitted and sliced into ½-inch strips to make ⅓ cup
1 scant teaspoon minced fresh rosemary or ¼ teaspoon crumbled dried rosemary
⅛ teaspoon salt, if desired

1. In a shallow bowl, combine flour and pepper. Dredge pork in seasoned flour and shake off excess. (Dredge just before browning or flour coating will become gummy.)
2. In a 10-inch skillet, heat olive oil over medium-high heat. Lightly brown meat on all sides; transfer to platter.
3. Add ¼ cup vermouth to skillet; turn heat to high, scraping any fragments that cling to bottom of pan. Cook, stirring constantly with wooden spoon until vermouth is reduced to about 1 tablespoon, about 1 minute. Add shallot and cook, stirring constantly, until barely tender, about 30 seconds. Remove pan from heat.
4. Arrange apple slices in bottom of skillet; arrange prunes over

apples. Place tenderloin on top of fruit mixture. Sprinkle rosemary over pork. Cover pan and simmer over medium heat just until apple slices start to exude their juices, about 5 minutes. Spoon some of the fruit mixture over pork and continue cooking, covered, basting pork with fruit frequently, for 25 minutes. If pan juices evaporate during cooking, add an additional tablespoon or more of vermouth.

5. Transfer pork to cutting board, cover loosely with foil, and let rest for 10 minutes before slicing.

6. To serve, slice tenderloin into ½-inch slices; arrange in a single row down center of platter in a slightly overlapping pattern. Spoon fruit mixture around pork; serve immediately.

Pork Scaloppine

The tomato mushroom sauce enhances the flavorful essence of these tender medallions.

SERVES 2

1 large ripe tomato (8 ounces)

2 tablespoons Wondra flour

¼ teaspoon freshly milled black pepper

One 8-ounce pork tenderloin, well trimmed of fat and any connecting membrane, sliced into ¼-inch rounds

2 teaspoons olive oil

¼ cup dry vermouth

½ cup scallions, cut into ½-inch lengths

¼ pound medium mushrooms, wiped, trimmed, and thinly sliced

1½ teaspoons minced fresh rosemary or ½ teaspoon crumbled dried rosemary

⅛ teaspoon salt, if desired

1. Plump fresh tomato in 1 quart boiling water for 1 minute. Rinse under cold water, core tomato, and peel skin with a small paring knife. Cut in half crosswise; gently squeeze each half and discard most of the seeds. Cut tomato into ½-inch cubes and place in strainer with bowl underneath to drain thoroughly; discard liquid.
2. In a shallow bowl, combine flour and pepper. Lightly dredge each pork medallion in seasoned flour and shake off excess. (Dredge just before sautéing or the flour coating will become gummy.)
3. In a 10-inch skillet, heat oil over medium-high heat. Sauté pork, turning once, until lightly golden on both sides, about 1½ minutes on each side; transfer to plate.
4. Add vermouth to skillet; turn heat to high, scraping any fragments that cling to bottom of pan with a wooden spoon. Cook until vermouth is reduced by half, about 30 seconds. Add scallions and cook, stirring constantly, until crisp tender, about 1 minute. Stir in drained cubed tomato. Cook, stirring constantly, until there are no tomato juices left in bottom of pan, about 1 minute. Add mushrooms and continue cooking, stirring constantly for an additional minute.
5. Turn heat down to medium and return pork to pan. Cook, stirring and spooning vegetable mixture over medallions for an additional 5 minutes. Stir in rosemary; season with salt and cook for an additional 30 seconds.
6. Transfer pork to platter and spoon vegetable mixture and sauce over top; serve immediately.

Glazed Roast Pork with Fruit Stuffing

The accent of dried fruit complements the pork's sweetness. When it is carved, each loin slice will be decorated with circles of stuffing, making a handsome presentation. There will be ample leftovers for another meal or you may wish to invite a favorite couple who enjoy pork.

SERVES 4 TO 6

½ cup well packed dried
apricots (3 ounces), cut
into ¼-inch dice
½ cup (2 ounces) seedless
dark raisins, loosely
packed
1½ cups apple cider,
preferably fresh

1½ teaspoons grated lemon
rind
¼ teaspoon ground allspice
One 2½-pound boneless
center-cut pork loin roast

1. Place apricots and raisins in a 1½-quart saucepan. Add cider, cover pan, and bring to a boil. As soon as cider comes to a boil, remove pan from heat, uncover, and let cool to room temperature. Drain fruit in strainer set over a bowl. Press fruit with the back of a spoon; reserve liquid (you should have about 1 cup reserved liquid after pressing fruit). In a small bowl, combine fruit with lemon rind and allspice; set aside.
2. Adjust rack to center of oven and preheat to 400 degrees.
3. Trim top layer of fat from roast, leaving a ⅛-inch layer. Place pork on a board, fat side facing down. Using a metal spatula, spread fruit mixture in an even layer over pork, leaving a ¼-inch border of meat on all four sides. Roll meat into a cylinder (like a jelly roll) and tie at 1-inch intervals; tie lengthwise once. Do not tie tightly or the twine will cut into the meat during cooking. Place roast on a rack in a roasting pan.
4. Place meat in preheated oven and roast for 30 minutes. Remove from oven and drain off any fat from pan.

5. Reduce oven temperature to 350 degrees. Pour reserved liquid over pork. Return to oven and roast, basting every 15 minutes with pan juices, until pork is a glossy brown color, about 50 minutes. Transfer roast to platter, cover loosely with foil, and let stand for 15 minutes before slicing.

6. Using a metal spoon, skim off any surface fat from roasting pan. Add 3 tablespoons hot water to pan and place over medium heat. Scrape bottom of pan with wooden spoon to loosen any glaze that might be stuck. Strain pan juices through a small strainer into a small saucepan. Keep warm over low heat.

7. Remove twine from roast and carve into ½-inch slices; arrange slices on a platter in a slightly overlapping pattern. Spoon about 3 tablespoons of pan juices on top of pork. Serve the remaining juices separately.

N O T E : The leftover roast makes excellent sandwiches. Remove from refrigerator 1 hour before making sandwiches. It is especially delicious when thinly sliced and served on lightly toasted homemade Old-fashioned Sesame Oatmeal Bread (page 289) with a thin layer of hot mustard, and topped off with a layer of watercress.

⫷⫷

LAMB

Broiled Lamb Steaks with Thyme

Broiling either in the oven or on an outdoor grill produces the most succulent lamb steaks. To avoid spattering and smoking when cooking, the meat should be well trimmed of fat. See bottom of recipe for grilling method.

S E R V E S   2

2 center-cut lamb steaks cut from leg, each ½ inch thick (1¼ pounds total weight), well trimmed of fat

2 teaspoons olive oil

1 tablespoon minced fresh thyme or 1½ teaspoons crumbled dried thyme

⅛ teaspoon freshly milled black pepper

1 tablespoon fresh lemon juice, strained

1. Place lamb steaks on a flat plate. With your fingers, rub 1 teaspoon olive oil on both surfaces of each steak. (Rubbing a little oil on surface of steaks will prevent them from sticking to the rack when broiling or when placed on heated grill.) With your fingertips, press thyme into both surfaces of steaks. Let the steaks rest at room temperature for 1 hour to allow the flavor of the thyme to penetrate the meat.

2. Remove broiler rack and pan from oven and preheat broiler for 15 minutes.

3. Place steaks on rack over broiler pan. Position broiler pan 4 inches from heat source. Broil until surface of meat is seared and lightly browned, about 3 minutes. Turn steaks and continue broiling on second side, 2 minutes for medium rare, 3 minutes for medium, and 5 minutes for well done.

4. Remove steaks from broiler pan (or grill) and place on a cutting board. With a sharp knife, carve around the leg bone (small round bone); discard bone. Slice the boned steak down center. Repeat with remaining steak. Season both sides of halved steaks with pepper.
5. Place steaks on platter, spoon lemon juice over steaks, and serve immediately.

NOTE: To grill lamb steaks, preheat charcoal grill until coals have turned a gray ashy color. Preheat gas or electric grill according to manufacturer's suggested time. Sear steaks on both sides, about 1 minute on each side, turning meat with long-handled tongs. Approximate cooking time after searing is 2 minutes on each side for medium rare, 3 minutes on each side for medium, and 4 minutes on each side for well done.

Lamb Shoulder Chops with Mustard and Dill

This tangy combination keeps the chops juicy and moist when broiling and adds a special zip to the lamb.

SERVES 2

2 lamb shoulder chops, each ½ inch thick (1¼ pounds total weight), well trimmed of fat

2 teaspoons Dijon mustard

1 tablespoon minced fresh dill or 1 teaspoon crumbled dillweed

⅛ teaspoon freshly milled black pepper

Several short sprigs of fresh dill (optional garnish)

1. Place chops on a flat plate. Spread mustard over both surfaces of each chop. With fingertips, press dill into both surfaces of chops. Let chops stand at room temperature for one hour to allow the mustard and dill flavors to penetrate the meat.
2. Remove broiler rack and pan from oven and preheat broiler for 15 minutes. Lightly grease broiler rack.
3. Place chops on prepared rack over broiler pan. Position broiler pan 4 inches from heat source. Broil until surface of meat is seared and lightly browned, about 3 minutes. Turn chops and continue broiling on second side, 2 minutes for medium rare, 3 minutes for medium, and 5 minutes for well done.
4. Transfer to platter and season with pepper; garnish with fresh dill and serve immediately.

Piquant Grilled Lamb Chops

These tasty chops may also be broiled in a preheated oven 4 inches from the heat source. If raspberry vinegar is unavailable, you can substitute white wine vinegar.

SERVES 2

3 tablespoons raspberry vinegar
1 teaspoon minced garlic
1½ teaspoons minced fresh marjoram or ½ teaspoon crumbled dried marjoram
4 loin lamb chops, each 1 inch thick (1¼ pounds total weight), well trimmed of fat

⅛ teaspoon freshly milled black pepper
Several curly parsley sprigs (optional garnish)

1. Place vinegar, garlic, and marjoram in a small bowl; stir with fork to combine.
2. Place chops in a single layer in shallow dish. Spoon marinade over chops, turning once to coat completely; marinate at room temperature for 30 minutes.
3. Preheat charcoal grill until coals have turned a gray ashy color. Preheat gas or electric grill according to manufacturer's suggested time.
4. Remove chops from marinade and gently blot dry with paper towel; discard marinade.
5. Lightly brush the grill rack with a little vegetable or olive oil to prevent chops from sticking while grilling.
6. Place chops on grill about 4 inches from heat source. Sear meat on both sides, about 1 minute on each side, turning meat with long-handled tongs. Approximate cooking time after searing is 2 minutes on each side for medium rare, 3 minutes on each side for medium, and 4 minutes on each side for well done.
7. Place chops on platter, season with pepper, garnish with parsley sprigs, and serve immediately.

⋘

Rack of Lamb

The crusty bread crumb and parsley coating seals in natural juices while it provides a handsome presentation.

SERVES 2

One 6-rib rack of lamb (about 1¼ pounds total weight)
1 teaspoon Dijon mustard
1 teaspoon olive oil
1 teaspoon minced garlic (mince to a paste)
1½ teaspoons minced fresh thyme or ½ teaspoon crumbled dried thyme
1½ teaspoons minced fresh rosemary or ½ teaspoon crumbled dried rosemary

¼ teaspoon freshly milled black pepper
½ cup fresh bread crumbs, preferably made from whole wheat bread
1 tablespoon minced Italian parsley leaves
½ bunch watercress, tough ends trimmed (garnish)
1 small lemon, cut into wedges (garnish)

1. Ask your butcher to make ½-inch cuts between the ribs so that carving will be easier. Have him also trim about 2 inches of fat and meat from between ribs to dress up the rack. Trim all the fat from the top of the meat.
2. Combine mustard, olive oil, garlic, thyme, rosemary, and pepper in a small bowl. Rub marinade all over meat; place rack in a shallow bowl and cover with plastic wrap. Refrigerate for at least 3 hours or overnight.
3. When ready to roast, adjust rack to center of oven and preheat to 375 degrees.
4. Wrap each exposed bone end of the chops with foil to prevent burning while roasting.
5. Place lamb meat side down on a rack in roasting pan. Roast until meat thermometer registers 140 degrees for medium rare, about 35 minutes, or 145 degrees for medium, about 45 minutes.

6. While lamb is roasting, combine bread crumbs and parsley in a small bowl; set aside.
7. Remove lamb from oven and turn it over (meat side up). Firmly press crumb mixture over top of lamb. Return to oven and bake until crumb mixture is lightly browned and crusty, about 10 minutes. Remove foil from bone ends and let rack rest for 10 minutes before serving (this will make carving easier).
8. Place rack of lamb on an oval platter and garnish with a border of watercress and lemon wedges. Carve between ribs to serve.

Braised Lamb Shanks

The savory blending of herbs, wine, lemon, and broth gives this hearty winter dish its full-bodied flavor. It happens to be one of my husband John's favorites. Plain cooked rice (either white or brown) would be an excellent accompaniment to the lamb shanks because there will be ample sauce from the shanks to spoon over the rice as well.

SERVES 2

2 lamb shanks (about 1½ pounds total weight), well trimmed of fat and any attached membrane
2 tablespoons Wondra flour
¼ teaspoon freshly milled black pepper
2 teaspoons olive oil
⅓ cup minced onion
⅓ cup minced carrot
⅓ cup minced celery, strings removed
½ cup dry white wine

1 teaspoon minced garlic
1½ teaspoons grated lemon rind
½ cup unsalted chicken broth, preferably homemade (page 51)
1 tablespoon minced fresh thyme or 1 teaspoon crumbled dried thyme
2 small bay leaves
1 tablespoon minced Italian parsley leaves (garnish)

1. Adjust rack to center of oven and preheat to 350 degrees.
2. Combine flour and pepper in a shallow bowl. Dredge lamb shanks in seasoned flour. (Dredge just before searing or flour coating will become gummy.)
3. In a 10-inch ovenproof sauté pan, heat oil over high heat. Sear lamb shanks on all sides until lightly golden. Transfer to a plate.
4. Turn heat down to medium and add onion, carrot, and celery. Sauté, stirring constantly until soft but not brown, and scraping any fragments that cling to bottom of pan, about 3 minutes. (If vegetables start to stick to bottom of pan while sautéing, add about 2 tablespoons of the wine to loosen.) Add garlic and lemon rind; mix well. Add wine, turn heat to high, and cook, stirring constantly, until slightly reduced, about 2 minutes. Add broth, thyme, and bay leaves to pan; cook until broth comes to a boil. Remove pan from heat and place shanks on top of vegetable mixture.
5. Cover pan and bake for 30 minutes. Remove pan from oven and spoon half of the vegetable mixture over shanks. Continue to cook, covered, basting frequently with pan juices until meat is very tender when pierced with fork, about 35 minutes. The meat is finished cooking when it almost falls from the bone.
6. Transfer lamb shanks to platter; discard bay leaves from sauce. Spoon sauce over lamb shanks and garnish with minced parsley; serve immediately.

N O T E : The lamb shanks may be cooked up to 3 hours before serving; keep covered after cooking and baste frequently with pan juices. When ready to serve, reheat in 300-degree oven for 20 minutes.

Lamb Stew

Nothing better on a cold winter day than a hearty dish of stew. A mixed green salad will round out this hearty one-dish meal.

SERVES 2

1 tablespoon olive oil
1 center-cut lamb steak 1 inch thick, cut from leg (1¼ pounds total weight), well trimmed of fat, cut into 1-inch cubes, and center round bone discarded
½ cup chopped yellow onion
½ teaspoon minced garlic
½ cup coarsely chopped canned tomatoes, juice included
1 bay leaf
1½ teaspoons minced fresh thyme or 1 teaspoon crumbled dried thyme

1 large carrot (4 ounces), trimmed, peeled, and sliced diagonally into ½-inch pieces
2 medium-sized white potatoes (8 ounces total weight), peeled and cut into 1½-inch cubes
1 cup frozen tiny green peas, defrosted and well drained
⅛ teaspoon salt, if desired
⅛ teaspoon freshly milled black pepper
2 teaspoons minced Italian parsley leaves (garnish)

1. In a 3-quart dutch oven, heat oil over medium heat. Add meat and sauté, stirring constantly, until very lightly golden. Transfer to plate with a slotted spoon. Add onion and garlic and sauté, stirring constantly, scraping any fragments that cling to bottom of pan with wooden spoon, until onion is barely tender, about 1 minute. Add tomatoes and thyme. Return meat to pan and bring to a boil over high heat, stirring constantly. Turn heat to low and cook, covered, stirring frequently until meat is very tender when pierced with the tip of a knife, about 40 minutes. (Watch cooking liquid; if it starts to evaporate, add about 2 tablespoons hot water.)
2. Add carrots and mix well. Cook over low heat, covered, until carrots are barely tender when tested with a fork, about 5 minutes.

Add potatoes and continue cooking, covered, stirring once or twice until potatoes are done, about 10 minutes. Add peas and cook an additional 2 minutes. Season with salt and pepper; remove from heat.
3. When ready to serve, remove bay leaf, transfer stew to platter, and garnish with minced parsley; serve immediately.

N O T E : Stew can be prepared up to 4 hours before serving and reheated over very low heat when ready to serve.

POULTRY

I can still remember my childhood days when poultry was served every Sunday, most often chicken. Each Saturday morning I would walk to the market, holding my father's hand with my left hand and pulling my little wagon with my right. After my father made his choice of chickens, either broilers or fryers, the farmer would tie the legs and wings in place with twine and place the bound chickens in my wagon for the walk home. I distinctly remember two different occasions when the chickens broke loose and I had to go running down the street to catch them. After the chickens were killed and plunged in boiling water, my job was to pluck and singe the feathers. How I dreaded that job. But the taste of those free-range birds was my reward. No matter how they were prepared—broiled, roasted, grilled, or sautéed—that taste was memorable.

Very few people today, however, are fortunate enough to get barn-yard-reared (free-range) freshly killed poultry. Instead, poultry must be bought in butcher shops or supermarkets.

While most of the recipes in this chapter call for boneless, skinless poultry, here are a few suggestions on selecting and preparing the poultry before cooking it.

- *When buying packaged poultry, either whole, parts, or boneless, skinless breasts, always check the expiration date. Make sure the outer wrapping on the package is completely sealed.*
- *The skin of whole birds or cut-up parts should look smooth and there should be no discoloration.*
- *Some birds have a few small feathers still attached, especially around the vent and wings. These feathers can easily be removed by hand or with tweezers. If there are any hairs on the flesh, carefully pass the birds over a low flame (either a gas burner or a candle) to singe them off.*
- *Poultry is extremely perishable and should be used within two days of purchase.*
- *Wash poultry as soon as you get it home, or soak it in cold water with a little lemon juice. Rinse whole, parts, or boneless, skinless breasts thoroughly and blot dry with paper towel.*

- *If you are not going to use it the same day, rub a cut lemon all over the poultry. The acid in the lemon will keep it fresh-smelling. Place in a nonaluminum bowl, cover with plastic wrap, and refrigerate overnight.*
- *Before cooking poultry, either whole or parts, be sure to remove any traces of fat. While this book includes just a few recipes in which poultry is cooked with the skin on, I suggest that you remove the skin before eating.*
- *Many of the recipes for chicken (whole, parts, and boneless, skinless breasts), turkey cutlets, and Rock Cornish hens are interchangeable. There are many in this chapter for you to choose from so use your imagination in the preparation of poultry for your table.*

≪≪

Roast Chicken with Rosemary

Placing the herbed mixture under the skin will help retain natural moisture and add distinctive flavoring to the chicken, a flavor that is not lost when the skin is later removed. See bottom of recipe for suggestions for leftover.

SERVES 4

1 whole frying chicken
(about 3 pounds)
1 teaspoon minced garlic
1½ teaspoons minced fresh
rosemary or ½ teaspoon
crumbled dried rosemary
¼ teaspoon freshly milled
black pepper

½ teaspoon dry mustard
2 teaspoons unsalted
margarine, softened
1 lemon (4 ounces), washed,
dried, and cut in half
crosswise
1 small bunch curly parsley
(optional garnish)

1. Adjust rack to center of oven and preheat to 350 degrees.
2. Remove fat from rear cavity of the chicken. Cut off wing tips at the first joint and discard. Rinse chicken under cold water and blot dry inside and out with paper towel. Place chicken on work surface with breast side up. Using your index finger, gently loosen skin from flesh of chicken breast, thighs, and upper portion of leg. Be careful not to puncture skin; set aside.
3. In a small bowl, combine garlic, rosemary, pepper, mustard, and softened margarine. Mix with spoon until herb mixture is a smooth paste.
4. With one hand, gently pull back the skin at one side of the neck to expose half of the breast flesh. With your other hand, rub half of the herbed mixture over breast and leg area; repeat same process on the other half of chicken. Pat the skin back in place. Rub outside of bird with ½ lemon. Squeeze the other half inside chicken and leave in cavity. Truss chicken with kitchen twine or simply tie legs and wings in place with twine.
5. Place chicken on rack in roasting pan, breast side up. Roast until skin is nicely browned and crisp, about 1 hour. To test for done-

Trussing Chicken With Twine

1. *Place chicken on its back on work surface. Cut a piece of kitchen twine approximately 45 to 50 inches in length (using a generous length of twine will simplify the job when it comes to pulling tightly and excess will be cut off after knotting). Place center of twine underneath its tail.*

2. *Cross the twine ends over tail and loop each end over and around the opposite drumstick.*

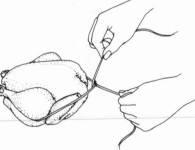

3. *Pull both ends of the twine away from the bird to draw the drumstick and tail tightly over the vent.*

4. *Pull twine under legs and up along sides of thigh and over wings. Make sure that wings are secure under twine as you pull.*

5. *Knot at top of neck and cut off excess twine.*

ness, remove chicken from roasting rack with two forks and tip it up on its tail over a white plate. If the juices that run out are a pale yellow color, the chicken is done. If the juices are a pale pink color, cover chicken with a loose tent of foil, return to oven, and roast for an additional 10 to 15 minutes. Test for doneness once again.

6. Transfer chicken to platter and let rest for 10 minutes before carving.
7. Skim off any surface fat from roasting pan. Add ½ cup water to pan and place over medium-high heat. Cook pan juices, scraping any fragments that cling to bottom of pan. Strain pan juices through a strainer set over a small pan; keep warm over low heat.
8. Remove twine from chicken and discard lemon from rear cavity.
9. Quarter chicken and place on serving platter. Garnish with parsley and serve with pan juices.

N O T E : Leftover chicken makes a delicious meal when added to pasta for a salad. See Pasta Salad with Chicken and Broccoli (page 93). For another variation, you may want to try Chicken Soup with Herbs (page 56).

⫷⫷⫷

Chicken Breast with Potatoes and Red Pepper

Simplicity is the keynote to this tasty one-dish meal. While the chicken and vegetables cook together, the flavors mingle, producing succulent juices for basting.

SERVES 2

1 large whole chicken breast, halved, including wings (1 pound 6 ounces total weight)

1 medium yellow onion (6 ounces), peeled and sliced into ¼-inch rounds

2 medium-sized all-purpose white potatoes (12 ounces), peeled and sliced into ½-inch rounds

¼ teaspoon freshly milled black pepper, divided

1 large red bell pepper (8 ounces), halved, cored, seeded, and sliced lengthwise into ½-inch strips

⅛ teaspoon salt, if desired

1½ teaspoons minced fresh sage or ½ teaspoon crumbled dried sage

2 teaspoons olive oil

1. Thoroughly wash chicken breasts in cold water and blot dry with paper towel. Clip wings at first joint and discard. Trim any fat that is attached to breast. Place breasts on work surface with skin side up. Slip your fingertips under the skin to loosen. Peel off skin carefully to avoid tearing the meat. Use knife to cut away skin and any connecting membrane; discard skin.

2. Adjust rack to center of oven and preheat to 350 degrees. Lightly grease bottom and sides of a 2-quart ovenproof casserole. Place sliced onions in a single layer in casserole. Arrange sliced potatoes in single layer over top of onions and sprinkle with ⅛ teaspoon pepper.

3. Arrange pepper strips in single layer over potatoes. Place breasts, skinned side up, on top of peppers; sprinkle with remaining ⅛

teaspoon pepper, salt, and sage. Drizzle olive oil over top of breasts.

4. Cover casserole and bake until potatoes are tender when tested with the tip of a fork, about 40 minutes. Using a bulb baster, baste chicken with juices from bottom of casserole. Continue cooking, uncovered, basting with pan juices every 5 minutes, until chicken is golden brown, about 20 minutes.

5. Use 2 large serving spoons to lift each portion onto dinner plates. Spoon a little of the pan juices on top of chicken and serve immediately.

Curried Braised Chicken with Tomato, Green Pepper, and Raisins

This winter fare just bursts with the flavor of curry. Cooked white or brown rice would be an excellent accompaniment, since there will be ample sauce to spoon over.

SERVES 2

- 1 whole chicken breast (1 pound 4 ounces)
- 2 tablespoons Wondra flour
- ¼ teaspoon freshly milled black pepper
- 1 tablespoon olive oil
- ½ cup dry white wine, divided
- ½ cup minced red onion

- 1 medium-sized green pepper (5 ounces), halved, cored, seeded, and cut into ¼-inch dice to make ¾ cup
- 1 teaspoon minced garlic
- ½ teaspoon curry powder

1 cup canned whole peeled tomatoes, including juice, coarsely chopped

2 tablespoons dark seedless raisins

⅛ teaspoon salt, if desired

1. Wash breast in cold water and blot dry with paper towel. Grasp the top of the breast on each side of the breastbone and bend the breast backward until the breastbone snaps. With the aid of a sharp knife, remove bone and attached cartilage. Split breast lengthwise down the middle and cut each halved breast crosswise (4 pieces total). Slip your fingertips under the skin to loosen. Peel off skin carefully to avoid tearing the meat. Use knife to cut away skin, any connecting membrane, and fat; discard skin.

2. In a shallow bowl, combine flour and pepper. Lightly dredge chicken pieces in seasoned flour (dredge just before sautéing or flour coating will become gummy).

3. In a 10-inch sauté pan, heat oil over medium-high heat. Place chicken, skinned side down, in pan and sauté until lightly golden on both sides, about 2 minutes on each side. Transfer chicken to platter. Discard any oil or pan drippings.

4. Add ¼ cup wine to pan and turn heat to high, scraping any fragments that cling to bottom of pan with wooden spoon. Turn heat to medium and stir in onion and diced pepper. Cook vegetables, stirring constantly until they are soft, about 5 minutes. Stir in garlic and cook, stirring constantly until soft, about 1 minute. Stir in remaining ¼ cup wine, curry, tomatoes, and raisins. Bring sauce to a boil, uncovered, stirring once or twice.

5. Return chicken to pan skinned side up and spoon sauce over pieces. Simmer, partially covered, over low heat, stirring and spooning sauce over chicken frequently, until chicken is tender, about 30 minutes. Season with salt and remove from heat. (Chicken can be cooked up to 2 hours before serving, then covered and reheated over low heat.)

6. To serve, arrange on a platter and spoon some sauce over chicken; serve remaining sauce separately. Or you can present both chicken and sauce on a bed of cooked rice.

⇚

Removing Fillets and Tendons from Chicken Breast Halves

Place each halved chicken breast on a cutting board with the skinned side down so that the tubular fillet, along the outer edge of each breast half, faces up. Grasp halved breast in one hand and its fillet in the other. Pull gently until they come apart.

To remove the tough white tendon running along the underside of tubular fillets, hold knife against tendon. With the other hand, grab the end of the tendon firmly with your index finger and thumb (you can get a better grip on the tendon if you hold it firmly with a small piece of paper towel) and pull tendon out against the blade.

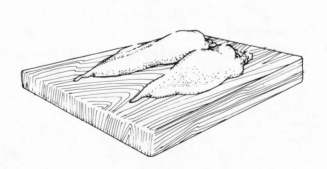

Chicken Breast with Piquant Vinegar Sauce

Deglazing the pan with white wine vinegar adds flavor and body to the sauce.

SERVES 2

1 whole boneless, skinless chicken breast (10 ounces), split in half
1 tablespoon olive oil
2 tablespoons minced shallots
3 tablespoons imported white wine vinegar
¾ cup unsalted chicken broth, preferably homemade (page 51)

2 teaspoons minced Italian parsley leaves
⅛ teaspoon salt, if desired
⅛ teaspoon freshly milled black pepper

1. Adjust oven rack to middle of oven and preheat to 200 degrees.
2. Wash chicken breast and blot dry with paper towel. Trim off any excess fat. Remove fillets and tendons from under breast halves. See directions, page 170. Place halved breasts between wax paper and lightly pound until each piece is about ½-inch thick. Slice each halved breast lengthwise into 2 even pieces.
3. In a 10-inch skillet, heat oil over medium heat. Sauté breast pieces and fillets, turning once with metal spatula, until lightly golden, about 2 minutes on each side. (If chicken starts to stick to bottom of pan, loosen gently with metal spatula.) Remove pan from heat and transfer chicken to ovenproof platter; cover loosely with a tent of foil. Place in oven while making sauce.
4. Add shallots to pan and sauté over medium heat until lightly golden, scraping any fragments that cling to bottom of pan with wooden spoon, about 30 seconds. Add vinegar and turn heat to high. Cook, stirring constantly until vinegar is reduced to 1 teaspoon and shallots are lightly glazed, about 1 minute. Stir in broth and continue cooking, stirring once or twice, until broth is reduced to about ¼ cup and sauce is slightly thickened, about 2 to

3 minutes. Stir in parsley. Season with salt and pepper; remove from heat. Stir in any juices that have accumulated on platter. Spoon sauce over chicken breasts; serve immediately.

Chicken Breast with Artichoke Hearts

A savory and nutritious accompaniment to this chicken dish would be Brown Rice Pilaf (page 112).

SERVES 2

> 1 whole boneless, skinless chicken breast (10 ounces), split in half
> 2 tablespoons Wondra flour
> ¼ teaspoon freshly milled black pepper
> 1 tablespoon olive oil
> ½ cup thinly sliced red onion
> ¼ cup Madeira wine

> One 9-ounce package frozen artichoke hearts, defrosted and well drained
> 1½ teaspoons minced fresh lemon thyme or ½ teaspoon dried lemon thyme
> ⅛ teaspoon salt, if desired

1. Wash chicken and blot dry with paper towel. Trim off any excess fat. Remove fillets and tendons from under breast halves. See directions, page 170. Holding knife at a slight angle, slice breasts and fillets crosswise into 2-inch pieces. (You will be slicing on a bias and cutting against the grain.)
2. In a shallow bowl, combine flour and pepper. Lightly dredge chicken pieces in seasoned flour and shake off excess. (Dredge just before sautéing or flour coating will become gummy.)
3. In a 10-inch skillet, heat oil over medium high heat. Add chicken and sauté, turning once, until lightly golden on both sides, about 2 minutes on each side. Using tongs, transfer chicken to plate.

4. Turn heat down to medium, add onion, and cook, stirring constantly and scraping any fragments that cling to bottom of pan. Add wine, turn heat to high, and cook, stirring constantly until wine has reduced to half, about 1 minute. Stir in artichoke hearts, turn heat down to medium, and cook, partially covered, stirring frequently until they are barely tender when tested with the tip of a knife, about 3 minutes. Stir in lemon thyme. Return chicken to pan and spoon artichoke mixture on top. Continue cooking over low heat, partially covered, for an additional 2 minutes. Season with salt and remove from heat.
5. Transfer chicken to platter and spoon artichoke mixture around chicken; serve immediately.

Chicken Breast with Lemon Caper Tarragon Sauce

The delicate taste of sautéed chicken breast is enhanced with a hint of sharpness from the lemon caper tarragon sauce, adding vigor to this dish.

S E R V E S   2

1 whole boneless, skinless chicken breast (10 ounces), split in half
1 tablespoon olive oil
1 tablespoon fresh lemon juice
½ cup unsalted chicken broth, preferably homemade (page 51)
2 teaspoons nonpareil capers, thoroughly rinsed and drained

1½ teaspoons minced fresh tarragon or ½ teaspoon crumbled dried tarragon
1 teaspoon arrowroot or cornstarch
1 tablespoon water
⅛ teaspoon salt, if desired
⅛ teaspoon freshly milled black pepper

1. Adjust rack to middle of oven and preheat to 200 degrees.
2. Wash chicken breast and blot dry with paper towel. Trim off any excess fat. Remove fillets and tendons from under breast halves. See directions, page 170. Place fillets and breast halves between wax paper and lightly pound until each piece is about ¼ inch thick.
2. In a 10-inch skillet, heat oil over medium heat. Sauté chicken, turning once with metal spatula, until lightly golden, about 1½ minutes on each side. (If chicken starts to stick to bottom of pan, loosen gently with metal spatula.) Remove pan from heat and transfer chicken to an ovenproof serving platter. Cover loosely with a tent of foil and place in oven while making sauce.
3. Discard any oil remaining in the skillet. Add lemon juice and broth to pan; bring to a boil over high heat, scraping any fragments that cling to bottom of pan with a wooden spoon. Turn heat to low, stir in capers and tarragon, and cook, stirring constantly, for 30 seconds.
4. In a small bowl, dissolve arrowroot or cornstarch in water. Stir into sauce and continue cooking over low heat until slightly thickened, about 30 seconds. Season with salt and pepper; remove from heat. Stir in any juices that have accumulated on serving dish. Spoon sauce over chicken and serve immediately.

⫷⫷⫷

Spicy Broiled Chicken Strips

For an attractive presentation, arrange Shredded Zucchini with Garlic (page 245) in an outer border on platter; fill center with these spicy morsels of chicken.

SERVES 2

1 whole boneless, skinless chicken breast (10 ounces)
1 small tomato (4 ounces), halved, cored, seeded, but not peeled, cut into 1-inch cubes
2 teaspoons olive oil
1 tablespoon apple cider vinegar

¼ teaspoon fennel seeds
¼ teaspoon ground cinnamon
½ teaspoon Tabasco sauce
1 teaspoon Worcestershire sauce
1 small clove garlic, peeled and halved

1. Wash chicken breast and blot dry with paper towel. Trim off any excess fat. Remove fillets and tendons from under breast. See directions, page 170. Cut fillets in half crosswise; set aside. Split breast in lengthwise. Cut pieces lengthwise into strips about ½ inch wide. Place chicken strips in low shallow bowl.
2. In food processor fitted with metal blade, place tomato, oil, vinegar, fennel seeds, cinnamon, Tabasco, and Worcestershire. Turn machine on and drop garlic, one piece at a time, through the feed tube. Stop machine once or twice and scrape down inside work bowl with plastic spatula. Run machine until tomato and garlic are finely minced and marinade is a smooth creamy consistency, about 1 minute.
3. Pour marinade over chicken and stir to coat thoroughly. Cover with plastic wrap and marinate in refrigerator for at least 3 hours. Remove from refrigerator ½ hour before broiling.
4. Adjust broiler pan 6 inches from heat source and preheat oven on broil setting for 15 minutes.
5. In a shallow baking pan, place chicken strips in a single layer, about ½ inch apart. Spoon any remaining marinade over chicken.

Broil chicken until meat turns white and strips feel firm to the touch, about 4 to 6 minutes.

6. Transfer chicken to a platter. Spoon pan juices over chicken; serve immediately. (If some of the pan juices stick to bottom of pan, add 1 tablespoon hot water and stir with a spoon to loosen.)

Poached Chicken with Apricot Sauce

The apricot sauce lightly coats the chicken breast while the grapes add a stylish touch to this flavorful entrée.

SERVES 2

1 whole boneless, skinless chicken breast (10 ounces), split in half
¼ cup water
One 5½-ounce can apricot nectar
2 teaspoons fresh lemon juice
⅛ teaspoon freshly grated nutmeg
1½ teaspoons minced fresh mint or ½ teaspoon crumbled dried mint

1½ teaspoons cornstarch
1 tablespoon water
⅛ teaspoon salt, if desired
⅛ teaspoon freshly milled white pepper
½ cup small seedless green grapes, washed, blotted dry with paper towel, and sliced in half lengthwise

1. Adjust rack to center of oven and preheat to 200 degrees.
2. Wash chicken and blot dry with paper towel. Trim off any excess fat. Place chicken in single layer in a 10-inch skillet.
3. In a bowl, combine ¼ cup water and apricot nectar and pour over chicken. Cover pan and bring to a boil over medium heat. As soon

as diluted nectar reaches a boil, reduce heat to low. Poach chicken, covered, spooning nectar over chicken frequently until chicken is cooked and feels springy to the touch, about 15 to 20 minutes. Using a pair of tongs, transfer chicken to an ovenproof serving platter. Cover loosely with a tent of foil. Place in oven while making sauce.

4. Add lemon juice to pan and bring to a boil over high heat. Cook, stirring constantly until sauce is reduced to about half, about 3 minutes. Stir in nutmeg and mint.

5. In a small bowl, mix cornstarch with 1 tablespoon water and stir until dissolved. Add to sauce and cook over low heat, stirring constantly until slightly thickened, about 30 seconds. Season with salt and pepper. Stir in grapes and remove from heat. Spoon sauce and grapes over and around chicken; serve immediately.

Stir-fried Chicken Breast and Romaine

With this classic Chinese stir-fry technique, the chicken stays moist and tender while the romaine retains its natural color and crisp texture. Serve with cooked white rice.

SERVES 2

1 small whole boneless, skinless chicken breast (6 ounces), split in half

1. Wash chicken and blot dry with paper towel. Trim off any excess fat. Remove fillet and tendons from under breast halves. See directions, page 170. Holding knife at a slight angle, slice breasts and fillets crosswise into ½-inch pieces. (You will be slicing on a bias and cutting against the grain.)

Marinade

2 teaspoons cornstarch
1 teaspoon sugar

2 teaspoons low-sodium light
soy sauce (Kikkoman Lite)
1 tablespoon water

1. Place all the marinade ingredients in a shallow bowl. Stir marinade with a fork until cornstarch is dissolved and mixture is smooth.
2. Add chicken and toss well to coat each piece. Marinate chicken at room temperature for 15 minutes. (Chicken may also be covered with plastic wrap and placed in refrigerator to marinate for up to 3 hours before stir-frying. Remove from refrigerator ½ hour before cooking and stir chicken once again to coat with marinade.)

To Assemble and Cook

1 medium-sized head romaine
lettuce (12 ounces)
1 tablespoon vegetable oil,
preferably corn oil
1 teaspoon minced garlic

½ cup unsalted chicken broth,
preferably homemade (page
51)
1 teaspoon cornstarch
1 tablespoon water

1. Using a pair of kitchen shears, trim tops of any bruised outer leaves from romaine. Separate leaves and wash several times in cold water. Drain well and blot thoroughly dry with paper towel, or spin dry in salad spinner. Stack leaves, about 6 at a time, and cut crosswise into ½-inch pieces; repeat with remaining greens. (Greens may be prepared up to 3 hours before cooking. Place in plastic bag and refrigerate until needed.)
2. Heat wok or heavy 12-inch skillet over high heat for 1 minute. When a drop of water sizzles immediately on contact with pan, slowly pour in 2 teaspoons oil and swirl pan to coat surface. Turn heat down to medium-high. To stir-fry, add chicken and toss lightly with long metal spatula. Cook, stirring and lightly tossing constantly until meat turns white, about 1 to 1½ minutes. Transfer chicken to platter with spatula.
3. Add remaining teaspoon of oil and swirl pan once again to coat.

Reduce heat to medium. Add garlic and stir-fry just until it starts to sizzle, about 3 seconds. Add romaine and stir fry for 30 seconds. Stir in broth, cover pan, turn heat to high, and cook for 1 minute.

4. In a small bowl, combine cornstarch with water and stir until cornstarch is dissolved.

5. Return chicken to pan, turn heat down to medium-high, and stir to combine. Pour cornstarch mixture into pan and continue stirring until sauce thickens and glaze coats the chicken and romaine. Transfer to platter and serve immediately.

Stir-fried Chicken Strips with Carrot and Zucchini

Traditionally, this dish is served with 2 cups cooked white rice, but I prefer brown rice (see recipe on page 110) as an accompaniment. The nutty flavor of the brown rice truly complements the stir-fried chicken and vegetables. Cook brown rice 1 hour before you start to stir-fry.

SERVES 2

1   small whole boneless, skinless chicken breast (6 ounces), split in half

1. Wash chicken breast and blot dry with paper towel. Trim off any excess fat. Remove fillets and tendons from under breast halves. See directions, page 170. Cut fillets in half crosswise. Cut each halved breast in half lengthwise and then once again in half crosswise. Cut all pieces lengthwise again into matchstick-size shreds, about ⅛ inch thick.

Marinade

2 teaspoons cornstarch
1 teaspoon sugar
2 teaspoons low-sodium light
  soy sauce (Kikkoman Lite)

2 teaspoons dry sherry
1 tablespoon water

1. Place all the marinade ingredients in a shallow bowl. Stir marinade with a fork until cornstarch is dissolved and mixture is smooth.
2. Add chicken and toss well to coat each piece. Marinate chicken at room temperature for 15 minutes.

To Assemble and Cook

1 medium-sized carrot (4 ounces), trimmed, peeled, and thinly sliced diagonally to make ½ cup
1 medium-sized zucchini (6 ounces)
1 tablespoon vegetable oil, preferably corn oil

¼ cup thinly sliced scallions
⅛ teaspoon red pepper flakes
½ cup unsalted chicken broth, preferably homemade (page 51)
1 teaspoon cornstarch
1 tablespoon water

1. Cook carrot in 2 cups boiling water until barely tender, about 2 minutes. Transfer to strainer, refresh under cold water, blot dry with paper towel, and place in a deep bowl.
2. Scrub zucchini under cold running water until the skin feels clean and smooth. Trim both ends. Cut zucchini lengthwise in half and then slice diagonally into ½-inch pieces. Add to bowl with carrots.
3. Heat wok or heavy 12-inch skillet over high heat for 1 minute. When a drop of water sizzles immediately on contact with pan, slowly pour in 2 teaspoons oil and swirl pan to coat surface. Turn heat down to medium. To stir-fry, add chicken and toss lightly with a long metal spatula. Cook, stirring and lightly tossing constantly to separate the shreds, until meat turns white, about 1 to 1½ minutes. Transfer chicken to platter with spatula.
4. Add remaining teaspoon of oil and swirl pan once again to coat. Turn heat to medium-high, add scallions and pepper flakes, and

stir-fry for 5 seconds. Add carrots and zucchini and continue to stir-fry for 30 seconds. Stir in broth, turn heat to high, and continue to stir-fry just until zucchini pieces are barely tender, about 1 minute.

5. In a small bowl, combine cornstarch with water and stir until cornstarch is dissolved.
6. Return chicken to pan and stir to combine over high heat. Pour cornstarch mixture into pan and continue to stir-fry until glaze coats the chicken and vegetables, about 30 seconds. Transfer to platter and serve immediately.

Chicken Salad with Yogurt Mint Dressing

Chicken tossed with grapes and pineapple and enveloped in this silky dressing makes a most refreshing salad to serve during hot weather. Whole Wheat Cinnamon Muffins (page 330) or Blueberry Muffins (page 325) would be an excellent accompaniment.

SERVES 2

1 whole chicken breast (about 1 pound 4 ounces)
1 small yellow onion (3 ounces), peeled and cut into 2-inch wedges
1 small carrot (2 ounces), trimmed, scrubbed, and cut into 2-inch pieces.

1 small celery rib (2 ounces), trimmed, scrubbed, and cut into 2-inch pieces
3 parsley stems
4 whole peppercorns

1. Wash chicken breast in cold water and place in a 3½-quart saucepan. Place onion, carrot, and celery pieces around chicken. Add parsley and peppercorns. Add enough cold water to pan to cover

chicken by 1 inch. Partially cover pan and slowly bring to a boil over low heat. As soon as liquid reaches a boil, simmer chicken over low heat for 30 minutes. Remove from heat, cover pan, and let chicken cool in broth to room temperature.

2. Skin and bone chicken. Cut breast into 1-inch cubes; set aside. Strain broth through a strainer set over a bowl. Save broth or freeze for another meal. (Chicken may be cooked one day before making salad. After skinning and boning, place in a 1½-quart wide-mouth jar, completely cover with strained broth to keep chicken pieces moist, and refrigerate overnight.)

Yogurt Mint Dressing

1½ tablespoons mayonnaise, preferably homemade (page 263)

3 tablespoons low-fat yogurt

2 teaspoons fresh lemon juice, strained

½ teaspoon honey, preferably orange blossom

⅛ teaspoon salt, if desired

⅛ teaspoon freshly milled white pepper

1½ teaspoons minced fresh mint or ½ teaspoon crumbled dried mint

Place all of the dressing ingredients in a small bowl. Beat with fork or whisk to combine.

To Assemble

¼ cup thinly sliced celery, strings removed

½ cup red seedless grapes, washed, blotted dry with paper towel, and sliced in half lengthwise

½ cup canned unsweetened Dole pineapple tidbits, thoroughly drained

1 medium-sized head Belgian endive (2 ounces)

1 tablespoon toasted slivered almonds (optional garnish)

1. In a deep bowl, place chicken, sliced celery, grapes, and pineapple; toss lightly with two forks to combine. Pour dressing over salad and lightly toss to combine. Cover with plastic wrap and refrigerate for 2 hours. (Salad may be made up to 4 hours before serving.)
2. Separate leaves from Belgian endive; wipe each leaf with a damp cloth to remove sand. (Endive may be cleaned up to 3 hours before serving salad; place in plastic bag, seal tightly, and refrigerate until needed.)
3. When ready to serve, arrange endive leaves in an outer border on platter. Lightly toss salad once again, spoon in center, and garnish with toasted almonds.

Oven-barbecued Chicken Thighs

To many, barbecuing means cooking outdoors on a grill. This indoor version bakes in the oven in 50 minutes with an authentic zippy hot sauce.

SERVES 2

¼ cup minced yellow onion
1½ tablespoons ketchup
2 teaspoons light brown sugar
¼ teaspoon dry mustard
¼ teaspoon red pepper flakes
2 tablespoons distilled white vinegar

½ cup apple juice
4 large chicken thighs (1 pound 4 ounces total weight), see Note
Curly parsley sprigs (garnish)

1. In a 1½-quart saucepan, combine onion, ketchup, brown sugar, mustard, pepper flakes, vinegar, and apple juice. Bring mixture to a boil over high heat. Turn heat to medium and cook, uncovered,

stirring frequently until barbecue sauce is slightly thickened, about 6 minutes. Remove from heat and let cool to room temperature.

2. Wash chicken thighs and blot dry with paper towel. Place thighs on work surface with skin side up. Slip your finger tips under the skin to loosen. Peel off skin carefully to avoid tearing the meat. Use knife to cut away any connecting membrane. Discard skin. Trim off any membrane or bits of fat that may still be attached to the thighs.

3. Place chicken in a single layer in a shallow 1½-quart ovenproof casserole. Spoon 4 tablespoons barbecue sauce over chicken; reserve remaining ¼ cup sauce. Cover chicken with plastic wrap and marinate in refrigerator for at least 2 hours, turning chicken twice. Return chicken to room temperature 15 minutes before cooking. Arrange thighs meaty sides down in casserole.

4. Adjust rack to center of oven and preheat to 350 degrees.

5. Cook chicken, covered, in preheated oven for 25 minutes, basting once with sauce. Remove chicken from oven and turn oven temperature up to 375 degrees. Turn thighs meaty side up. Spoon reserved barbecue sauce over chicken. Return to oven and continue cooking, uncovered, basting frequently until thighs are golden and glazed, about 25 minutes. Transfer to platter and spoon sauce over chicken. (If some of the sauce sticks to bottom of pan, add 1 teaspoon hot water and stir to loosen with a spoon.) Garnish with parsley sprigs and serve immediately.

NOTE: If you cannot find four large chicken thighs at the market, purchase 4 whole legs weighing approximately 2 pounds 8 ounces. Place the whole leg on a board with skin side down. With a chef's knife, cut firmly down through the joint between the drumstick and thigh to separate the two pieces. Wrap drumsticks in plastic wrap, place in plastic bag, seal tightly, and freeze for another meal.

⋘

Peachy Drumsticks with Orange Sauce

The slight hint of ginger adds zest to the orange sauce. A spicy accompaniment to this dish is Barley Pilaf with Raisins (page 118).

SERVES 2

4 large chicken legs (1 pound 4 ounces total weight)

One 8¾-ounce can (Del Monte) sliced yellow cling peaches in heavy syrup

½ cup fresh orange juice, strained

2 teaspoons low-sodium soy sauce (Kikkoman Lite)

2 teaspoons cornstarch

½ teaspoon powdered ginger

1. Adjust rack to center of oven and preheat to 350 degrees.
2. Wash chicken legs and blot dry with paper towel; place chicken legs on work surface. Starting at top of leg, slip your fingertips under the skin to loosen. Peel off skin carefully, using a pair of kitchen shears to snip the skin and any connecting membrane to avoid tearing the meat; discard skin. Trim off any membrane or bits of fat that may still be attached to leg. Place chicken legs in a single layer in a 1½-quart ovenproof casserole.
3. Drain peaches in a strainer set over a bowl. Reserve ¼ cup of the syrup; discard remaining syrup.
4. In a small saucepan, place ¼ cup peach syrup, orange juice, soy sauce, cornstarch, and ginger. Stir with whisk until cornstarch is completely dissolved. Cook, uncovered, over medium heat, whisking constantly, until sauce is slightly thickened, about 1 to 2 minutes.
5. Spoon orange sauce over chicken. Cook, covered, in preheated oven for 20 minutes. Remove chicken from oven and turn oven temperature up to 375 degrees.
6. Return chicken to oven and continue cooking, uncovered, basting and turning legs every 5 minutes until lightly golden and glazed, about 20 minutes longer. Add peaches to casserole and spoon some of the sauce over them. Continue cooking, uncovered, just until peaches are heated, about 2 minutes.

Broiled Rock Cornish Game Hen

To ensure that bird will turn crisp, brown without burning, and cook through evenly, broil 6 inches from the heat source. Always remove the wing tips so that protruding wings will not char during the time it takes the breast to cook.

SERVES 2

1 Rock Cornish game hen
(about 1½ pounds)
2 tablespoons fresh lemon
juice, strained
½ teaspoon minced garlic
½ teaspoon Dijon mustard
1½ teaspoons minced fresh
savory or ½ teaspoon
crumbled dried savory

¼ teaspoon freshly milled
black pepper
2 teaspoons olive oil
Several curly parsley
sprigs (garnish)

1. Rinse hen under cold water and blot dry inside and out with paper towel. Trim any fat from rear cavity. Place hen on work surface with breast side down. Using kitchen shears, snip through one side of neck down backbone. Snip along other side of backbone down to the tail; discard backbone. Turn hen over and clip wing tips off at the first joint. Grasp the top of the breast on each side of the breastbone and bend the breast backward until the breastbone snaps. Carefully remove the bone and attached cartilage using your fingers and a small sharp knife. With breast side down, slice hen in half lengthwise.
2. Place lemon juice, garlic, mustard, savory, and pepper in a small bowl. Using a fork or small whisk, beat to combine. Add oil a little at a time and whisk to thoroughly combine marinade.
3. Place split hen in a shallow bowl. Using your hands, rub marinade into both surfaces of hen. Cover with plastic wrap and marinate in refrigerator for at least 3 hours, turning twice in marinade. Remove from refrigerator ½ hour before broiling.
4. Remove broiler rack and pan from oven and preheat broiler for 15 minutes. Lightly grease broiler rack.

5. Using a narrow metal spatula or the back of a knife, scrape marinade off both surfaces into bowl; reserve marinade. Blot hen dry with paper towel.

6. Place hen, skin side down, on prepared rack over broiler pan and position hen 6 inches from heat source. Broil until lightly golden, about 15 minutes. Remove from oven and brush half of the reserved marinade over surface. Return to oven and continue broiling until golden brown, about 15 minutes longer. Remove from oven and, using long-handled tongs, carefully turn the hen skin side up. (Using tongs will prevent piercing the flesh and letting the juices run out). Return to oven and broil until skin is a light golden color, about 15 minutes more. Remove from oven and baste with remaining marinade. Return to oven and broil until the skin has turned a deep golden brown, about 15 minutes longer.

7. To test for doneness, place split hen on a white plate with skin side down. Using a small knife, make a slit about ½ inch deep into the thickest part of the thigh. If the juices that run out are pale yellow, the bird is done. If the juices are pink, turn oven temperature down to 375 degrees, cover pan with a loose tent of foil and place in oven. Cook for an additional 10 minutes. Test for doneness once again.

8. Place split hen on a platter, garnish with parsley, and serve immediately.

⇜

Glazed Rock Cornish Game Hen

The delicate taste of these glazed Cornish game hens are enhanced by the light honey orange sauce made with the pan juices.

S E R V E S 2

1 Rock Cornish game hen (about 1½ pounds)
1 large clove garlic, split in half
¼ cup fresh orange juice, strained
2 teaspoons low-sodium light soy sauce (Kikkoman Lite)
2 teaspoons honey, preferably orange blossom
¼ teaspoon ground ginger
1 teaspoon apple cider vinegar
Several curly parsley sprigs (optional garnish)

1. Adjust rack to center of oven and preheat to 350 degrees.
2. Rinse hen under cold water and blot dry inside and out with paper towel. Thoroughly rub surface of hen with split garlic, then place garlic in rear cavity. Truss hen with kitchen twine or simply tie legs and wings in place with twine.
3. Place orange juice, soy sauce, honey, ginger, and vinegar in a small bowl. Beat with a fork or small whisk to combine; set aside.
4. Place hen on rack in roasting pan breast side up. Roast until skin is a very light golden color, about 50 minutes. To test for doneness, remove hen from roasting rack with two forks and tip it up on its tail over a white plate. If the juices that run out are pale yellow, the hen is done. If the juices are pale pink, cover hen with a loose tent of foil, return to oven, and roast for an additional 10 minutes. Test for doneness once again.
5. Remove pan from oven and pour off any drippings in bottom of pan. If using foil, discard.
6. Whisk glaze once again. Turn hen breast side down on rack. Brush with half of the glaze and bake until bottom surface is glazed, about 5 minutes. Remove from oven and turn hen breast side up. Brush with remaining glaze and bake until top surface of hen is glazed, about 5 to 7 minutes.

7. Transfer hen to platter and let rest for 10 minutes before serving.
8. Add ¼ cup water to pan and place over medium high heat. Cook pan juices, scraping any fragments that cling to bottom of pan with wooden spoon. Pour sauce through a strainer set over a small pan; keep warm over low heat.
9. Remove twine from hen and discard garlic from rear cavity. Place hen on a serving platter and garnish with parsley. Serve sauce separately.

Turkey Cutlets with Mushrooms and Tarragon

Deglazing the pan with dry vermouth enriches the sauce of this mushroom-and tarragon-garnished entrée.

SERVES 2

2 turkey cutlets (8 ounces total weight), each ¼ inch thick	¼ pound medium-sized mushrooms, wiped, trimmed, and sliced in half
2 teaspoons Wondra flour	1½ teaspoons minced fresh tarragon or ½ teaspoon crumbled dried tarragon
¼ teaspoon freshly milled black pepper	
1 tablespoon olive oil	
¼ cup dry vermouth	⅛ teaspoon salt, if desired
1 large shallot (2 ounces), peeled and thinly sliced to make ¼ cup	2 teaspoons minced Italian parsley leaves (garnish)

1. Holding knife at a slight angle, slice each cutlet crosswise into 2 pieces. (You will be slicing on a bias and cutting against the grain.)
2. In a shallow bowl, combine flour and pepper. Lightly dredge each

piece of turkey in seasoned flour and shake off excess. (Dredge just before sautéing or the flour coating will become gummy.)

3. In a 10-inch skillet, heat oil over medium-high heat. Sauté turkey pieces, turning once, until lightly golden on both sides, about 1½ minutes on each side. Transfer turkey to a plate.

4. Add vermouth and turn heat to high, scraping any fragments that cling to bottom of pan with wooden spoon. Cook until vermouth is reduced by half, about 1 minute. Stir in shallots and sauté until crisp tender, about 1 minute. Stir in mushrooms and sauté just until they start to exude their juices, about 2 minutes. Stir in tarragon and mix well to combine. Return turkey to pan and cook, spooning mushrooms and pan juices over turkey for an additional 30 seconds. Season with salt; remove from heat.

5. Transfer to platter, garnish with minced parsley, and serve immediately.

Turkey Cutlets with Tomato Sauce

The slight hint of lemon rind in the bread crumb coating adds a distinctive taste to these cutlets.

S E R V E S 2

2 tablespoons Wondra Flour	2 turkey cutlets (8 ounces total weight), each ¼ inch thick
⅛ teaspoon freshly milled black pepper	
1 large egg	1 tablespoon olive oil
1½ teaspoons cold water	¼ cup Tomato Basil Sauce (page 75)
½ cup fine dry bread crumbs	
1 teaspoon minced Italian parsley leaves	1 teaspoon minced Italian parsley leaves (garnish)
1 teaspoon finely grated lemon rind	

1. In a shallow bowl, combine flour and pepper. In another shallow bowl beat egg and cold water with a fork. On a flat plate, combine bread crumbs, parsley, and lemon rind. Dredge cutlets in seasoned flour, dip in beaten egg, and then thoroughly coat with bread crumb mixture. Refrigerate cutlets in a single layer on a plate lined with waxed paper for at least 1 hour (chilling prevents coating from coming off during sautéing.)
2. In a 12-inch skillet, heat oil over medium-high heat. Sauté the cutlets on one side until lightly golden, about 2 minutes. Turn the cutlets, partially cover the skillet, and sauté on second side until cutlets feel firm but springy to the touch, about 2 minutes more. Transfer cutlets to serving platter.
3. While cutlets are sautéing on second side, heat Tomato Basil Sauce over low heat.
4. Spoon 2 tablespoons of the sauce over each cutlet and garnish each with a little minced parsley; serve immediately.

FISH AND SEAFOOD

❮❮❮

A fish-eating society has been evolving during the past ten years. I attribute this to people being more aware of healthy eating habits and to the improved marketing and distribution of fresh fish and seafood.

When you add fresh fish to your diet, you are adding taste, variety, and valuable nutrients. Fresh fish has little waste and loses little of its food value when cooked properly. It is high in protein, low in calories, and a source of important vitamins and minerals. Because of its nutritional value, fish is often referred to as nature's most nearly perfect food, ideal for people of all ages from young toddlers to senior citizens.

With today's efficient cross-country transportation in refrigerated trucks and planes, it is possible to purchase fresh fish and seafood of the highest quality at local supermarkets or fish markets.

All over the country, people are developing a new appreciation for fish, are learning how to handle it more comfortably and cook it with imagination and style. Whether it be broiled, grilled, baked, poached, or oven-fried, whether served hot or cold, fish and shell fish are indispensable to today's cook, especially to those who are in a hurry or do not want to spend hours in the kitchen. Many cuts of meat, notably beef and pork, require longer periods of cooking to become tender, but all fish and seafood are by contrast naturally tender and require relatively brief cooking times.

Most of my childhood summer vacations were spent with my family at the New Jersey shore. As we sat on the beach, we could see the fishing boats come into the inlet of the Manasquan River. It was always fun to go down to the fishing pier and watch the sea captains and crew unload the catch of the day. Like any curious child, I enjoyed looking at the fish with their clear protruding eyes and black pupils, bright red gills, and shiny, tightly adhering scales. Naturally, my inquisitive instinct always prompted me to touch the fish and feel the firm elastic flesh spring back when pressed with my finger. I can still remember the faintly sweet, appetizing aroma of the sea as the fish were sorted, cleaned, and packed in ice to be shipped to restaurants or local markets. Little did I know then that I was being taught my first lesson in using my eyes and nose to sharpen my sea sense in selecting fresh fish.

The following pointers are offered to help sharpen your sea sense:

- *Remember, freshness is the key to quality. When a recipe requires a particular fish that is not available fresh, substitute another appropriate fresh fish, if possible, or choose a different recipe.*
- *Watch closely when your fish seller picks up the fish. The flesh of the fillet should be white or almost translucent and should appear firm and resilient. If the fillets have a yellow tinge along the cut surface, the fish is spoiling.*
- *Do not purchase fish that is prewrapped. In selecting fresh fish, the first thing to do is smell the fish. There should be no smell at all or a mild fresh aroma like seawater or seaweed. Reject any fish that has a fishy odor—this is an early sign of decomposition.*
- *Always make the fish store or fish department in the supermarket your last stop when shopping so that your purchase is unrefrigerated for the shortest possible time. When you get home, unwrap fish immediately, thoroughly wash in cold water, and pat dry with paper towel.*
- *Fresh fish should be eaten the same day of purchase. If the fish must be stored, cover it loosely with plastic wrap and keep it in the coldest part of your refrigerator, but no longer than two days.*

The recipes in this chapter offer flavorful opportunities to create dishes that should be just right to introduce you to a culinary pleasure you may have been missing.

⫷⫷⫷

Cod Stew

This stew has a tantalizing mild and subtle flavor. The careful layering of ingredients adds to its delicate appeal. Broccoli with Garlic and Lemon (page 228) would be an excellent accompaniment to this hearty one-dish meal.

SERVES 2

1 skinless fillet of cod about 1 inch thick (12 ounces)
1 tablespoon olive oil
1 medium-sized yellow onion (5 ounces), peeled, halved, and cut into ½-inch slices
2 large celery ribs (4 ounces), strings removed and cut into 2-inch lengths
1 large Idaho potato (8 ounces), peeled and sliced into ½-inch rounds

⅛ teaspoon salt, if desired
¼ teaspoon freshly milled black pepper, divided
½ cup canned whole peeled tomatoes, coarsely chopped, juice included
2 medium bay leaves, broken in half
2 tablespoons water

1. Rinse fillet with cold water and blot dry with paper towel. Cut fillet crosswise into 4 even pieces; set aside.
2. Drizzle 1 teaspoon olive oil in bottom of a 3-quart dutch oven. Place onion in a single layer in pan. Arrange celery in a single layer on top of onion. Place sliced potatoes on top of celery in a single layer and sprinkle with salt and ⅛ teaspoon pepper. Place cut cod fillet in a single layer on top of potatoes. Place ½ bay leaf on top of each piece of fillet. Spoon chopped tomato on top of fish and season with remaining ⅛ teaspoon pepper. Drizzle remaining 2 teaspoons olive oil over tomatoes and add water to bottom of pan.
3. Cover pan and cook over medium-low heat, basting frequently with cooking liquid, until potatoes are cooked when tested with the tip of a fork, about 30 to 40 minutes. Check cooking liquid frequently; if the dutch oven is not a heavy one, you may have to add a few more teaspoons of water to keep mixture moist. Remove from heat and discard bay leaves.

4. Use two large serving spoons to carefully lift portions into individual bowls. Spoon a little of the pan juices on top and serve immediately.

Poached Fish Rolls in Tomato Wine Sauce

Turbot is a delicate, sweet-tasting fish that is a member of the flatfish or flounder family. If turbot is unavailable, you may substitute fillets of lemon sole.

SERVES 2

2 skinless fillets of turbot, each ¼ inch thick (about 8 ounces total weight)
2 teaspoons olive oil
½ teaspoon minced garlic
½ cup canned whole peeled tomatoes, finely chopped including juice (can be chopped in food processor fitted with metal blade)

⅓ cup dry white wine
¼ teaspoon dry mustard
1 small bay leaf
1 scant teaspoon minced fresh thyme or ¼ teaspoon crumbled dried thyme
⅛ teaspoon salt, if desired
⅛ teaspoon freshly milled black pepper

1. Wash fillets under cold water and blot dry with paper towel. Place fillets on a work surface. Cut each fillet in half lengthwise. With skinned side down, and starting from broad end, roll each piece jelly roll fashion into a cylinder.
2. Adjust rack to center of oven and preheat to 200 degrees.
3. In a 10-inch skillet, heat oil over medium-low heat. Add garlic and sauté until very lightly golden, about 1 minute. Add tomato, wine, mustard, and bay leaf. Bring sauce to a boil and cook for 1 minute,

stirring constantly with a wooden spoon. Turn heat down to low. Arrange fish rolls seam side down in single layer in pan. Cover pan and poach rolls, basting frequently, until easily flaked when tested with a toothpick, about 6 to 7 minutes. Remove from heat.

4. Using two forks, carefully transfer rolls to an ovenproof serving platter. Place in oven to keep warm while finishing sauce.

5. Turn heat to high and cook sauce, stirring constantly, until slightly thickened, about 1½ to 2 minutes. Stir in thyme. Season with salt and pepper and remove from heat. Remove bay leaf from sauce. Spoon sauce over fish rolls and serve immediately.

Broiled Flounder with Thyme

Nothing is better than a piece of simply broiled fish. The bread crumb coating on the surface of the fillet will keep fish moist during broiling.

SERVES 2

1 skinless fillet of flounder ½ inch thick (about 12 ounces)

1 tablespoon dry bread crumbs

⅛ teaspoon salt, if desired

⅛ teaspoon paprika

1 scant teaspoon minced fresh thyme or ¼ teaspoon crumbled dried thyme

2 teaspoons olive oil

1 tablespoon fresh lemon juice, strained

1. Remove broiler rack and pan from oven and preheat broiler for 15 minutes. Lightly grease broiler rack.

2. Wash fillet in cold water and thoroughly blot dry with paper towel. Slice fillet in half crosswise and place pieces about 2 inches apart on prepared rack.

3. In a small bowl, combine bread crumbs, salt, paprika, and thyme. Using a small pastry brush, evenly spread 1 teaspoon oil over

entire surface of each half of the fillet. Sprinkle bread crumb mixture on top of fish.

4. Position broiler pan so that the fish will be 5 inches from heat source. Broil until surface of fish is lightly golden and barely flakes when tested with a fork, about 7 to 8 minutes. (The fish does not have to be turned.)
5. Remove from oven and transfer to platter. Spoon lemon juice over each portion and serve immediately.

Broiled Halibut Steaks with Herbs

Marinating the halibut before cooking adds subtle flavor and will keep steaks juicy and moist while broiling. Swordfish or salmon steaks may be substituted for the halibut.

SERVES 2

2 halibut steaks, each about 1 inch thick (12 ounces total weight)
¼ cup fresh lemon juice, strained
1 teaspoon minced garlic
1 scant teaspoon minced fresh oregano or ¼ teaspoon crumbled dried oregano

1½ teaspoons snipped fresh dill or ½ teaspoon crumbled dried dillweed

1. Rinse steaks under cold water and blot dry with paper towel. Place steaks in a single layer in a shallow dish.
2. Place lemon juice, garlic, oregano, and dill in a small bowl. Beat with fork or small whisk to combine marinade. Spoon marinade

over fish and turn the steaks once to coat thoroughly. Marinate at room temperature for 30 minutes.

3. Remove broiler rack and pan from oven and preheat broiler for 15 minutes. Lightly grease broiler rack.

4. Using a pair of tongs, lift steaks out of marinade. Scrape marinade off steaks with the back of a knife; reserve marinade for basting.

5. Place steaks about 2 inches apart on prepared rack. Position broiler pan so that the fish will be 5 inches from heat source. Broil steaks, basting once with half of the reserved marinade, until surface is golden, about 5 minutes. Remove broiler pan and carefully turn steaks with a wide metal spatula. Spoon remaining marinade over steaks and broil until second side is golden, about 5 minutes. To test for doneness, slip a small knife between the bone and the flesh; if the fish is sufficiently cooked, the flesh will separate easily from the bone. Transfer to platter and serve immediately.

Broiled Monkfish with Mustard and Chives

This fish was once called the "poor man's lobster" because of its sweet flavor. This recipe is equally as good with tilefish, grouper, or sea bass fillets.

SERVES 2

1 skinless monkfish fillet 1 inch thick (12 ounces)

¼ teaspoon freshly milled white pepper

2 teaspoons Dijon mustard, divided

1 tablespoon unsalted margarine, melted

1 tablespoon minced chives

1. Preheat oven on broil setting for 15 minutes. Lightly grease a shallow ovenproof baking dish large enough to hold the monkfish; set aside.
2. Wash fillet in cold water and thoroughly blot dry with paper towel.
3. Rub pepper into both surfaces of fish. Place fillet in prepared pan. Using a small pastry brush, brush surface of fish with 1 teaspoon mustard. Spoon 1½ teaspoons melted margarine over fish.
4. Position broiler pan so that the fish will be 5 inches from the heat source. Broil fillet until very lightly golden, about 3 to 4 minutes. Remove from oven and carefully turn fish with a wide metal spatula. Brush surface with remaining mustard and spoon remaining melted margarine over top. Return to oven and broil until second side of fish is lightly golden and barely flakes when tested with a fork, about 4 to 5 minutes.
5. Remove from oven and sprinkle chives over surface; serve immediately.

Poached Salmon with Dill Sauce

Poaching the salmon steaks in this mild vegetable and wine mixture (court boullion) will keep them very moist. The court boullion will be transformed into a delicate dill sauce to gracefully dress these steaks. The Grapefruit Salad with Watercress Dressing (page 252) would be an excellent accompaniment to this entrée.

S E R V E S   2

2 salmon steaks, each about 1 inch thick (12 ounces total weight)
2 teaspoons unsalted margarine
¼ cup minced yellow onion
¼ cup minced carrot
¼ cup minced celery, strings removed
¼ teaspoon freshly milled black pepper
1 to 1½ cups dry white wine

1. Wash steaks in cold water and thoroughly blot dry with paper towel; set aside.
2. In a 10-inch sauté pan, melt margarine over medium heat. Add onion, carrot, and celery; cover pan and cook, stirring once or twice, until soft but not brown, about 5 minutes. Remove pan from heat; spread vegetable mixture evenly in bottom of pan.
3. Place steaks in single layer on top of vegetable mixture and season with pepper. Add 1 cup of wine to pan (wine should barely cover top of steaks; add more if necessary). Cover pan and bring court boullion to a slow boil over medium heat. As soon as it comes to a boil, turn heat to low. Poach salmon, covered, until steaks turn a light pink color all the way through, about 8 to 10 minutes. After 8 minutes of poaching, remove pot lid and with the tip of a small sharp knife, gently separate the flesh as its thickest point. If the interior of the flesh is opaque (light pink) and barely begins to flake, the fish is done.
4. Adjust rack to center of oven and preheat to 200 degrees.
5. Using 2 wide spatulas, carefully transfer steaks to an ovenproof platter. Spoon 1 tablespoon of the court boullion on top of steaks (to keep steaks moist) and place in preheated oven to keep warm while making sauce.
6. Pour court boullion through strainer set over a bowl; reserve solids in strainer. Measure ½ cup strained liquid and combine with solids from strainer; reserve for sauce. Discard remaining liquid.
7. Transfer mixture to blender or food processor fitted with metal blade. Run machine nonstop until vegetables are finely puréed, stopping machine once or twice to scrape inside work bowl with plastic spatula. Transfer to a 1½-quart saucepan.

Dill Sauce

1 teaspoon arrowroot
1 tablespoon cold water
1½ teaspoons minced fresh dill or ½ teaspoon crumbled dried dillweed
2 teaspoons minced Italian parsley leaves

⅛ teaspoon freshly milled black pepper
6 sprigs watercress, tough lower stems discarded (garnish)

1. To complete the dill sauce, dissolve arrowroot in cold water in a small bowl and stir into puréed mixture in saucepan. Cook over medium-low heat, stirring constantly, until slightly thickened, about 3 minutes. Stir in dill and parsley. Season with salt and pepper and remove from heat.
2. Spread 2 tablespoons of heated sauce on individual plates. Remove steaks from oven and place in center of plates. With your fingertips, slightly overlap steak tails. Spoon 2 tablespoons sauce on top of each steak. Place 3 sprigs of watercress in cavity just above overlapped tails; serve immediately.

Sautéed Scallops with Mushroom Herb Sauce

The sauce adds tantalizing flavor to the tender sautéed scallops. A good addition to this entrée would be Rice with Zucchini (page 107).

SERVES 2

2 large ripe plum tomatoes (8 ounces total weight)
½ pound sea scallops
2 tablespoons Wondra flour
¼ teaspoon freshly milled black pepper
1 tablespoon olive oil
¼ cup thinly sliced scallions
6 medium-sized mushrooms (3 ounces), trimmed, wiped, and thinly sliced to make 1 cup
¼ cup dry vermouth

1 scant teaspoon minced fresh thyme or ¼ teaspoon crumbled dried thyme
1½ teaspoons minced fresh basil or ½ teaspoon crumbled dried basil
⅛ teaspoon salt, if desired
1 tablespoon fresh lemon juice, strained
1 tablespoon minced Italian parsley leaves

1. Plump fresh tomatoes in 1 quart boiling water for 1 minute. Rinse under cold water, core tomatoes, and peel with a small paring knife. Cut tomatoes in half lengthwise. Gently squeeze each half and discard most of the seeds. Cut tomatoes into ½-inch cubes and place in strainer over a bowl to drain thoroughly; discard juice.

2. Wash scallops in cold water and thoroughly blot dry with paper towel. If scallops are more than 1 inch in diameter, slice in half crosswise.

3. In a shallow bowl, combine flour and pepper. Lightly dredge scallops in seasoned flour and shake off excess. (Dredge just before sautéing or the flour coating will become gummy.)

4. In a 10-inch skillet, heat oil over medium-high heat. Sauté scallops, turning once, just until they are lightly golden and feel slightly firm to the touch, about 1½ minutes on each side. Using a slotted spoon, transfer scallops to a plate.

5. Turn heat down to medium, add scallions, and cook until crisp tender, about 1 minute, scraping any fragments that cling to bottom of pan with wooden spoon. Turn heat to high, add mushrooms, and sauté, stirring constantly, just until they begin to exude their juices, about 30 seconds. Add vermouth, stirring constantly until liquid in pan is reduced by half, about 30 seconds. Stir in diced tomatoes, thyme, and basil. Continue cooking over high heat, stirring constantly until very little liquid is left in bottom of pan and sauce is slightly thickened, about 1 minute.

6. Return scallops and any accumulated juices on plate to pan. Cook mixture, stirring constantly, over medium-high heat, until scallops are heated through, about 30 seconds. Season with salt; stir in lemon juice and parsley. Remove from heat. Transfer to platter and serve immediately.

<<<

Cleaning Shrimp

Using a sharp pair of kitchen shears, cut shell down back of shrimp to tail (you will be exposing the black intestinal vein as you cut). Peel off shell to tail. With your thumb and index finger pinch tail and pull off remaining tail shell (this will leave tail meat intact). Under cold running water lift out intestinal vein with fingers and discard. Wash shrimp in cold water and thoroughly blot dry with paper towel.

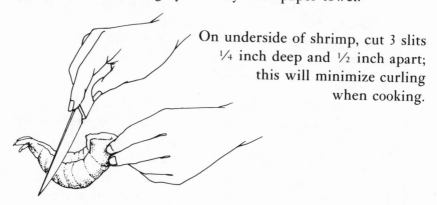

On underside of shrimp, cut 3 slits ¼ inch deep and ½ inch apart; this will minimize curling when cooking.

Speedy Shrimp Scampi

This delectable scampi recipe is simple to prepare and can be on the table in a matter of minutes.

SERVES 2

1 tablespoon olive oil
½ teaspoon minced garlic
½ pound medium-sized shrimp, shelled and deveined (see directions for shelling and cleaning, page 205)
1 tablespoon lemon juice, strained
2 tablespoons dry white wine

1 tablespoon dry bread crumbs
⅛ teaspoon salt, if desired
⅛ teaspoon freshly milled black pepper
2 teaspoons minced Italian parsley
2 lemon wedges (optional garnish)

1. In a 10-inch skillet, heat oil over low heat. Add garlic and sauté, stirring constantly with a wooden spoon until very lightly golden, about 1 minute. Add shrimp, turn heat to medium-high, and sauté, stirring constantly until they turn pink, about 1½ minutes. Turn heat to high; stir in lemon juice and wine. Cook, stirring constantly just until blended, about 20 seconds. Stir in bread crumbs and cook, stirring constantly until crumbs absorb most of the pan juices. Season with salt and pepper; stir in minced parsley and remove from heat.
2. Transfer to individual serving plates and garnish each plate with a lemon wedge; serve immediately.

⋘

Shrimp and Snow Pea Salad

An eye-catching, delicious salad that can be served as a main course for lunch or supper. An excellent first course for this entrée would be a cup of Chilled Cucumber Soup (page 57).

SERVES 2

1 tablespoon fresh lemon juice

½ pound medium-sized shrimp, shelled and deveined (see directions for shelling and cleaning, page 205)

In a 12-inch skillet, bring 2 cups water to a boil with lemon juice. Place shrimp in pan in single layer and cover. Bring to a boil. As soon as water reaches a boil, uncover and cook shrimp just until they turn pink, about 2 minutes. Drain in strainer and cool to room temperature. Blot shrimp dry with paper towel and transfer to bowl.

Dressing

1 tablespoon minced scallion, green part only (reserve white part for garnish)
2 teaspoons fresh lemon juice, strained
¼ teaspoon Dijon mustard

⅛ teaspoon sugar
⅛ teaspoon freshly milled white pepper
1 tablespoon olive oil, preferably extra virgin

1. Place all the dressing ingredients except oil in a small bowl. Stir with a fork or small whisk to combine. Add oil a little at a time and whisk thoroughly to incorporate.
2. Pour dressing over shrimp and toss lightly. Cover with plastic wrap and refrigerate for 2 hours (do not marinate any longer or shrimp will become soggy).

To Assemble

16 snow peas (about 3 ounces)   1 tablespoon thinly sliced
                                  scallion (white part only)

1. Using a small paring knife, slice through the stem end of each snow pea but do not sever the string. Holding the pod between your index finger and thumb, peel the stem end and attached string down the pod. On opposite end, remove the little tip and repeat to pull off second string. Thoroughly wash snow peas in cold water and transfer to strainer to drain. Blanch snow peas in 1 quart boiling water just until they start to puff up, about 1 minute. Transfer to a strainer, refresh under cold water, and blot dry with paper towel. (Snow peas can be prepared up to 3 hours before serving. Place on small plate lined with paper towel, cover with plastic wrap, and refrigerate until needed.)
2. When ready to serve, arrange 8 snow peas in an outer border on two salad plates. Toss shrimp in dressing again and spoon into center of each plate; garnish with scallion and serve.

⫷

Poached Red Snapper with Tomato Dill Sauce

The assertive flavoring of this sauce enhances the poached snapper. It is equally delicious with fillet of sole sliced to a thickness of 1/2 inch so that poaching time will be the same. This recipe is an adaptation of one developed by my daughter Amy for a popular Manhattan restaurant.

SERVES 2

Tomato Dill Sauce

2 teaspoons olive oil
1/2 teaspoon minced garlic
1/2 cup canned whole peeled tomatoes, well drained and finely chopped (can be chopped in food processor fitted with metal blade)

1/8 teaspoon sugar
1 scant teaspoon minced fresh dill or 1/4 teaspoon crumbled dried dillweed
1/8 teaspoon salt, if desired
1/8 teaspoon freshly milled black pepper

First, prepare sauce; in a small saucepan, heat oil over medium heat. Add garlic and sauté, stirring constantly with wooden spoon until very lightly golden, about 30 seconds. Add tomatoes and sugar. Turn heat to high and bring sauce to a boil, stirring constantly. As soon as sauce reaches a boil, turn heat down to low. Cook, partially covered, stirring frequently, until sauce is slightly thickened, about 5 to 7 minutes. Stir in dill; season with salt and pepper. Cover pan and remove from heat. (Sauce may be made up to 2 hours before poaching fish. Reheat, covered, over low heat just before serving.)

⋘

To Assemble and Cook

2 medium-sized limes (6 ounces total weight), ends trimmed and each sliced into 6 thin rounds

2 unskinned boneless red snapper fillets, each about ½ inch thick (12 ounces total weight)

½ cup dry white wine

½ to ¾ cup water, approximately

1 tablespoon minced Italian parsley leaves (garnish)

1. Line bottom of a 10-inch sauté pan with lime slices. Place fillets on top of lime slices skin side down. Add wine and enough water to pan to barely cover top of fillets. Cover pan and bring liquid to a low boil over medium-low heat. As soon as liquid comes to a low boil, turn heat to low. Poach fillets, covered, just until they are firm and opaque and barely begin to flake when tested with a toothpick, about 5 minutes.

2. Using a slotted spatula or two forks, transfer fillets to individual dinner plates with skinned side down. Spoon heated sauce over fillets, garnish with minced parsley, and serve immediately.

Tuna and Orange Salad

This salad is alive with the flavor of mint. It is an excellent one-dish meal for lunch, especially when served with homemade Cornmeal and Wheat Muffins (page 326).

S E R V E S 2

1 large navel orange (10 ounces)

One 6½-ounce can water-packed solid white albacore tuna

1 tablespoon snipped fresh chives or thinly sliced scallions (green part only)

1½ teaspoons minced fresh mint or ½ teaspoon crumbled dried mint

2 teaspoons minced Italian parsley leaves

⅛ teaspoon salt, if desired

⅛ teaspoon freshly milled black pepper

1 tablespoon olive oil, preferably extra virgin

4 medium-sized lettuce leaves (optional garnish)

1. With sharp knife, cut a small slice from top and bottom of orange. With tip of knife, divide orange skin into 8 sections. Peel each section, removing most of the white membrane as you peel. With a vegetable peeler, remove all the white membrane from orange. Cut out each orange segment, removing its protective membrane as you cut. Cut each segment in half and place to a strainer set over a bowl for at least 15 minutes to drain off excess juice; reserve 1 tablespoon juice for dressing.
2. Place tuna in another strainer and thoroughly rinse under cold water. Drain well and break into bite-sized pieces.
3. Place orange segments, tuna, chives or scallions, mint, and parsley in a bowl. Lightly toss with two forks to combine.
4. Place reserved tablespoon of orange juice, salt, and pepper in a small bowl. Beat with a fork or small whisk to combine. Add oil a little at a time and whisk thoroughly to incorporate. Pour dressing over salad and toss lightly with two forks to combine.
5. Arrange lettuce on salad plates. Spoon salad on top and serve.

Oven-fried Fillet of Sole

Baking in the upper portion of the oven will help keep the sole moist without losing its crunchy coating.

SERVES 2

2 skinless fillets of lemon or gray sole (12 ounces total weight)
¼ cup low-fat or skim milk
½ cup dry bread crumbs
1 teaspoon grated lemon rind
½ teaspoon minced garlic
1 tablespoon minced Italian parsley leaves

1½ teaspoons minced fresh oregano or ½ teaspoon crumbled dried oregano
¼ teaspoon freshly milled black pepper
2 teaspoons olive oil
2 lemon wedges (garnish)

1. Adjust rack to top shelf of oven and preheat to 450 degrees. Lightly grease bottom of a shallow 9- by 13- by 2-inch baking pan; set aside.
2. Wash fillets in cold water and thoroughly blot dry with paper towel.
3. Place milk in a shallow bowl. On a flat plate, combine bread crumbs, lemon rind, garlic, parsley, oregano, and pepper. Dip fillets in milk and then dredge in bread crumb mixture. Place fillets in prepared pan and drizzle 1 teaspoon oil over each fillet.
4. Bake in preheated oven until surface of fish is lightly golden and barely flakes when tested with a fork, about 5 to 7 minutes depending on thickness of fish. The fish does not have to be turned.
5. Using a wide metal spatula, transfer fillets to platter, garnish with lemon wedges, and serve immediately.

⫷⫷⫷

Swordfish and Cucumber Kebabs with Basil Dressing

Cucumber not only provides an unusual flavor addition when threaded with swordfish, but will help keep the fish moist during broiling. The cucumber must be parboiled so the swordfish and cucumber grill at the same rate.

S E R V E S   2

Basil Dressing

1 tablespoon low-fat yogurt

1 tablespoon mayonnaise, preferably homemade (page 263)

1½ teaspoons minced fresh basil or ½ teaspoon crumbled dried basil

2 drops Tabasco sauce

Place all of the dressing ingredients in a small bowl and stir with a fork to combine. Cover with plastic wrap and refrigerate for at least 2 hours. (Dressing may be made up to 4 hours before preparing fish.) Remove dressing from refrigerator just before placing kebabs on grill.

To Assemble and Grill

1 swordfish steak, 1 inch thick (14 ounces)

1 large cucumber (10 ounces)

3 tablespoons fresh lime juice

1 tablespoon imported white wine vinegar

1 teaspoon minced garlic

2 medium bay leaves, crumbled

1. Trim away and discard the skin from swordfish. Cut the steak into 1½- by 1-inch rectangles. Place pieces of fish in a shallow dish.
2. Peel cucumber, slice in half lengthwise, and trim ends. Using a melon scoop or a teaspoon, scrape out seeds. Slice halved cucumber crosswise into 1-inch pieces. Blanch cucumber in 1 quart boiling water for 2 minutes. Transfer to strainer, refresh under cold

water, drain thoroughly, and blot dry with paper towel. Transfer to dish with swordfish.

3. Place lime juice, vinegar, garlic, and bay leaves in a small bowl. Stir with fork to combine marinade. Spoon marinade over fish and cucumber pieces; turn to coat thoroughly. Marinate at room temperature for 1 hour, turning pieces once more to coat.

4. Preheat charcoal grill until coals have turned a gray ashy color. Preheat gas or electric grill according to manufacturer's suggested time.

5. Beginning and ending each kebab with a piece of cucumber, thread the fish and cucumber pieces alternately onto two 12-inch metal skewers. Push the pieces close together as you thread. Discard any remaining marinade in dish.

6. Lightly brush the grill rack with a little vegetable or olive oil to prevent kebabs from sticking while grilling.

7. Place the kebabs on grill 4 inches from the heat source. Grill the kebabs, turning frequently, until the fish is firm and lightly golden on all sides, about 7 minutes. To ensure that the pieces brown evenly on all sides, loosen the kebabs every two minutes with a wide metal spatula and turn them with long-handled tongs that have long gripping ends.

8. Grasp the handle of each skewer with a towel and hold one kebab over each dinner plate. Using a 2-pronged fork, push the fish and cucumber pieces off the skewer onto individual plates. Spoon basil dressing over kebabs and serve immediately.

⫷⫷⫷

Broiled Swordfish Steaks

Purchase steaks that are at least ¾ of an inch thick so that they will remain juicy while cooking. Leaving the outer skin on the steak will protect the flesh from breaking while broiling.

SERVES 2

2 swordfish steaks, each about ¾ inch thick (12 ounces total weight)
1 teaspoon finely grated orange rind
¼ cup orange juice, strained

2 teaspoons low-sodium light soy sauce (Kikkoman Lite)
½ teaspoon powdered ginger
3 drops Tabasco sauce
½ medium-sized navel orange, sliced into 4 wedges (garnish)

1. Rinse steaks under cold water and blot dry with paper towel. Place steaks in a single layer in a shallow dish.
2. Place orange rind, juice, soy sauce, ginger, and Tabasco sauce in a small bowl; beat with fork or small whisk to combine marinade. Spoon marinade over fish and turn the steaks once to coat thoroughly. Marinate at room temperature for 30 minutes or cover with plastic wrap and refrigerate up to 2 hours, turning steaks once in marinade.
3. Remove broiler rack and pan from oven and preheat broiler for 15 minutes. Lightly grease broiler rack.
4. Remove steaks from marinade and place 2 inches apart on prepared broiler rack; reserve marinade for basting.
5. Position broiler pan 5 inches from heat source. Broil steaks, basting once with marinade, until surface of steaks is lightly golden, about 4 minutes. Turn steaks with a wide metal spatula and continue broiling, basting once with marinade, until second side is lightly golden, about 4 to 5 minutes. When done, steaks should feel firm to the touch and barely flake when tested with the tip of a knife. Transfer to platter, garnish with orange wedges, and serve.

⋘

Baked Trout with Shallots, Orange, and Watercress

The sautéed shallots and orange juice not only keep these tender fillets moist while baking but add to the lovely final presentation.

SERVES 2

2 teaspoons olive oil
2 tablespoons minced shallots
3 tablespoons fresh orange juice, strained
2 unskinned fillets of brook or rainbow trout (about 12 ounces total weight)
¼ teaspoon freshly milled black pepper
2 tablespoons minced watercress leaves, tough stems discarded

2 teaspoons grated orange rind
Several watercress leaves, tough stems discarded (garnish)
1 small navel orange, halved and cut into ½ inch slices (garnish)

1. Adjust rack to upper third of oven and preheat to 375 degrees. Lightly grease a shallow baking pan; set aside.
2. In a small saucepan, heat olive oil over low heat. Add shallots and cook, covered, until they are soft but not brown, about 2 minutes. Remove from heat and stir in 2 tablespoons orange juice. (If shallots start to stick to bottom of pan while cooking, stir in a little of the 2 tablespoons orange juice to loosen.)
3. Wash fillets in cold water and thoroughly blot dry with paper towel. Place fillets in prepared pan skin side down. Sprinkle surface of fillets with pepper. Spoon shallot mixture over fillets.
4. Bake fillets in preheated oven until fish barely flakes when tested with the tip of a knife, about 8 to 10 minutes. Remove from oven.

5. In a small bowl, combine minced watercress and orange rind.
6. Transfer fillets to platter and spoon remaining 1 tablespoon of orange juice over them. Sprinkle watercress–orange rind mixture over fillets. Garnish platter with an outer border of watercress leaves and orange slices; serve immediately.

VEGETABLES

≪←

The colorful bounty of local farms during early summer through late fall always presents a challenge to me when I shop for vegetables during their natural seasons. Today, many supermarkets offer a dazzling variety of fresh produce, as do specialty markets. The wide range of vegetables available to us throughout the year provides unending and exciting combinations of color, texture, and taste.

Fresh vegetables are used exclusively in this chapter, with the exception of the tiny green peas available in the frozen food section of most supermarkets.

Vegetables should never be overcooked. The recipes in this chapter do not, of course, cover every possible method of cooking a vegetable, nor do they mention every vegetable you might encounter, but they will provide helpful hints on how to select many vegetables for purchase, and explain how to prepare them in unusual and imaginative ways.

Baked Acorn Squash Rings

Select a hard acorn squash that has no cracks or blemishes for this late fall and winter favorite.

SERVES 2

1 large acorn squash (about 1 pound)
1½ tablespoons dark rum, preferably Myers's
2 teaspoons unsalted margarine, melted

1 tablespoon light brown sugar, firmly packed
⅛ teaspoon freshly grated nutmeg

1. Wash and dry squash. Cut off 1 inch from top and bottom of squash; discard ends. Slice squash into 4 even rounds, each about ½ inch thick. Using a small knife, cut out fibre and seeds from center of rings and discard.
2. Adjust rack to center of oven and preheat to 375 degrees. Lightly grease bottom of a 9- by 13- by 2-inch ovenproof baking dish.
3. Place squash rings in a single layer in prepared pan. With a fork, prick top of each round at ¼-inch intervals. Brush rum over squash and let stand at room temperature for 15 minutes to absorb liquor.
4. Brush each round evenly with melted margarine.
5. In a small bowl, combine brown sugar and nutmeg. Carefully sprinkle mixture on top of each round.
6. Bake in preheated oven until tender when tested with fork, about 25 to 30 minutes. Arrange in a slightly overlapping pattern on platter and serve immediately.

≪≪

Asparagus and Tomatoes

Peeling the asparagus stalks will ensure even cooking.

SERVES 2

1 pound large asparagus
(about 12 spears)
2 well-ripened plum
tomatoes (4 ounces total
weight)
2 teaspoons olive oil
2 large scallions, washed,
trimmed, sliced
lengthwise and then cut
crosswise into 1-inch
pieces to make ½ cup

1½ teaspoons minced fresh
basil or ½ teaspoon
crumbled dried basil
⅛ teaspoon salt, if desired
⅛ teaspoon freshly milled
black pepper

1. Wash asparagus several times in cold water to get rid of sand. Using a sharp knife, cut off woody ends at base of spears. With a vegetable peeler, peel up from base of spears, leaving tips intact. Cut off asparagus tips, leaving about 2 inches of spear, and reserve. Cut asparagus stalks in half lengthwise and then slice crosswise into 2-inch lengths.
2. Plump fresh tomatoes in 1 quart boiling water for 1 minute. Rinse under cold water. When cool enough to handle, core tomatoes and peel skins with a small paring knife. Cut tomatoes in half lengthwise. Gently squeeze each half and discard most of the seeds. Place on plate and slice lengthwise into ½-inch strips.
3. In a 10-inch skillet, heat oil over medium heat. Add scallions and cook, partially covered, until lightly golden, about 2 minutes. Stir in tomatoes and any accumulated juices from plate. Cook, covered, until barely tender when tested with fork, about 1 minute. Stir in asparagus bottoms and cook, covered, stirring once or twice until barely tender when tested with the tip of a knife, about 3 minutes. Stir in asparagus tips and basil. Continue cooking, covered, stir-

ring once or twice until tips are tender, about 3 minutes. (If to-mato-scallion mixture starts to stick to bottom of pan, stir in 2 teaspoons of water to loosen.) Season with salt and pepper; remove from heat. Transfer to platter and serve immediately.

Artichokes with Green Dipping Sauce

Artichokes are now available year-round but are more plentiful February through May. Select large artichokes with tightly packed leaves. Artichokes with open, spreading leaves are tough. During late fall and the early winter months, do not be discouraged from buying artichokes that have bronze-tipped outer petals. This is a result of frost, and growers refer to such artichokes as being "winter-kissed." They may look unattractive, but will have a more intense flavor and I think are the best-tasting artichokes of all. In spring, the leaves should be bright green. Discoloration is a sign of age or damage. Cook artichokes only in an enameled, glass, or stainless steel-lined pan. They will discolor if cooked in aluminum or cast-iron saucepans.

SERVES 2

2 large artichokes (about 1
   pound 4 ounces total
   weight)

½ lemon
2 tablespoons lemon juice

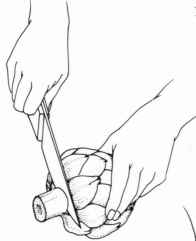

1. Wash artichokes in cold water. Cut off the stem flush with the base so that the artichokes will stand upright when placed in saucepan.

Hold one artichoke in the palm of your hand and snap off any small or discolored leaves at the base.

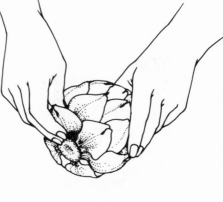

Place the artichoke on a cutting board and cut off about 1 inch from top. Rub the cut edge with cut lemon to prevent discoloration.

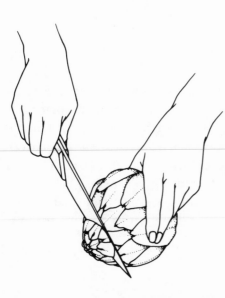

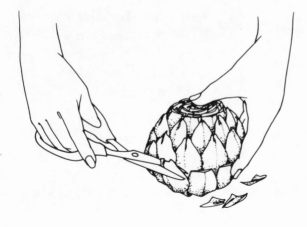

With a pair of kitchen shears, snip off about ½ inch from tip of each leaf.

Rub the cut edges with lemon. Repeat with other artichoke.

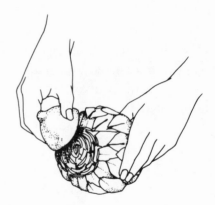

2. Place artichokes upright in a 3½-quart saucepan (or one large enough that the two artichokes will fit in snugly when placed in pan). Pour in enough water to reach 3 inches up the sides of the pan. Add lemon juice to water. Cover pan and bring to a boil over high heat. As soon as water reaches a boil, turn heat down to medium and cook artichokes, covered, until a petal near center pulls out easily, about 30 to 45 minutes. Remove from pan, drain artichokes upside down on a platter lined with paper towel, and let cool to room temperature.

⋘

Green Dipping Sauce

1 ½ tablespoons mayonnaise,
  preferably homemade
  (page 263)
  3 tablespoons low-fat yogurt
  ½ teaspoon Dijon mustard
  1 tablespoon minced green
  pepper

1 tablespoon minced fresh
  chives
1 tablespoon minced Italian
  parsley leaves
⅛ teaspoon salt, if desired
⅛ teaspoon freshly milled
  white pepper

While artichokes are cooking, make dipping sauce. In a small bowl, combine all of the ingredients and whisk with a fork to mix well. Transfer sauce to a small bowl for dipping.

To Eat

1. Place artichokes on individual plates.
2. To eat artichokes, pull off outer petals one at a time. Dip base of petal into sauce; pull through teeth to remove soft, pulpy portion of petal; discard remaining petal. Continue until all petals have been removed. Spoon out fuzzy center (the choke) at base and discard. The bottom or heart of the artichoke is entirely edible, and it happens to be the best part. Cut into small pieces and dip into sauce.

Broccoli with Garlic and Lemon

A good vegetable any time of year. When selecting broccoli, make sure the buds are tightly closed. The tips may be tinged with purple but not yellow, which is a sign of age.

SERVES 2

1 small bunch broccoli (10 ounces)
2 teaspoons olive oil
½ teaspoon minced garlic
1 tablespoon fresh lemon juice, strained

⅛ teaspoon salt, if desired
⅛ teaspoon freshly milled black pepper
2 teaspoons grated lemon rind (garnish)

1. Remove florets from broccoli, leaving about ½ inch of stems. Cut or break florets into 1-inch pieces. Wash in cold water, drain, and set aside. Remove and discard the large coarse leaves from stems and cut off about ½ inch of tough lower part of stalk. Wash thoroughly and peel stalks with a vegetable peeler. Cut stalks in half lengthwise. (If stalks are more than 1 inch in diameter, cut into quarters.) Cut halved or quartered stalks into 1-inch pieces.
2. Bring 2 quarts of water to a boil. Add broccoli stalks and cook until almost tender when tested with a fork, about 3 minutes. Add florets and continue cooking about 4 minutes longer, until florets tender when tested with fork. Drain thoroughly in a colander. Transfer broccoli to platter.
3. While broccoli is cooking, heat oil in a small saucepan over low heat. Add garlic and sauté until lightly golden, about 1 minute. Remove from heat and stir in lemon juice. Spoon garlic mixture over broccoli. Season with salt and pepper. Garnish with lemon rind and serve immediately.

⋘

Parsleyed Baby Carrots

Sweet-tasting baby carrots always make a beautiful presentation. I frequently use them as a garnish for broiled chicken, lamb, or fish.

SERVES 2

12 small baby carrots (8 ounces total weight), see Note

2 teaspoons unsalted margarine

2 teaspoons minced Italian parsley leaves

⅛ teaspoon salt, if desired

⅛ teaspoon freshly milled white pepper

1. Wash carrots and peel lightly with a vegetable peeler. Trim tops of carrots so that they are all the same size. Cook in 1 quart boiling water until barely tender when tested with fork, about 3 minutes. Transfer to colander and rinse under cold water. Blot dry with paper towel. (Carrots may be prepared up to this point 4 hours in advance, placed in bowl, and covered with plastic wrap.)
2. In a 10-inch skillet, melt margarine over medium-high heat. Add carrots and cook, stirring once or twice with wooden spoon, until heated, about 1½ minutes. Stir in parsley and season with salt and pepper. Transfer to platter and serve immediately.

NOTE: If baby carrots are unavailable, use 4 medium-sized carrots (8 ounces total weight), trimmed, peeled, and cut into strips ½ inch wide by 3 inches long.

⟪⟪⟪

Marinated Eggplant

Select glossy, firm, unblemished eggplant for this tangy marinated vegetable. For best flavor, serve at room temperature. It can also be served as an appetizer on unsalted crackers. Eggplant can be made up to 3 days before serving and stored, covered, in refrigerator until needed.

SERVES 2 AS VEGETABLE,
4 AS APPETIZER

1 small eggplant (12 ounces)
1 tablespoon olive oil
1 large clove garlic, peeled and split in half
1½ tablespoons imported white wine vinegar
1½ teaspoons minced fresh basil or ½ teaspoon crumbled dried basil
⅛ teaspoon salt, if desired
⅛ teaspoon freshly milled black pepper

1. Remove broiler pan and preheat oven at broil setting. Line broiler pan with a single sheet of aluminum foil.
2. Wash eggplant and blot dry with paper towel. Trim both ends of eggplant but do not peel. Slice eggplant crosswise into 1-inch rounds. Cut each round in half and then into ½-inch wedges, like a pie.
3. Lightly brush both sides of each wedge with olive oil. Arrange wedges in single layer in broiler pan.
4. Position broiler pan 3 inches from heat source. Broil until lightly golden on both sides, about 3 minutes on each side. (Watch carefully so wedges do not burn.)
5. Rub a small serving bowl with split garlic clove and leave garlic in bowl. Add eggplant and any accumulated pan juices to bowl. Add vinegar and basil. Season with salt and pepper; toss lightly. Cover with plastic wrap and let cool to room temperature. Remove garlic and toss once again just before serving.

≪≪

Escarole au Gratin

A very hearty vegetable dish for winter when escarole is abundant. This dish can be assembled up to 3 hours before baking. Add bread crumb topping just before baking. See variations at bottom of recipe.

SERVES 2

1 medium-sized head escarole (12 ounces)

Discard any wilted or bruised leaves from escarole. Separate leaves and cut off and discard about 1 inch of tough bottom ends of greens. Slice greens into 2-inch lengths and wash several times in lukewarm water to get rid of grit. Place escarole in a 5-quart saucepan and cover. Do not add water; the final rinse water clinging to leaves will be sufficient to steam them. Cook, covered, over medium-high heat until leaves are limp, about 5 minutes. Transfer to colander and drain thoroughly. When cool enough to handle, thoroughly squeeze out excess moisture with your hands; set aside.

Velouté Sauce

2 teaspoons unsalted margarine

2 teaspoons flour

¾ cup unsalted chicken broth, preferably homemade (page 51)

⅛ teaspoon freshly grated nutmeg

⅛ teaspoon salt, if desired

⅛ teaspoon freshly milled white pepper

Prepare sauce: in a 1½-quart saucepan, melt margarine over low heat. When margarine begins to froth, add the flour. Mix well with a wire whisk and cook over medium heat, whisking constantly, until golden, Add chicken broth and turn heat to low. Cook, whisking constantly, until thick and creamy, about 3 to 4 minutes. Stir in nutmeg and season with salt and pepper; remove sauce from heat.

To Assemble and Cook

2 tablespoons freshly grated   2 tablespoons dry bread
  Parmesan cheese   crumbs

1. Adjust rack to center of oven and preheat to 375 degrees. Lightly grease bottom and sides of a shallow 2½-cup ovenproof casserole.
2. In a small bowl, combine Parmesan cheese with bread crumbs for topping.
3. Arrange escarole in prepared casserole to form a shallow level layer. Spoon velouté sauce over top, spreading evenly with a narrow metal spatula. Sprinkle bread crumb mixture over top.
4. Bake in preheated oven until golden brown crust has formed on top, about 30 minutes; serve immediately.

VARIATIONS

Romaine au Gratin

Substitute 1 medium-sized head of romaine lettuce (12 ounces) for the escarole. Follow same cleaning and cooking procedures as for escarole.

Carrots au Gratin

Substitute 4 medium-sized carrots (8 ounces total weight) for the escarole. Wash carrots, trim ends, and peel lightly with a vegetable peeler. Slice carrots into thin 2- by ½-inch strips. Boil in 2 cups boiling water until barely tender when tested with fork, about 3 minutes. Transfer to strainer, refresh under cold water, and blot dry with paper towel. Arrange in two layers in prepared casserole. Spoon velouté sauce and bread crumb topping over carrots; bake as directed for escarole.

⫷

Celery au Gratin

Substitute 4 large celery ribs [8 ounces total weight] for the escarole. Cut off leaves and trim bottoms of stalks. Using a vegetable peeler, remove coarse strings. Wash celery and cut into thin 2- by ½-inch strips. Cook in 2 cups boiling water until tender when tested with fork, about 8 minutes. Transfer to strainer, refresh under cold water, and blot dry with paper towel. Arrange in two layers in prepared casserole. Spoon velouté sauce and bread crumb topping over celery; bake as directed for escarole.

Green Beans with Carrots and Tarragon

Make this beautiful combination when you can find crisp, tender, young beans about ¼ inch wide and no more than 5 inches in length.

SERVES 2

2 medium-sized carrots (4 ounces total weight)
¼ pound green beans
2 teaspoons olive oil
1 tablespoon minced shallots

1½ teaspoons minced fresh tarragon or ½ teaspoon crumbled dried tarragon
⅛ teaspoon salt, if desired
⅛ teaspoon freshly milled black pepper

1. Wash carrots, trim, and peel lightly with a vegetable peeler. Cook in 1 quart boiling water until barely tender when tested with a fork, about 4 minutes. Transfer to strainer and rinse under cold water. Blot dry with paper towel and cut into ¼-inch by 4-inch strips (the same size as green beans).
2. Wash green beans, trim both ends, and cook in 1 quart boiling

water until barely tender when tested with a fork, about 4 to 5 minutes. Drain in a strainer, rinse under cold water, and blot dry with paper towel. (Vegetables may be prepared up to this point 3 hours in advance, combined in a bowl, and covered with plastic wrap.)

3. In a 10-inch skillet, heat oil over medium heat. Add shallots and cook, partially covered, stirring frequently with wooden spoon until lightly golden, about 2 minutes. Add carrots and green beans and continue cooking, stirring constantly until vegetables are heated through, about 1 minute. Stir in tarragon and cook for an additional 20 seconds. Season with salt and pepper; remove from heat. Transfer to platter and serve immediately.

Minted Green Beans

Green beans harmonize beautifully with chives or scallions, mint, and extra virgin olive oil. This dish is at its best when served at room temperature.

SERVES 2

6 ounces green beans
1 tablespoon olive oil, preferably extra virgin
1 tablespoon snipped fresh chives or thinly sliced scallion (green part only)
1½ teaspoons minced fresh mint or ½ teaspoon crumbled dried mint

⅛ teaspoon sugar
⅛ teaspoon salt, if desired
⅛ teaspoon freshly milled black pepper

1. Wash green beans and trim both ends. (If beans are more than 5 inches in length, slice in half diagonally.) Boil green beans in 3 quarts boiling water until tender when tested with a fork, about

5 minutes. Drain in colander, rinse under cold water, and blot dry with paper towel.
2. Transfer to serving bowl, drizzle olive oil over top, and toss lightly. Add chives or scallions, mint, and sugar. Season with salt and pepper; lightly toss again. Cover with plastic wrap and set aside to cool to room temperature. Toss lightly once again just before serving.

Two-minute Mushrooms

Select small white button mushrooms no larger than 1 inch in diameter, with tight-fitting stems, for this very fast sauté.

SERVES 2

½ pound small white mushrooms
2 teaspoons olive oil
½ teaspoon minced garlic
⅛ teaspoon salt, if desired

⅛ teaspoon freshly milled black pepper
2 teaspoons minced Italian parsley leaves

1. Wipe mushrooms with a damp cloth. Cut off stems and save for another purpose or discard.
2. In a 10-inch skillet, heat oil over low heat. Add garlic and sauté, stirring constantly with wooden spoon until very lightly golden, about 1 minute.
3. Add mushroom caps and turn heat to high; quickly toss with wooden spoon until caps are well coated with oil and garlic. Cook, stirring constantly, just until mushrooms begin to exude their juices, about 1 to 2 minutes. Season with salt and pepper. Stir in parsley and remove from heat. Transfer to platter and serve immediately.

Peas with Mushrooms

A great combination to make on those days when you are too busy to cook.

SERVES 2

2 teaspoons olive oil
2 tablespoons thinly sliced
 scallions, white part only
 (reserve green part for
 garnish)
1 cup tiny frozen peas,
 defrosted (see Note)
¼ pound medium-sized
 mushrooms, trimmed,
 wiped, and thinly sliced

⅛ teaspoon salt, if desired
⅛ teaspoon freshly milled
 black pepper
2 teaspoons thinly sliced
 scallions, green part only
 (garnish)

In a 10-inch skillet, heat oil over medium heat. Add white part of scallions and cook, stirring frequently, until lightly golden, about 2 minutes. Add peas and cook, partially covered, stirring frequently until crisp tender, about 1 minute. Turn heat to high, add mushrooms, and cook stirring constantly, just until they begin to exude their juices, about 1 to 2 minutes. Season with salt and pepper; remove from heat. Transfer to bowl and garnish with green part of scallions.

NOTE: To defrost frozen peas, place in strainer, and run under warm water, breaking block apart with your fingertips until peas are separated, about 30 seconds.

Grilled Potatoes

These potatoes go very well with any of the grilled recipes in this book. After parboiling, they can be grilled at the same time you are barbecuing your meat or fish.

SERVES 2

2 large Idaho potatoes (about
  1 pound)
2 teaspoons olive oil

⅛ teaspoon salt, if desired
⅛ teaspoon freshly milled
  black pepper

1. Scrub potatoes under cold running water with a stiff brush. Place in a 5-quart pot with enough water to cover by 2 inches. Cover pot and bring to a boil. Parboil potatoes, covered, until a fork can penetrate partway but meets firm resistance toward the center, about 6 minutes. Drain in colander. When potatoes are cool enough to handle, peel. Trim about ½ inch from each end of potato and discard. Slice each potato lengthwise into 3 even pieces. Place potatoes in a single layer on a plate. Lightly brush both surfaces of sliced potatoes with a little oil. (Brushing surfaces with a little oil will prevent them from sticking when placed on heated grill.)
2. Place potato slices on preheated grill about 4 inches from heat source. Cook until lightly golden on underside, about 3 minutes. Using a long spatula, turn potatoes and continue grilling until second side is lightly golden, about 3 minutes. Transfer to platter and season with salt and pepper; serve immediately.

Herbed Potato Salad

A wonderful salad to make during the summer months or whenever fresh herbs are available. For best flavor, serve warm or at room temperature.

SERVES 2

4 small red-skinned potatoes (about 12 ounces total weight)

1 tablespoon snipped fresh chives

1 tablespoon minced fresh basil

1 tablespoon minced Italian parsley leaves

1 tablespoon imported white wine vinegar

⅛ teaspoon salt, if desired

⅛ teaspoon freshly milled white pepper

1 tablespoon olive oil, preferably extra virgin

1. Scrub potatoes well with a vegetable brush. Place in a 2½-quart saucepan with enough water to cover by 2 inches. Cover pan and bring to a boil. As soon as water reaches a boil, uncover pot, reduce heat to medium-high, and cook until potatoes are tender when tested with the tip of a knife, about 15 to 20 minutes; if potatoes vary in size, remove small ones first to prevent overcooking. Transfer to colander and let stand just until cool enough to handle.
2. In the same bowl in which you plan to serve the salad, place chives, basil, parsley, vinegar, salt, and pepper. Stir with a fork or small whisk to combine. Add oil a little at a time and whisk to combine.
3. Peel potatoes and cut into 1-inch cubes. Transfer to bowl and toss with dressing (this must be done while the potatoes are still warm so they will absorb the full flavor of the dressing). Serve immediately or cover with plastic wrap and let come to room temperature. If serving at room temperature, toss again just before serving.

⋘

Savoy Cabbage and Potatoes

A great winter combination, especially satisfying when served with Oven-fried Pork Chops (page 141).

SERVES 2

1 small head of savoy
cabbage (12 ounces)
2 teaspoons olive oil
2 small white potatoes (8
ounces total weight),
peeled and cut into
1-inch cubes

1 to 2 tablespoons water
1 large clove garlic,
peeled and split in half
½ teaspoon sugar
⅛ teaspoon salt, if desired
⅛ teaspoon freshly milled
black pepper

1. Discard any bruised outer leaves from cabbage. Wash cabbage and blot dry with paper towel. Quarter, remove center core, and cut cabbage crosswise into ½-inch slices.
2. Drizzle oil in the bottom of a heavy 3½-quart saucepan. Place cabbage and potatoes in pan. Drizzle 1 tablespoon water over vegetables. Add garlic and and sprinkle sugar on top.
3. Cover pan and cook vegetables over medium-low heat until potatoes are tender when tested with a fork, about 35 minutes. After 15 minutes of cooking, check liquid in pan and add remaining tablespoon of water if needed. Season with salt and pepper; remove from heat. Remove garlic, transfer vegetables to a bowl, and serve. (This vegetable combination can be cooked up to two hours before serving and reheated over low heat.)

⫸⫸⫸

Yellow Squash with Red Pepper

Look for small, firm yellow squash that are no more than 5 inches in length for this versatile combination.

SERVES 2

2 small yellow squash
(about 6 ounces)
1 teaspoon olive oil
1 teaspoon unsalted
margarine
¼ cup thinly sliced red
onion
1 medium-sized red bell
pepper (5 ounces), washed,
halved, cored, seeded, and
sliced into ½-inch strips

1½ teaspoons minced fresh
basil or ½ teaspoon
crumbled dried basil
⅛ teaspoon salt, if desired
⅛ teaspoon freshly milled
black pepper

1. Scrub squash under cold running water until the skins feel smooth. Blot dry with paper towel and trim off both ends. Starting from bottom end, slice at a 20-degree angle into ½-inch diagonal slices; set aside.
2. In a 10-inch skillet, heat oil and margarine over low heat. Add onion and cook, partially covered, stirring frequently until soft but not brown, about 3 minutes. Add peppers, cover pan, and cook, stirring once or twice with wooden spoon until crisp tender, about 3 minutes. Stir in squash and continue cooking, covered, until squash is barely tender when tested with fork, about 3 minutes. Increase heat to high and continue cooking, uncovered, stirring constantly until squash is tender when tested with fork, about 2 minutes. Stir in basil. Season with salt and pepper; remove from heat. Transfer to platter and serve immediately.

⋘

Baked Tomatoes Provençale

This is my adaptation of a side dish I was once served at a little French restaurant in New York City.

SERVES 2

2 large firm ripe tomatoes (about 1 pound total weight)

1½ tablespoons mayonnaise, preferably homemade (page 263)

1½ tablespoons freshly grated Parmesan cheese

⅛ teaspoon freshly milled black pepper

2 tablespoons dry bread crumbs

2 teaspoons minced Italian parsley leaves

1. Adjust rack to upper third of oven and preheat to 375 degrees. Lightly grease a small baking sheet; set aside.
2. Wash tomatoes and blot dry with paper towel. Core tomatoes; slice off about ½ inch from top and bottom of each tomato and discard. Slice each tomato into 3 even rounds.
3. In a small bowl, combine mayonnaise, Parmesan cheese, and pepper. Using a small metal spatula, spread cheese mixture over each tomato slice.
4. In a small bowl, combine bread crumbs and parsley. Sprinkle bread crumb mixture over tomatoes.
5. Arrange tomatoes in a single layer in prepared pan. Bake in preheated oven until cheese mixture puffs a little and bread crumb mixture is lightly golden, about 20 minutes. Arrange in a single layer on platter and serve immediately.

≪≪-

Vegetable Kebabs

Take full advantage of your grill and make these vegetable kebabs while barbecuing any of the meat or fish dishes in this book.

SERVES 2

2 medium-sized yellow squash (about 8 ounces), washed and trimmed

1 large firm red bell pepper (about 8 ounces), washed, halved, cored, and seeded

6 medium-sized mushrooms (about 3 ounces)

1. Bring 2 quarts of water to a rolling boil. Add squash and cook, partially covered, until barely tender when tested with the tip of a knife, about 3 minutes. Transfer with a skimmer to a colander, refresh under cold running water, and blot dry with paper towel. When cool enough to handle, slice into 1-inch rounds and transfer to a shallow bowl.
2. Bring water in which squash was cooked back to a boil and blanch pepper for 2 minutes. Transfer to colander and refresh under cold running water; blot dry with paper towel. Slice peppers into 1- by 1½-inch pieces and add to bowl with squash.
3. Wipe mushrooms with a damp cloth. Cut off stems and save for another purpose or discard. Place mushrooms in bowl with other vegetables.

Marinade

2 teaspoons fresh lemon juice

1 tablespoon minced fresh oregano or 1 teaspoon crumbled dried oregano

⅛ teaspoon salt, if desired

¼ teaspoon freshly milled black pepper

1 tablespoon olive oil

In a small bowl, combine all the marinade ingredients except olive oil. Add oil a little at a time and whisk with fork or small whisk to combine. Drizzle marinade over vegetables and toss lightly with two forks to combine. Let vegetables marinate at room temperature for 1 hour, turning in marinade once.

To Assemble and Grill

1. Beginning and ending each kebab with a piece of red pepper, thread the vegetables alternately onto two 12-inch metal skewers. Push the pieces close together as you thread. Discard any remaining marinade.
2. Place kebabs on preheated grill 4 inches from heat source. Grill the kebabs, turning frequently with long-handled tongs that have long gripping ends, until peppers are tender and kebabs are evenly browned on all sides, about 7 minutes.
3. Grasp the handle of each skewer with a towel and, using a 2-pronged fork, push the vegetable pieces off the skewer onto individual plates.

Candied Yams with Pecans

Using dark corn syrup for the glaze provides a rich color as well as distinctive flavoring to the candied potatoes. This dish is an excellent accompaniment to Glazed Roast Pork with Fruit Stuffing (page 149).

SERVES 2

2 medium-sized yams (about 12 ounces total weight)

¼ cup dark corn syrup, preferably Karo

2 teaspoons unsalted margarine

¼ teaspoon ground cinnamon

⅛ teaspoon freshly ground nutmeg

1½ tablespoons finely chopped pecans

1. Lightly grease bottom and sides of a 8- by 8- by 2-inch baking dish; set aside.
2. Scrub potatoes well with a vegetable brush. Place in a 5-quart pot with enough water to cover by 2 inches. Cover pot, bring to a boil, and cook until potatoes are tender when pierced with the tip of a knife, about 25 to 30 minutes. Transfer to a colander and let stand until cool enough to handle. Peel skins with a small paring knife. Slice each potato in half lengthwise and place halves in a single layer, cut sides up, in prepared baking dish.
3. Adjust oven rack to center of oven and preheat to 350 degrees.
4. In a small saucepan, combine syrup with margarine. Bring to a boil over medium heat, stirring once or twice with wooden spoon. Reduce heat to low and simmer, stirring constantly, until thick and syrupy, about 2 minutes. Remove from heat and stir in cinnamon and nutmeg.
5. Spoon syrup over yams and bake in preheated oven, basting every 10 minutes, until potatoes are well glazed, about 30 minutes; remove from oven.
6. Turn oven to broil setting. Sprinkle pecans over top of potatoes. Place 6 inches from heat source and broil until nuts are lightly golden, about 2 to 3 minutes. (Watch carefully so that nuts do not burn.) Serve immediately.

⫷⫷⫷

Shredded Zucchini with Garlic

Select firm, medium-sized zucchini with a good deep color and unblemished skins for this dish. Be sure to squeeze out excess moisture from the zucchini shreds so that they will still be crunchy and crispy when served.

SERVES 2

2 medium-sized zucchini (8 ounces total weight)
1 tablespoon olive oil
½ teaspoon minced garlic

⅛ teaspoon salt, if desired
⅛ teaspoon freshly milled black pepper

1. Scrub zucchini under cold running water until the skins feel clean and smooth. Trim both ends. Cut into 1-inch lengths, place horizontally in food processor fitted with shredding disk, and use light pressure on pusher to grate. (If you do not have a food processor, leave zucchini whole and shred with the coarse side of a grater.) Place shredded zucchini in the center of a large piece of cheese cloth or a clean dish towel. Thoroughly squeeze out as much moisture as possible.
2. In a 10-inch skillet, heat oil over medium-high heat. Add garlic and zucchini. Sauté, turning zucchini with a wide metal spatula constantly, until they are barely tender but still crisp, about 2 minutes. Season with salt and pepper; remove from heat. Transfer to a platter and serve immediately.

≪≪←

SALADS

My students frequently ask at what point in the meal they should serve the salad. I tell them it is all a matter of preference. I always like a salad with the meal when serving meat, poultry, or fish, and after the main course when serving a pasta dish or good, hearty soup. The one thing I am obsessive about is always serving salad on a separate plate so that the delicate dressing does not mingle the entrée.

Green salads should not be tossed with dressing until they are ready to be served, since once dressed they rapidly go limp. (Certain other types of salads are mixed ahead of time and refrigerated while their flavors blend.) A good strategy is to prepare your dressing ahead of time.

Salads should always be exactly what they appear to be—bright, tempting, and as fresh as possible. In selecting greens for salads, look for crisp leaves with no signs of brown. The heavier the lettuce, whether it be romaine, Bibb, or iceberg, the more tightly packed it will be, giving you more leaves for your money. All recipes here will give you the measured amounts of greens needed for each salad. However, if purchasing a large head of romaine, you may want to trim off all the large outer leaves to save for Romaine au Gratin (page 232), and use the innermost tender leaves for salad. Salad leaves must be trimmed, washed, and dried either by absorbing the moisture with paper towels or a clean dish towel or by my favorite method—spinning dry in a salad spinner. If the greens are fresh and have been thoroughly dried after washing, you can hardly go wrong. After drying, I usually wrap them between two layers of paper toweling, lightly roll into a cylinder, place in a plastic bag, seal tightly, and store them in the refrigerator up to 24 hours before using. The leaves should be torn rather than cut to avoid bruising. For salads that require shredded greens a knife must be used, but postpone shredding until just before the greens are needed, since they wilt quickly after being cut.

Many meals call for nothing more complex than a mixed green salad tossed with a light, refreshing dressing such as a vinaigrette of good imported vinegar and a little extra virgin olive oil. Top-quality fruity extra virgin olive oil is the best choice as a dressing for simple salads. Just remember to use a ratio of 1 teaspoon vinegar to 1 tablespoon extra virgin olive oil, seasoned with a little salt and pepper, for a simple dressing—no further embellishment is needed.

≪≪

Chick-pea Salad

I can still remember sitting at my grandfather's table eating this salad. The onion was actually quartered and used as a scoop for the beans. Both were eaten at the same time, with crusty Italian bread. He always insisted that the skins be removed from the chick-peas. This crispy salad can be varied by using other beans, such as cannellini or red kidney beans. It is an excellent accompaniment to the Tuna and Orange Salad (page 211) or Broiled Flounder with Thyme (page 198).

SERVES 2

1 small red onion (about 4 ounces)
One 16-ounce can chick-peas, rinsed and well drained
1½ teaspoons imported red wine vinegar
1 scant teaspoon minced fresh oregano or ¼ teaspoon crumbled dried oregano

⅛ teaspoon salt, if desired
⅛ teaspoon freshly milled black pepper
1 tablespoon olive oil, preferably extra virgin
1 tablespoon minced Italian parsley leaves

1. Peel onion and slice in half. Slice into paper-thin slices. Place onion in a bowl, cover with 4 ice cubes and fill bowl with enough cold water to cover onion slices. Let soak for at least 1 hour, or cover with plastic wrap and refrigerate until needed. (Soaking the red onion will ensure crispness.) Just before assembling salad, drain onion slices in strainer and thoroughly blot dry with paper towel.
2. To remove skins from chick-peas, squeeze each one gently between thumb and forefinger to slip off the skin; discard skins.
3. Place vinegar, oregano, salt, and pepper in serving bowl. Stir with fork or small whisk to combine. Add oil, a little at a time, and whisk thoroughly to incorporate.
4. Add onion, chick-peas, and parsley to bowl, toss thoroughly with

dressing, and serve. (Salad may be completely assembled, covered with plastic wrap, and stored in refrigerator up to 2 hours. Toss once again before serving.)

Cucumber and Radish Salad

Creamy horseradish dressing adds zesty excitement to this crispy salad.

SERVES 2

1 small cucumber (about 6 ounces), washed, trimmed, peeled, and thinly sliced, to make 1½ cups

6 large radishes (about 4 ounces), washed, trimmed, and sliced paper-thin, to make ¾ cup

Creamy Horseradish Dressing (page 264)

Arrange cucumber slices in a circular outer border, with slices slightly overlapping, on individual salad plates. Arrange radish slices in the same manner in the center of the plates, slightly overlapping cucumber slices. (Salad can be prepared up to 2 hours before serving. Cover plates with plastic wrap and refrigerate until needed.) When ready to serve, spoon dressing over each portion and serve immediately.

Grapefruit Salad with Watercress Dressing

A superb winter salad to make when firm pink grapefruit are in season. This salad is an excellent accompaniment to any of the fish or seafood recipes in this book.

SERVES 2

2 medium-sized firm pink grapefruit (about 1½ pounds total weight)

1 medium-sized bunch watercress (6 ounces)

1. With a small sharp knife, cut a small section from the top and bottom of each grapefruit. With the tip of the knife, divide grapefruit skin into 6 sections. Peel each section, removing most of the white membrane as you peel. With a vegetable peeler, remove all the white membrane from grapefruit.
2. Place a medium-sized strainer over a bowl. Cut out each grapefruit segment, removing its protective membrane over the strainer to catch juice. Let grapefruit drain in strainer for at least 30 minutes; reserve juice for dressing.
3. Wash watercress several times in cold water, drain well, and blot dry with paper towel or spin dry in salad spinner. Remove tough lower stems. Measure out ¼ cup watercress and reserve it for dressing.
4. Arrange remaining watercress on two salad plates. Arrange slices of grapefruit in a circular pattern, slightly overlapping, on top of watercress.

Watercress Dressing

2 tablespoons grapefruit juice
1 tablespoon olive oil,
preferably extra virgin
¼ cup watercress, cut into
1-inch pieces
⅛ teaspoon Dijon mustard

1 teaspoon honey, preferably
orange blossom
⅛ teaspoon salt, if desired
⅛ teaspoon freshly milled
black pepper

1. Place all of the dressing ingredients in a blender or food processor fitted with metal blade. Run machine nonstop until watercress is finely minced and dressing is creamy, about 1 minute; stop machine once to scrape inside work bowl with plastic spatula. (Dressing may be made up to 1 hour before using; transfer to a small jar and refrigerate until needed.)
2. Spoon dressing over each salad and serve immediately.

Honeydew Waldorf Salad

A lovely salad for those hot summer days, this is enlivened with the pale pink, delicately flavored strawberry yogurt dressing. This salad goes extremely well with Broiled Rock Cornish Game Hen (page 186), Broiled Swordfish Steaks (page 215), or Shrimp and Snow Pea Salad (page 207).

SERVES 2

2 cups bite-sized pieces
honeydew melon
1 cup small red seedless
grapes, stemmed, washed,
and blotted dry with paper
towel
½ cup thinly sliced celery,
strings removed

2 tablespoons pecans,
coarsely chopped
3 tablespoons Strawberry
Yogurt Dressing (page 265)
4 medium-sized iceberg or
Bibb lettuce leaves
(garnish)

1. Place melon pieces in strainer set over a bowl. Place in refrigerator to drain thoroughly for at least 1 hour; discard liquid.
2. Combine melon, grapes, celery, and pecans in a bowl. Spoon dressing over salad and lightly toss with two spoons. Cover with plastic wrap and refrigerate salad up to 2 hours. (Do not chill any longer than this because the honeydew may exude more liquid, making for a soggy salad).
3. When ready to serve, arrange lettuce leaves on two salad plates. Spoon salad on lettuce leaves and serve immediately.

Green Bean and Zucchini Salad with Tarragon Dressing

Cooked green beans and crunchy raw zucchini tossed with tarragon dressing give this salad a new dimension in texture as well as flavor.

SERVES 2

¼ pound green beans

1 small zucchini (about 4 ounces)

1. Wash green beans and trim both ends. If green beans are more than 4 inches in length, slice diagonally in half crosswise. Cook beans in 2 quarts boiling water until tender when tested with fork, about 5 minutes. Drain in colander, rinse under cold water, and blot dry with paper towel.
2. Scrub zucchini and blot dry with paper towel. Trim ends and cut into 2-inch lengths. Slice each piece in half lengthwise and slice into ¼-inch julienne strips.

Tarragon Dressing

1 medium-sized clove garlic,
  peeled and split in half
1 teaspoon imported white
  wine vinegar
1½ teaspoons minced fresh
  tarragon or ½ teaspoon
  crumbled dried tarragon

⅛ teaspoon sugar
⅛ teaspoon salt, if desired
⅛ teaspoon freshly milled
  black pepper
1 tablespoon olive oil,
  preferably extra virgin

1. Thoroughly rub inside of serving bowl with split garlic and leave in bowl. Push garlic to one side and place remaining dressing ingredients except olive oil in serving bowl. Stir with fork or small wire whisk to combine. Add oil a little at a time and whisk to combine thoroughly.
2. Add zucchini to serving bowl and toss with dressing. Add green beans and toss once again. Cover with plastic wrap and refrigerate for at least 1 hour before serving. Remove garlic and toss once again just before serving.

⫷⫷

Mixed Green Salad with Mustard Vinaigrette

A good salad to serve during the winter months when Bibb or Boston lettuce is plentiful. Mustard and garlic add a snappy bite to the dressing.

SERVES 2

1 medium-sized head Bibb or Boston lettuce (about 7 ounces)
1 medium-sized head Belgian endive (2 ounces)
4 large radishes (3 ounces), washed, trimmed, and thinly sliced

4 medium-sized mushrooms (3 ounces), wiped, stems removed, and thinly sliced

1. Using a pair of kitchen shears, trim any bruised tips from lettuce. Separate leaves and wash greens several times in cold water. Drain well and gently blot dry with paper towel, or spin dry in salad spinner. Break into bite-sized pieces and place in salad bowl.
2. Halve Belgian endive lengthwise. Cut out bitter center core; wipe leaves with a dampened cloth to remove sand. Slice into ½-inch widths and add to salad bowl. Add radishes and mushrooms to bowl. (Salad ingredients can be prepared up to 2 hours before serving. Cover with plastic wrap and refrigerate until needed.)

Mustard Vinaigrette Dressing

1 teaspoon imported white wine vinegar
¼ teaspoon minced garlic
¼ teaspoon Dijon mustard
1½ teaspoons minced fresh basil or ½ teaspoon crumbled dried basil

⅛ teaspoon sugar
⅛ teaspoon salt, if desired
⅛ teaspoon freshly milled black pepper
1 tablespoon olive oil, preferably extra virgin

1. Place all of the dressing ingredients except olive oil in a small bowl and stir with fork or small whisk to combine. Add oil a little at a time and whisk until dressing is well combined.
2. Toss dressing with salad ingredients and serve immediately.

Lettuce and Carrot Salad

Easy to prepare and eye-catching. The horseradish dressing gives this salad its special, snappy taste.

SERVES 2

½ medium-sized head iceberg lettuce (about 6 ounces)
2 medium-sized carrots (5 ounces)
2 tablespoons snipped fresh chives or thinly sliced scallions (green part only)

Creamy Horseradish Dressing (page 264)

1. Remove center core from lettuce. Separate leaves and wash in cold water. Drain well and gently blot dry with paper towel or spin dry in salad spinner. Stack several leaves at a time and slice crosswise into ¼-inch strips. Place a mound of shredded lettuce on each salad plate.
2. Wash carrots, trim, and peel lightly with a vegetable peeler. Cut into 2-inch lengths, place horizontally in food processor fitted with shredding disk, and use firm pressure on pusher to grate. (If you do not have a food processor, leave carrots whole and shred on the coarse side of a grater.) Mound carrots in center of plate and garnish with chives or scallions.
3. Spoon dressing over each portion and serve immediately.

Orange and Kiwi Salad

A perfectly delightful highlight when served with either Broiled Rock Cornish Game Hen (page 186) or Broiled Flounder with Thyme (page 198). This colorful recipe was developed by David Wald, a dear friend and excellent cook.

SERVES 2

2 large navel oranges (1¼ pounds total weight)
2 kiwi fruit (3 ounces total weight)
2 teaspoons raspberry vinegar

⅛ teaspoon sugar
⅛ teaspoon salt, if desired
⅛ teaspoon freshly milled black pepper
1 tablespoon olive oil, preferably extra virgin

1. Cut a slice from top and bottom of oranges to expose the fruit. Peel the oranges and remove all the white membrane with a vegetable peeler. Slice crosswise into ¼-inch rounds. Place in strainer set over a bowl to drain thoroughly for at least 30 minutes; reserve 1 tablespoon juice for dressing.
2. Cut about ¼ inch from top and bottom of kiwi fruit. To remove the fuzzy brown skin, peel lengthwise with a vegetable peeler using a zigzag motion. Slice into ¼-inch rounds.
3. Arrange orange slices in a circular outer border, with slices slightly overlapping, on individual salad plates. Arrange kiwi slices in the same manner in center of the plates, slightly overlapping orange slices.
4. Place raspberry vinegar, 1 tablespoon reserved orange juice, sugar, salt, and pepper in a small bowl. Stir with fork or small whisk to combine. Add oil a little at a time and whisk until dressing is well blended.
5. Spoon dressing over fruit and serve immediately.

⫷⫷⫷

Red Onion and Tomato Salad

Serve this salad during the summer months when tomatoes are at their best and fresh basil is readily available.

S E R V E S 2

1 small red onion (about 4
ounces)
2 large, firm, ripe tomatoes
(about 1 pound total
weight)
⅛ teaspoon sugar
⅛ teaspoon freshly milled
black pepper

2 teaspoons freshly grated
Parmesan cheese
1 tablespoon olive oil,
preferably extra virgin
6 large basil leaves, sliced
into fine shreds (see Note)

1. Peel onion and slice into paper-thin rounds. Separate onion rings
and place in a bowl. Cover rings with 4 ice cubes and fill with
enough cold water to cover. Let soak for at least 1 hour or cover
with plastic wrap and refrigerate until needed. (Soaking the red
onion will ensure crispness when ready to serve.) Just before assembling salad, drain onion rings in strainer and blot thoroughly
dry with paper towel.
2. Wash tomatoes and blot dry with paper towel. Core tomatoes; slice
off about ½ inch from top and bottom of each tomato and discard.
Slice each tomato into 3 even rounds.
3. Arrange tomato rounds and onion rings in an overlapping pattern
on two salad plates.
4. Place sugar, pepper, and Parmesan cheese in a small bowl. Stir
with fork or small whisk to combine. Add oil a little at a time and
whisk thoroughly to incorporate.
5. Spoon dressing over the tomato and onion slices. Sprinkle basil
over the top and serve.

N O T E : To cut basil leaves into fine shreds, known as a chiffonade,
stack the leaves one on top of another. Starting from broad end of
leaves, roll the leaves into a tight cylinder. Place the cylinder on a

cutting board. Holding the cylinder tightly to keep its shape, cut crosswise through the roll at ¹⁄₁₆-inch intervals to produce find shreds. To prevent basil shreds from darkening, slice into chiffonade just before dressing salad.

Romaine and Strawberry Salad

The flavorful creamy dressing truly enhances this refreshing salad, which can be served with or after the meal. It is an excellent accompaniment to Peachy Drumsticks with Orange Sauce (page 185) or Lamb Shoulder Chops with Mustard and Dill (page 152).

SERVES 2

1 medium-sized head romaine lettuce (about 1 pound)
12 medium-sized ripe strawberries (6 ounces)

3 tablespoons Strawberry Yogurt Dressing (page 265)

1. Discard tough outer leaves from romaine. Break off the tender inner leaves and wash several times in cold water. Drain well and blot thoroughly dry with paper towel or spin dry in salad spinner. Break off the tough bottom ends of each leaf and discard. Place leaves between 2 layers of paper toweling; roll up and place in plastic bag and seal tightly. Refrigerate for at least 2 hours to crisp the romaine. (Greens may be refrigerated up to 24 hours before using.)
2. Rinse berries in cold water, drain thoroughly in strainer, and blot dry with paper towel or spin dry in salad spinner. To core the berries, gather up the leaves of each stem cap and with the tip of a small knife, cut a ¼-inch circle around the base of the cap. Pull the leaves and the white core will come out as well. Slice strawber-

ries in half lengthwise. Transfer, cut sides down, to a flat plate lined with paper towel. Cover with plastic wrap and refrigerate until needed. (Berries may be prepared up to 2 hours before assembling salad.)

3. When ready to serve, break greens into bite-sized pieces and place on two salad plates (preferably glass). Mound strawberries in center of each plate, cut sides down. Spoon 1½ tablespoons dressing on top of each salad and serve immediately.

Spinach Salad

A perfect salad for any season. The mellow tomato shallot dressing brings out its full flavor.

SERVES 2

1 medium-sized cucumber (about 8 ounces)	3 tablespoons Tomato Shallot Dressing (page 266)
½ pound spinach	

1. Trim ends and peel cucumber with a vegetable peeler. Slice in half lengthwise and scoop out seeds with a melon baller. Slice lengthwise into ¼-inch strips and then crosswise into 2½-inch pieces. Place in a small deep bowl, cover with ice cubes, and fill with enough cold water to cover. Place in refrigerator to crisp for at least 2 hours.

2. Wash spinach clusters several times in cold water until there is not a grain of sand left. Remove stems and discard. Blot dry with paper towel or spin dry in salad spinner. (Spinach may be prepared up to this point 2 hours before serving. Place in a plastic bag and refrigerate until needed.)

3. When ready to serve, stack about 8 spinach leaves at a time on a

cutting board and slice crosswise into ½-inch strips. Repeat with remaining leaves. Place a mound of spinach on each salad plate.
4. Drain cucumber strips in a strainer and blot thoroughly dry with paper towel. Mound strips in center of each plate.
5. Spoon 1½ tablespoons dressing on top of each salad and serve immediately.

Zucchini Salad

This salad is best when you can find small, firm zucchini at the market.

SERVES 2

3 small zucchini (12 ounces total weight)
3 tablespoons Tomato Shallot Dressing (page 266)

4 large-Bibb lettuce leaves
1 teaspoon minced Italian parsley leaves (garnish)

1. Scrub zucchini under cold running water until the skins feel clean and smooth. Trim both ends. Bring 1 quart of water to a rolling boil and add zucchini. When water returns to a boil, cook, uncovered, until barely tender when tested with the tip of a knife, about 3 minutes. Transfer to a colander and refresh under cold water. Blot dry with paper towel and cool to room temperature. Slice into ½ inch rounds and place in a small bowl. Toss with dressing. Cover with plastic wrap and refrigerate for at least 2 hours.
2. Wash lettuce leaves in cold water. Drain well; place between 2 layers of paper towel and gently blot dry.
3. Place 2 lettuce leaves on each salad plate. Toss zucchini again with dressing and spoon on top of greens. Garnish each with minced parsley and serve.

DRESSINGS

Food Processor Mayonnaise

This is the very first recipe I made when I purchased my first food processor, and I have been making it ever since. It is prepared in a matter of seconds, and once you taste it you may never buy mayonnaise again. You can also substitute fresh lemon juice or imported white wine vinegar for the apple cider vinegar. Remember: To form a perfect emulsion, the egg and oil must be at room temperature.

YIELDS 1 CUP

- 1 extra large egg, at room temperature
- 2 tablespoons apple cider vinegar
- 1 teaspoon sugar
- ½ teaspoon Dijon mustard
- ¼ teaspoon salt, if desired
- ½ teaspoon freshly milled white pepper
- ¾ cup olive oil, at room temperature

Insert metal blade in food processor. Combine all ingredients except oil in work bowl. Add 2 tablespoons oil and run machine nonstop for 30 seconds. Remove cover and scrape down the sides of work bowl with a plastic spatula. Replace cover and turn machine on. With the machine running, drizzle remaining oil through the feed tube in a very fine, steady stream; the mixture will emulsify and become thick. Using a rubber spatula, transfer mayonnaise to an 8-ounce airtight jar. Keep refrigerated until needed. Mayonnaise will keep up to 2 weeks in refrigerator.

Creamy Horseradish Dressing

This tangy, creamy dressing is alive with the flavor of horseradish. Besides using it on the two salads in this chapter for which it is recommended, you will find that it also makes an extraordinary contribution when spooned over cold, poached chicken breast or chilled, cooked shrimp.

YIELDS ABOUT ¼ CUP
SERVES 2

2 tablespoons low-fat yogurt
1 ½ teaspoons bottled
   horseradish, well drained
1 teaspoon apple cider
   vinegar
¼ teaspoon Dijon mustard

¼ teaspoon freshly milled
   black pepper
1 ½ teaspoons olive oil,
   preferably extra virgin

Place all of the above ingredients except oil in a small bowl and beat with a fork or small whisk to combine. Add oil a little at a time beating constantly with fork or whisk until dressing is creamy. (Dressing may be made up to 4 hours before serving; transfer to a small jar and refrigerate until needed. Whisk dressing once again before using.)

Strawberry Yogurt Dressing

Commercial yogurt tends to be watery, so it is very important that the yogurt be thoroughly drained before making dressing. In addition to the recipes for which it is specified, this dressing is also excellent spooned over any combination of the following fruits cut into bite-sized pieces: nectarines, cantaloupe, watermelon, or pineapple. Serve on a bed of Bibb or iceberg lettuce and garnish with thin slices of lime. Dressing can be stored in refrigerator in an airtight jar up to 8 days. Whisk with fork before spooning or tossing with different salads.

YIELDS ABOUT ⅔ CUP

½ cup low-fat yogurt
6 medium-sized ripe
   strawberries (6 ounces
   total weight), washed,
   hulled, blotted dry, and
   quartered, to make ⅓ cup
   well packed
2 tablespoons mayonnaise,
   preferably homemade
   (page 263)

1 teaspoon fresh lemon juice
1 teaspoon honey,
   preferably orange blossom
1½ teaspoons snipped fresh
   mint or ½ teaspoon
   crumbled dried mint
¼ teaspoon salt, if desired

1. Line a fine mesh strainer with a double thickness of dampened cheesecloth. Spoon yogurt into lined strainer set over a bowl. Place, uncovered, in refrigerator to drain thoroughly for at least 1½ hours. (Yogurt will exude as much as 2 tablespoons of liquid, and after draining it should be the consistency of whipped heavy cream.) Discard liquid. Using a rubber spatula, scrape yogurt from cheesecloth into food processor fitted with metal blade.

2. Add remaining ingredients to food processor. Run machine nonstop for 30 seconds. Remove cover and scrape down sides of work bowl with plastic spatula. Run for an additional 30 seconds until dressing is pale pink, with a smooth consistency. Transfer to airtight jar and refrigerate for at least 3 hours before using so that all the flavors meld together.

Tomato Shallot Dressing

Make sure you select an extremely well ripened tomato to bring out the full mellow flavoring of this dressing. Not only does it go well with spinach and zucchini, it also harmonizes very nicely when tossed with bite-sized salad greens such as Bibb or romaine lettuce. Dressing can be stored in the refrigerator in an airtight jar for up to 10 days. Whisk with fork before spooning or tossing with various salads.

YIELDS ABOUT ⅔ CUP

1 medium-sized very ripe
tomato (about 6 ounces)

1 tablespoon imported white
wine vinegar

2 tablespoons olive oil,
preferably extra virgin

1 tablespoon snipped fresh
basil or 1 teaspoon
crumbled dried basil

¼ teaspoon sugar

¼ teaspoon salt, if desired

¼ teaspoon freshly milled
black pepper

1 large shallot (2 ounces),
peeled and quartered

1. Plump tomato in 1 quart boiling water for 1 minute. Rinse under cold water. When cool enough to handle, core tomato and peel skin with a small paring knife. Cut in half crosswise and squeeze to discard most of the seeds. Place tomato on a plate and cut into 1-inch cubes.

2. Put tomato and any accumulated juices from plate in food processor fitted with metal blade. Add all the remaining ingredients except shallot to work bowl. Turn machine on and drop quartered shallot, one piece at a time, through the feed tube. Stop machine once and scrape down inside work bowl with plastic spatula. Run machine nonstop until shallot is finely minced and dressing is a smooth creamy consistency, about 1 minute. Transfer dressing to airtight jar and refrigerate until needed.

⋘

YEAST BREADS

《《

Today, all across the country people are becoming more aware of pure, wholesome, natural foods. One reflection of this trend is the resurgence in the popularity of making bread. There is nothing more delightful than the rich aroma of freshly made bread right from the oven. Once tasted, homemade bread truly spoils one for any other kind.

There are a variety of reasons why so many of us favor homemade bread. It is difficult to find commercially prepared bread that has no artificial flavoring or preservatives added. The incorporation of a variety of grains will also increase the natural fiber so important in our diet. The amount of salt and the quality of ingredients can also be monitored when we bake it ourselves.

One of the best things that this current enthusiasm has brought is the return of bread flour to supermarket shelves. After an absence of more than three decades, bread flour is readily available to the public and does not require trips to specialty shops for its purchase.

I remember going as a child to our local grocer to purchase flour for my mother, who baked bread no less than twice a week. At that time, bread flour was delivered to the grocer in 50- and 100-pound muslin sacks, some plain and some with printed patterns. My mother bleached and washed the plain ones, and the smaller pieces were saved for my first sewing lessons. I can still remember my mother and her friends gathered around the radio at night and adding fancy stitches to convert the sacks into dish towels while they listened to the "Lux Family Theatre." Whenever a schoolmate appeared in class with a spanking new, yet all too familiar print dress, I realized we were not the only ones for whom the grocer was saving empty flour sacks.

When I was married, some of the dish towels made by my mother and her friends were part of my trousseau. Several of these were large enough to be used for pastry cloths, and they continue to be used to this day.

There is nothing mysterious or difficult about making bread. The amount of time needed to make old-fashioned homemade bread is minimal, especially with the aid of today's modern appliances, the food processor and the electric mixer.

Good ingredients, recipes, and techniques make beautiful bread. Be-

fore you begin mixing any dough, I strongly advise that you read the Guide for Basic Yeast Breads, and Simple Techniques, which follows. Understanding the basics will save you time, make bread-making easier, and clear up any questions or problems that might arise in the bread-making process.

Guide for Basic Yeast Breads, and Simple Techniques

Bread Pans

Black steel loaf pans are best for baking bread. Breads baked in this type of pan always produce a very crisp crust. Breads baked in shiny metal pans may require more browning. When using glass pans reduce the required baking temperature 25 degrees, as breads bake faster in glass.

Flour

Flour is the basic ingredient in bread-making. Bread flour, because of its high gluten content, is best for basic bread-making. It is readily available in most supermarkets today, but if you cannot obtain it, unbleached all-purpose flour will yield an excellent bread. Whole wheat flour (sometimes referred to as graham flour) should be purchased in small quantities (2-pound bags) and refrigerated to keep from spoiling. Whole wheat flour works best when combined with bread flour or unbleached flour (which produces a stronger gluten network) to yield a higher volume, fine texture, and more satisfactory baked product. For enriched sweet breads, unbleached flour provides a lighter texture than bread flour. For more details on flour, see section on ingredients (page 32).

For successful bread-making, it is essential that flour and all dry ingredients be measured accurately into dry-ingredient measuring cups. (Such cups have no lip above the top measure.) If flour has been stored in a container for a period of time (about 2 months), stir it with a long wooden spoon to loosen before measuring.

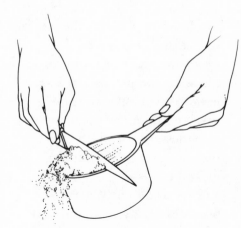

Scoop the flour from the storage container into dry-ingredient measuring cups and then level off with a narrow metal spatula or the straight edge of a knife. Do not shake, tap, or pack the flour down into the cup before leveling.

The room temperature, the humidity in the air, and the type flour selected will affect the amount of liquid that the flour will absorb to produce a dough of the right consistency. Bread flour will absorb more liquid than unbleached all-purpose flour. For this reason, all recipes will tell you to withhold some of the flour, checking the consistency of the dough first before adding any additional flour.

Yeast

All recipes in this book were developed using active dry yeast. When purchasing, always check the expiration date stamped on each package and use within the recommended time. When proofing yeast, be sure to use the size measuring cup specified in each recipe to allow expansion of the yeast mixture, which usually doubles in volume. Ideally, the temperature of the water should be between 105 degrees F. and 115 degrees F. You can test the water temperature with a candy or instant-read thermometer. If you do not own either of these thermometers, test by dropping a few drops of the warm water on the

inside of your wrist; the water should feel lukewarm. To proof the yeast (making sure it's alive and active), the sugar is mixed with the warm water first and then the yeast granules are sprinkled over the mixture. Stir mixture briefly to dissolve granules and set aside until mixture becomes foamy and doubles in volume, about 5 to 10 minutes. If yeast mixture does not foam after resting for 15 minutes, dispose of it and start over with another packet. (The yeast may have been killed by the heat of the water; on the other hand, if liquid is too cool, it can retard the growth.) Just before adding proofed yeast mixture to any bread recipe, whisk the mixture vigorously so that it will combine evenly with remaining ingredients.

Mixing and Kneading

FOOD PROCESSOR METHOD

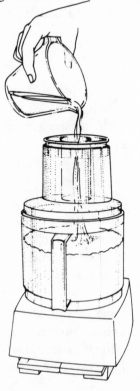

When you make bread dough in the food processor, the dry ingredients can be measured right into the work bowl. Remember to reserve the amount of flour specified in each recipe because you may not need the full amount. Be sure to pour yeast mixture and any other specified liquid through the feed tube with the machine running. This will avoid any leakage through the center shaft of the work bowl and help prevent dough from getting stuck under the metal blade. After all the liquid is added through the feed tube, the dough is kneaded by letting the machine run nonstop for 50 seconds. The dough will mass together and leave the sides of the work bowl. At this point the dough should be smooth, elastic, and slightly sticky to the touch. If the consistency of the dough is too wet or sticky (because of temperature and/or humidity) add reserved flour, 1 tablespoon at a time, and process for 5 seconds after each addition until the proper consistency is achieved. After you remove the dough from the processor, knead for a couple of minutes by hand on a clean, dry work surface until the dough feels nonsticky, satiny, and smooth. This small amount of kneading will result in a better bread product.

ELECTRIC MIXER AND HAND METHOD

Measure dry ingredients into large mixer bowl. Reserve the amount of flour specified in each recipe because you may not need the full amount. Add to the dry ingredients the proofed yeast mixture plus any other ingredients specified in each recipe. Beat the bread mixture until smooth, usually about 2 minutes. (Beating with the mixer helps develop the gluten to give bread more structure, and will also shorten the amount of time necessary to finish kneading dough by hand.) At this point, the dough will be extremely sticky. Add the reserved flour by hand (amount will be specified in each recipe), gradually stirring it in bit by bit just until the dough is a soft mass and pulls away from the sides of the bowl. The dough should feel somewhat sticky to handle, but stiff enough to hold its shape when turned out onto a lightly floured work surface. Do not be concerned if a small amount of dough sticks to the bottom of the bowl; just scrape it up and work it into the dough.

As you knead by hand, the dough will change from a rough, sticky mass into a nonsticky, satiny, smooth ball. You will feel the change taking place as kneading progresses. On a lightly floured work surface, press dough to flatten it. Rub a little flour on your hands. Pick up edge of dough farthest

from you and fold dough in
half toward you. With the
heels of both hands, push
dough away from you. Fold
dough once again and give a
quarter turn on the board. Repeat
pushing, folding, and turning until
dough is nonsticky, elastic, satiny,
and smooth, about 8 to 10 minutes. If dough
still feels sticky after 5 minutes of kneading, sprinkle about 1½
teaspoons of the remaining flour on the board under dough.
Lightly flour hands once again and continue kneading until dough
is the proper consistency.

First Rising

After kneading, shape the
dough into a ball and place
it in a greased ceramic or
glass bowl. (Do not use a
metal bowl; it conducts heat
and may cause the dough to
rise too rapidly.) Turn ball
in bowl to grease entire
surface. Cover bowl with plastic
wrap. Yeast dough needs a constant
warm, draft-free atmosphere for
uniform rising. I recommend putting it to raise in an oven. If you
have a gas oven with a gas pilot, no preheating is necessary. An
electric oven or a gas oven with an electric pilot should be preheated at lowest setting for 2 minutes and then turned off
immediately. Place bowl of dough in the center of a large bath
towel and fold ends loosely over top to cover. (Wrapping the bowl
in a towel will cushion the bottom and help insulate it from oven
rack.) Most doughs will rise and double in volume in about 1 to 1½
hours, depending on the type of flour used. To test the dough,
press two fingers into the risen dough close to the side of bowl. If
the indentation remains, the dough has risen sufficiently.

Placing bowl of dough in center of bath towel.

Testing risen dough.

Pulling edges of dough to the center.

Punching, Shaping, and Second Rising

After the dough has risen to twice its original size, punch it down. Punch your fist firmly into the center of the dough to expel any large gas bubbles. Pull the edges of the dough to the center and consolidate it in the bottom of the bowl. Remove dough to a clean, dry, lightly floured work surface. For a single loaf you will leave the dough in one solid mass; otherwise, you will divide it according to instructions in each recipe. Gently knead the dough once again for about 2 minutes. Reshape into ball, cover lightly with a towel, and allow to rest for at least 10 minutes. During this short rest period, the gluten mesh in the dough will relax a little, making dough easier to handle when shaping.

In shaping dough for a single loaf pan, roll to the size specified in each recipe. It is important that the rolled dough exactly match the length of the pan so that it will fit snugly in the pan for the second rising.

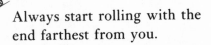

Always start rolling with the end farthest from you.

As you roll dough toward you, use your thumbs to seal to produce a compact cylinder.

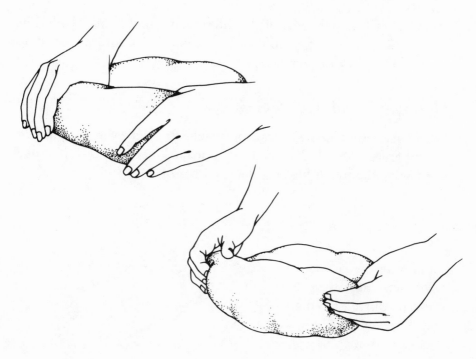

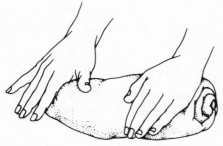

With the palms of your hands, gently roll the cylinder back and forth to even out the surface.

Pinch center seam and ends well to seal so they won't pop open in baking. Place the sealed loaf seam side down in the greased pan for second rising.

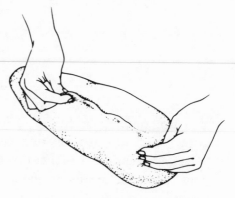

Cover the dough once again, and return it to the turned off oven for its second rising until doubled in volume, noting the specific time suggested in each recipe.

Finishing Bread and Baking

Remove risen, shaped loaf from oven. Preheat oven to specified temperature. Slash the top of the unbaked loaf with a single-edge razor or the metal blade of food processor.

Slashing the surface of loaf lets excess gas escape during baking and prevents the top of loaf from splitting in the oven.

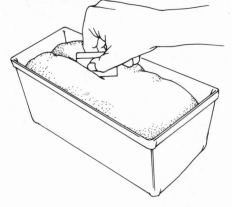

Unglazed bread will brown without a sheen. If you prefer a shiny, crisp crust, make a glaze by beating one egg (or 1 egg yolk) with 1 tablespoon water. Dip a pastry brush into glaze and apply it lightly to the surface of the bread, being careful not to let excess glaze drip onto pan.

You can then sprinkle top of loaf with 1 tablespoon sesame or poppy seeds, wheat germ, or rolled oats, if you like. Any remaining glaze may be placed in a covered jar and refrigerated for up to 5 days; whisk before using again.

Place the loaf in your oven, preheated to the temperature recommended for each recipe. Bake for the specified amount of time. Check to see if the top of loaf is well browned. Remove the bread onto a wire rack. Tap the bottom of loaf with your knuckles; if bread sounds hollow and hard, it is done. If not, return loaf to oven, without the pan, for an additional 5 to 10 minutes; test once again.

To Serve and Store

It is best to allow bread to cool to room temperature before serving. Cooled bread will be easier to slice without tearing or crumbling. Rolls cool faster and can be served warm. To reheat, place on a cookie sheet in a preheated 300-degree oven (or toaster oven) for 10 minutes before serving. Cooling bread on a wire rack will let air circulate around bread, which helps the crust to remain crisp.

To store bread or rolls, place in a tightly sealed plastic bag and refrigerate. Bread stored in this manner will stay fresh up to 5 days. To freeze, wrap bread in plastic wrap, then place in a plastic bag and seal tightly. Rolls should be placed in a double plastic bag before freezing. Bread and rolls can be frozen for up to 3 months. To defrost, remove wrappings and let bread or rolls thaw at room temperature (bread about 3 hours and rolls about 1 hour). Place defrosted bread in a preheated 350-degree oven for 10 minutes to crisp before serving, if desired.

Wheat Germ Bread

This bread always brings rave notices with every bite. It is also wonderful for sandwiches and toast.

YIELDS 1 LOAF

2 tablespoons sugar
¾ cup warm water (105 degrees F. to 115 degrees F.)
One ¼-ounce package active dry yeast
2¾ to 3 cups bread flour or unbleached all-purpose flour
¼ cup wheat germ

¼ cup nonfat dry milk powder
½ teaspoon salt
2 tablespoons unsalted margarine at room temperature, cut into 8 pieces
1 extra large egg at room temperature, lightly beaten

In a 2-cup glass measure, stir 1 tablespoon sugar into warm water. Sprinkle yeast over water and stir briefly until completely dissolved. Set aside until foamy, about 5 to 10 minutes.

FOOD PROCESSOR METHOD

1. Fit food processor with metal blade. Put 2¾ cups bread flour or unbleached flour in work bowl; reserve remaining ¼ cup. Add wheat germ, dry milk, remaining 1 tablespoon sugar, and salt to work bowl; process for 10 seconds to combine. Add margarine and process for another 10 seconds.
2. Using a fork or small whisk, beat yeast mixture briefly. Turn machine on and pour yeast mixture through feed tube; process until blended, about 10 seconds. Stop machine and scrape down inside work bowl with plastic spatula.
3. With machine running, slowly drizzle lightly beaten egg through feed tube. Process for 50 seconds. (Dough will form a mass, and is kneaded by spinning in machine for this period of time.) At this point, dough should feel smooth, elastic, and just slightly sticky to the touch. If dough feels wet, gradually add reserved flour 1 table-

spoon at a time and process for 5 seconds after each addition until dough is the proper consistency.

4. Transfer dough to a clean, dry work surface. Knead until dough is smooth and satiny, about 2 minutes. Shape dough into a ball.

ELECTRIC MIXER AND HAND METHOD

1. In large mixer bowl, put 2½ cups bread flour or unbleached flour; reserve remaining ½ cup. Add wheat germ, dry milk, remaining 1 tablespoon sugar, and salt. Run mixer at low speed for 30 seconds to combine.

2. Using a fork or small whisk, beat yeast mixture briefly and pour into flour mixture. Add margarine and lightly beaten egg; blend at low speed until moistened, about 30 seconds. Turn machine off and scrape inside bowl with spatula. Turn speed to medium and beat until smooth, about 2 minutes. At this point dough will be extremely sticky. Clean off any sticky dough attached to beaters and add to bowl. Remove bowl from stand. With your hand, gradually stir in reserved flour a little at a time (starting with ¼ cup and then adding 2 tablespoons at a time), just until the dough is a soft mass and pulls away from the sides of the bowl.

3. Transfer dough to a lightly floured work surface. Rub a little flour on your hands and knead the dough until smooth, elastic, and satiny, about 8 to 10 minutes. If dough still feels sticky after 5 minutes of kneading, sprinkle 1½ teaspoons of flour on board under dough. Lightly flour hands once again and continue kneading until dough is the proper consistency. Shape dough into a ball.

FIRST RISING

1. Adjust rack to center of oven, set oven to lowest temperature for 2 minutes, and then turn off. If you have a gas oven with a gas pilot light, no preheating is necessary.

2. Lightly grease bottom and sides of a 2½-quart bowl with ½ teaspoon unsalted margarine, softened. Place dough in greased bowl, turning ball to coat entire surface with margarine. Cover bowl with plastic wrap. Place bowl in center of bath towel and fold ends loosely over top to cover. Transfer to oven and let dough rise until double in bulk, about 1 hour.

SHAPING AND SECOND RISING

1. Lightly grease bottom and sides of an 8½- by 4½- by 3-inch loaf pan; set aside.
2. Using a closed fist, punch risen dough down in center. Gently pull the outside edges of dough to center.
3. Transfer dough to a clean, dry work surface. Knead dough gently for 30 seconds. Shape into a ball and cover with a dish towel. Let dough rest for 10 minutes before shaping into loaf (letting the dough rest briefly will make rolling and shaping easier).
4. Gently pat down dough with fingertips to flatten into a rectangle. Roll dough into a sheet about 10 inches long by 8 inches wide. Starting at the far narrow edge, roll up jelly roll fashion toward you, sealing with your thumbs as you roll. Pinch seam and ends of dough firmly with fingertips to seal well. Place seam side down in greased pan. Lightly cover with plastic wrap and place a dish towel loosely on top. Return to turned off oven and let dough rise again until doubled, about 1 hour. (Dough should be about ½ inch above rim of pan when doubled.)

TO BAKE

1 egg   1 tablespoon wheat germ
1 tablespoon water

1. Leave rack in center of oven and preheat to 375 degrees.
2. With a single-edge razor blade or the metal blade from the food processor, cut a slash about ¼ inch deep down center top of loaf.
3. In a small bowl, beat egg with water. Lightly brush top of loaf with glaze and sprinkle with wheat germ.
4. Bake in preheated oven until the top is well browned, about 30 to 35 minutes. Remove loaf from pan to a wire rack and tap the bottom with your knuckles. If the bread sounds hollow and hard, it is done; if not, return loaf to oven, without its pan, for an additional 5 to 7 minutes; test again. Transfer to wire rack and cool to room temperature before serving, storing, or freezing.

≪≪

Mini Dill Breads

These savory loaves fill the kitchen with a pleasing aroma while baking. Serve them with lunch or dinner. They also make very welcome gifts.

YIELDS 3 LOAVES

1 tablespoon sugar

½ cup plus 2 tablespoons warm water (105 degrees F. to 115 degrees F.)

One ¼-ounce package active dry yeast

2¾ to 3 cups bread flour or unbleached all-purpose flour

¼ cup nonfat dry milk powder

3 tablespoons minced fresh dill or 1 tablespoon dried dillweed

½ teaspoon salt

1 extra large egg white at room temperature (reserve yolk for glaze)

1 extra large egg at room temperature

2 tablespoons olive oil

In a 2-cup glass measure, stir sugar into warm water. Sprinkle yeast over water and stir briefly until completely dissolved. Set aside until foamy, about 5 to 10 minutes.

FOOD PROCESSOR METHOD

1. Fit food processor with metal blade. Put 2¾ cups bread flour or unbleached flour in work bowl; reserve remaining ¼ cup. Add dry milk, dill or dillweed, and salt to work bowl; process for 10 seconds to combine.

2. With a fork or small whisk, beat yeast mixture briefly. Turn machine on and pour yeast mixture through feed tube; process until blended, about 10 seconds. Stop machine and scrape down inside work bowl with plastic spatula.

3. In glass measure, place egg white, whole egg, and oil; whisk briefly to combine. With machine running, slowly drizzle egg mixture through feed tube. Process for 50 seconds. (Dough will form a mass, and is kneaded by spinning in machine for this period of

time.) At this point, dough should feel smooth, elastic, and just slightly sticky to the touch. If dough feels wet, gradually add reserved flour 1 tablespoon at a time and process for 5 seconds after each addition until dough is the proper consistency.

4. Transfer dough to a clean, dry work surface. Knead until dough is smooth and satiny, about 2 minutes. Shape dough into ball.

ELECTRIC MIXER AND HAND METHOD

1. In large mixer bowl, put 2½ cups bread flour or unbleached flour; reserve remaining ½ cup. Add dry milk, dill or dillweed, and salt. Run machine at low speed for 30 seconds to combine.

2. Using a fork or small whisk, whisk yeast mixture briefly and pour into flour mixture. Add egg white, whole egg, and oil; blend at low speed until moistened, about 30 seconds. Turn machine off and scrape inside bowl with rubber spatula. Turn speed to medium and beat until smooth, about 2 minutes. At this point dough will be extremely sticky. Clean off any sticky dough attached to beaters and add to bowl. Remove bowl from stand. With your hands, gradually stir in reserved flour a little at a time (starting with ¼ cup and then adding 2 tablespoons, at a time), just until the dough is a soft mass and pulls away from the sides of the bowl.

3. Transfer dough to a lightly floured work surface. Rub a little flour on your hands and knead the dough until smooth, elastic, and satiny, about 8 to 10 minutes. If dough still feels sticky after 5 minutes of kneading, sprinkle about 1½ teaspoons flour on board under dough. Lightly flour hands once again and continue kneading until dough is the proper consistency. Shape dough into a ball.

FIRST RISING

1. Adjust rack to center of oven, set at lowest temperature for 2 minutes, and then turn off. If you have a gas oven with a gas pilot light, no preheating is necessary.

2. Lightly grease bottom and sides of a deep 2½-quart bowl with ½ teaspoon olive oil. Place dough in greased bowl, turning ball to coat entire surface with oil. Cover bowl loosely with plastic wrap. Place bowl in center of bath towel and fold ends loosely over top

to cover. Transfer to oven and let dough rise until double in bulk, about 1 hour.

SHAPING AND SECOND RISING

1. Lightly grease bottom and sides of three 5- by 2½- by 2½-inch loaf pans; set aside.
2. Using a closed fist, punch risen dough down in center. Gently pull the outside edges of dough to center.
3. Transfer dough to a clean, dry work surface. Divide dough into 3 equal pieces; knead each piece briefly. Shape each into a ball and cover with a dish towel. Let dough rest for 10 minutes before shaping into loaves (letting the dough rest briefly will make shaping easier). Take one ball of dough and leave remaining pieces covered with towel. With your hands, pat dough into a rectangle about 7 inches long and 5 inches wide. Starting at the far narrow edge, roll up jelly roll fashion toward you, sealing with your thumbs as you roll. Pinch seam and ends of dough firmly with fingertips to seal well. Place seam side down in greased pan; repeat with remaining dough. Lightly cover each pan with plastic wrap. Place pans 1 inch apart in turned off oven. Loosely cover all three with one dish towel. Let dough rise again until doubled, about 45 minutes. (Dough should be about ½ inch above rims of pans when doubled.)

TO BAKE

1 egg yolk   1 tablespoon water

1. Leave rack in center of oven and preheat to 375 degrees.
2. With a single-edge razor blade or the metal blade from the food processor, cut a slash about ¼ inch deep down center top of each loaf.
3. In a small bowl, beat egg yolk with water. Lightly brush top of each loaf with glaze.
4. Bake in preheated oven until the top of each loaf is well browned, about 20 to 25 minutes. Remove loaves from pans onto wire rack and tap the bottom of each with your knuckles. If the loaves sound hollow and hard, they are done; if not, return loaves to oven

without their pans for an additional 3 to 4 minutes; test again. Transfer to wire rack and cool to room temperature before serving, storing, or freezing.

Three-grain Rolls

Whole wheat flour, wheat germ, and brown sugar add natural goodness to these crusty rolls. They're great for breakfast, brunch, lunch, or dinner.

YIELDS 16 ROLLS

2 tablespoons plus 1 teaspoon light brown sugar

1 cup warm water (105 degrees F. to 115 degrees F.)

One ¼-ounce package active dry yeast

2 ¼ to 2 ¾ cups bread flour or unbleached all-purpose flour

½ cup whole wheat flour

¼ cup wheat germ

½ teaspoon salt

2 tablespoons olive oil

In a 2-cup glass measure, stir 1 teaspoon brown sugar into warm water. Sprinkle yeast over water and stir briefly until completely dissolved. Set aside until foamy, about 5 to 10 minutes.

FOOD PROCESSOR METHOD

1. Fit food processor with metal blade. Place 2 ½ cups bread flour or unbleached flour in work bowl; reserve remaining ¼ cup. Add all of the whole wheat flour, the wheat germ, the remaining 2 tablespoons brown sugar, and salt to work bowl; process until combined, about 10 seconds.

2. Using a fork or small whisk, beat yeast mixture briefly. Turn machine on and pour yeast mixture through feed tube; process until blended, about 10 seconds. Stop machine and scrape down inside work bowl with spatula.

3. With machine running, slowly drizzle oil through feed tube. Process for 50 seconds. (Dough will form a mass and is kneaded by spinning in machine for this period of time.) At this point, dough should feel smooth, elastic, and just slightly sticky to the touch. If dough feels wet, gradually add reserved flour 1 tablespoon at a time and process for 5 seconds after each addition until dough is the proper consistency.

4. Transfer dough to a clean, dry work surface. Knead until dough is smooth and satiny, about 2 minutes. Shape dough into a ball.

ELECTRIC MIXER AND HAND METHOD

1. In large mixer bowl, put 2 cups bread flour or unbleached flour; reserve remaining ¾ cup. Add all the whole wheat flour, the wheat germ, the remaining 2 tablespoons brown sugar, and salt. Run machine at low speed for 30 seconds to combine.

2. Using a fork or small whisk, beat yeast mixture briefly and pour into flour mixture. Add oil; blend at low speed until moistened, about 30 seconds. Turn machine off and scrape inside bowl with a rubber spatula. Turn speed to medium and beat until smooth, about 2 minutes. At this point dough will be extremely sticky. Clean off any sticky dough from beaters and add to bowl. Remove bowl from stand. With your hand, gradually stir in reserved flour a little at a time (starting with ¼ cup and then adding 1 tablespoon at a time), just until the dough is a soft mass and pulls away from the sides of the bowl.

3. Transfer dough to a lightly floured work surface. Rub a little flour on your hands and knead the dough until smooth, elastic, and satiny, about 8 to 10 minutes. If dough still feels sticky after 5 minutes of kneading, sprinkle about 1½ teaspoons of flour on board under dough. Lightly flour hands once again and continue kneading until dough is the proper consistency. Shape dough into a ball.

FIRST RISING

1. Adjust rack to center of oven, set oven to lowest temperature for 2 minutes, and then turn off. If you have a gas oven with a gas pilot light, no preheating is necessary.
2. Lightly grease bottom and sides of a deep 2½-quart bowl with ½ teaspoon olive oil. Place dough in greased bowl, turning ball to coat entire surface with oil. Cover bowl with plastic wrap. Place bowl in center of a bath towel and fold ends loosely over top to cover. Transfer to oven and let dough rise until double in bulk, about 1 hour.

SHAPING AND SECOND RISING

1. Lightly grease bottom of a large cookie sheet or jelly roll pan; set aside.
2. Using a closed fist, punch risen dough down in center. Gently pull the outside edges of dough to center.
3. Transfer dough to a clean, dry work surface. With your hands, roll dough into a rope about 16 inches long. Divide dough into 16 equal pieces. Knead each piece briefly. Cover with a dampened towel and let rest for 10 minutes. Take one piece of dough and leave remaining pieces covered with towel. Roll dough between the palm of your hands to form a ball. Transfer to greased baking sheet and repeat with remaining pieces of dough, placing rolls 2 inches apart. Lightly cover with dampened towel. Return to turned off oven and let rolls rise again until doubled, about 30 minutes.

TO BAKE

1 egg   1 tablespoon water

1. Leave rack in center of oven and preheat to 375 degrees.
2. Using a sharp pair of kitchen shears, snip a small, shallow cross on top of each roll.
3. In a small bowl, beat egg with water. Lightly brush the top of each roll with glaze, taking care not to get glaze on baking sheet.
4. Bake in preheated oven until rolls are glossy and evenly browned, about 20 to 25 minutes. Transfer rolls to wire rack and cool for 10 minutes if serving immediately. (Cool to room temperature if storing or freezing.)

Old-fashioned Sesame Oatmeal Bread

The combination of oats and toasted sesame seeds adds a rich, nutlike, old-fashioned flavor to this bread.

YIELDS 1 LOAF

1 cup water

½ cup old-fashioned oats, preferably Quaker

2 tablespoons unsalted margarine at room temperature, cut into 8 pieces

¼ cup unhulled sesame seeds

3 tablespoons light brown sugar

½ cup warm water (105 degrees F. to 115 degrees F.)

One ¼-ounce package active dry yeast

2½ to 3 cups bread flour or unbleached all-purpose flour

½ teaspoon salt

1. In a 1½-quart saucepan, bring 1 cup water to a boil over high heat. Remove from heat and add oats and margarine; stir until margarine is completely melted. Set aside and cool oatmeal mixture, uncovered, to lukewarm.
2. Place sesame seeds in a 10-inch skillet. Toast over medium heat, stirring constantly, until lightly golden, about 2 minutes. Stir toasted seeds into oatmeal mixture.
3. In a 2-cup glass measure, stir 1 tablespoon light brown sugar into ½ cup warm water. Sprinkle yeast over water and stir briefly until completely dissolved. Set aside until foamy, about 5 to 10 minutes.

FOOD PROCESSOR METHOD

1. Fit food processor with metal blade. Put 2½ cups bread flour or unbleached flour into work bowl; reserve remaining ½ cup. Add the remaining 2 tablespoons light brown sugar and salt to work bowl; process for 5 seconds to combine.
2. Add cooled oatmeal mixture and process until blended, about 20

seconds. Stop machine and scrape down inside work bowl with plastic spatula.

3. Using a fork or small whisk, beat yeast mixture briefly. Turn machine on and pour yeast mixture through feed tube. Process for 50 seconds. (Dough will form a mass and is kneaded by spinning in machine for this period of time.) At this point, dough should feel smooth, elastic, and just slightly sticky to the touch. If dough feels wet, gradually add reserved flour, 1 tablespoon at a time, and process for 5 seconds after each addition until dough is the proper consistency.

4. Transfer dough to a clean, dry work surface. Knead until dough is smooth and satiny, about 2 minutes. Shape dough into a ball.

ELECTRIC MIXER AND HAND METHOD

1. In large mixer bowl, put 2½ cups bread flour or unbleached flour; reserve remaining ½ cup. Add the remaining 2 tablespoons light brown sugar and salt. Run machine at low speed for 30 seconds to combine.

2. Using a fork or small whisk, stir yeast mixture briefly and pour into flour mixture. Add oatmeal mixture; blend at low speed until moistened, about 30 seconds. Turn machine off and scrape inside bowl with spatula. Turn speed to medium and beat until smooth, about 2 minutes. At this point dough will be extremely sticky. Clean off any sticky dough attached to beaters and add to the bowl. Remove bowl from stand. With your hand, gradually stir in reserved flour a little at a time (starting with ¼ cup and then 2 tablespoons at a time), just until the dough is a soft mass and pulls away from the sides of bowl.

3. Transfer dough to a lightly floured work surface. Rub a little flour on your hands and knead the dough until smooth, elastic, and satiny, about 8 to 10 minutes. If dough still feels sticky after 5 minutes of kneading, sprinkle about 1½ teaspoons of flour on board under dough. Lightly flour hands once again and continue kneading until dough is the proper consistency. Shape dough into a ball.

FIRST RISING

1. Adjust rack to center of oven, set oven to lowest temperature for 2 minutes, and then turn off. If you have a gas oven with a gas pilot light, no preheating is necessary.
2. Lightly grease bottom and sides of a deep 2½-quart bowl with ½ teaspoon unsalted margarine, softened. Place dough in greased bowl, turning ball to coat entire surface with margarine. Cover bowl with plastic wrap. Place bowl in center of bath towel and fold ends loosely over top to cover. Transfer to oven and let dough rise until double in bulk, about 1 hour.

SHAPING AND SECOND RISING

1. Lightly grease bottom and sides of an 8½- by 4½- by 3-inch loaf pan; set aside.
2. Using a closed fist, punch risen dough down in center. Gently pull outside edges of dough to center.
3. Transfer dough to a clean, dry work surface. Knead dough gently for 30 seconds. Shape into a ball and cover with a dish towel. Let dough rest for 10 minutes before shaping into loaf (letting the dough rest briefly will make rolling and shaping easier).
4. Gently pat down dough with fingertips to flatten into a rentangle. Roll dough into a sheet about 10 inches long by 8 inches wide. Starting at far narrow edge, roll up jelly roll fashion toward you, sealing with your thumbs as you roll. Pinch seam and ends of dough firmly with fingertips to seal well. Place seam side down in greased pan. Lightly cover with plastic wrap and place a dish towel loosely on top. Return to oven and let dough rise again until doubled, about 1 hour. (Dough should be about ½ inch above rim of pan when doubled.)

TO BAKE

| 1 egg | 1 tablespoon sesame seeds |
| 1 tablespoon cold water | |

1. Leave rack in center of oven and preheat to 375 degrees.
2. With a single-edge razor blade or the metal blade from the food processor, cut a slash about ¼ inch deep down center top of loaf.

3. In a small bowl, beat egg with water. Lightly brush top of loaf with glaze and sprinkle with sesame seeds.
4. Bake in preheated oven until the top is well browned, about 30 to 35 minutes. Remove loaf from pan to a wire rack and tap the bottom with your knuckles. If the bread sounds hollow and hard, it is done; if not, return loaf to oven, without its pan, for an additional 5 to 7 minutes; test again. Transfer to wire rack and cool to room temperature before serving, storing, or freezing.

Whole Wheat Bread

High in fiber, this loaf has wholesome texture with good flavor and color. One of my favorite breakfasts is a slice of this bread toasted and spread with homemade Raisin Spread (page 332).

YIELDS 1 LOAF

2 tablespoons plus 1 teaspoon light brown sugar
1 cup warm water (105 degrees F. to 115 degrees F.)
One ¼-ounce package active dry yeast
1¼ to 1½ cups bread flour or unbleached all-purpose flour
1½ cups whole wheat flour
¼ cup nonfat dry milk powder
½ teaspoon salt
2 tablespoons unsalted margarine at room temperature, cut into 8 pieces.

In a 2-cup glass measure, stir 1 teaspoon brown sugar into warm water. Sprinkle yeast over water and stir briefly until completely dissolved. Set aside until foamy, about 5 to 10 minutes.

FOOD PROCESSOR METHOD

1. Fit food processor with metal blade. Put 1¼ cups bread flour or unbleached flour in work bowl; reserve remaining ¼ cup. Add all of the whole wheat flour, dry milk, the remaining 2 tablespoons light brown sugar, and salt to work bowl; process until combined, about 10 seconds. Add margarine and process for 10 seconds.

2. Using a fork or small whisk, stir yeast mixture briefly. Turn machine on and pour yeast mixture through feed tube. Process for 50 seconds. (Dough will form a mass and is kneaded by spinning in machine for this period of time.) At this point, dough should feel smooth, elastic, and just slightly sticky to the touch. If dough feels wet, gradually add reserved flour 1 tablespoon at a time and process for 5 seconds after each addition until dough is the proper consistency.

3. Transfer dough to a clean, dry work surface. Knead until dough is smooth and satiny, about 2 minutes. Shape dough into a ball.

ELECTRIC MIXER AND HAND METHOD

1. In large mixer bowl, put 1 cup bread flour or unbleached flour; reserve remaining ½ cup. Add all the whole wheat flour, dry milk, the remaining 2 tablespoons light brown sugar, and salt. Run machine at low speed for 30 seconds to combine.

2. Using a fork or small whisk, stir yeast mixture briefly and pour into flour mixture. Add margarine; blend at low speed until moistened, about 30 seconds. Turn machine off and scrape inside bowl with a rubber spatula. Turn speed to medium and beat until smooth, about 2 minutes. At this point dough will be extremely sticky. Clean off any sticky dough from beaters and add to bowl. Remove bowl from stand. With your hand, gradually stir in reserved flour a little at a time (starting with ¼ cup and then 1 tablespoon at a time), just until the dough is a soft mass and pulls away from the sides of bowl.

3. Transfer dough to a lightly floured work surface. Rub a little flour on your hands and knead the dough until smooth, elastic, and satiny, about 8 to 10 minutes. If dough still feels sticky after 5 minutes of kneading, sprinkle about 1½ teaspoons of flour on board under dough. Lightly flour hands once again and continue

kneading until dough is the proper consistency. Shape dough into a ball.

FIRST RISING

1. Adjust rack to center of oven, set oven to lowest temperature for 2 minutes, and then turn off. If you have a gas oven with a gas pilot light, no preheating is necessary.
2. Lightly grease bottom and sides of a deep 2½-quart bowl with ½ teaspoon unsalted margarine, softened. Place dough in greased bowl, turning ball to coat entire surface with margarine. Cover bowl with plastic wrap. Place bowl in center of a bath towel and fold ends loosely over top to cover. Transfer to oven and let dough rise until double in bulk, about 70 minutes.

SHAPING AND SECOND RISING

1. Lightly grease bottom and sides of an 8½- by 4½- by 3-inch loaf pan; set aside.
2. Using a closed fist, punch risen dough down in center. Gently pull the outside edges of dough to center.
3. Transfer dough to a clean, dry work surface. Knead dough gently for 30 seconds. Shape into a ball and cover with a dish towel. Let dough rest for 10 minutes before shaping into loaf (letting the dough rest briefly will make rolling and shaping easier).
4. Gently pat down dough with fingertips to flatten into a rectangle. Roll dough into a sheet about 10 inches long by 8 inches wide. Starting at far narrow edge, roll up jelly roll fashion toward you, sealing with your thumbs as you roll. Pinch seam and ends of dough firmly with fingertips to seal well. Place seam side down in greased pan. Lightly cover with plastic wrap and place a dish towel loosely on top. Return to turned off oven and let dough rise again until doubled, about 1 hour. (Dough should be just level with top rim of pan when doubled.)

TO BAKE

1. Leave rack in center of oven and preheat to 375 degrees.
2. With a single-edge razor blade or the metal blade from the food processor, cut a slash about ¼ inch deep down center top of loaf.
3. Bake in preheated oven until the top is well browned, about 35 to

40 minutes. Remove loaf from pan to wire rack and tap the bottom with your knuckles. If the bread sounds hollow and hard it is done; if not, return loaf to oven, without its pan, for an additional 3 to 5 minutes; test again. Transfer to wire rack and cool to room temperature before serving, storing, or freezing.

Yogurt Wheat Bread

Yogurt is the special ingredient that keeps this bread moist and light. The bread is an excellent accompaniment to any meal. It's also nice for sandwich-making or toasting.

YIELDS 1 LOAF

1 tablespoon sugar

⅔ cup warm water (105 degrees F. to 115 degrees F.)

One ¼-ounce package active dry yeast

1¾ to 2 cups bread flour or unbleached all-purpose flour

1 cup whole wheat flour

½ teaspoon salt

½ cup low-fat yogurt, room temperature

1 tablespoon olive oil

In a 2-cup glass measure, stir sugar into warm water. Sprinkle yeast over water and stir briefly until completely dissolved. Set aside until foamy, about 5 to 10 minutes.

FOOD PROCESSOR METHOD

1. Fit food processor with metal blade. Put 1¾ cups bread flour or unbleached flour in work bowl; reserve remaining ¼ cup. Add all of the whole wheat flour and salt; process until combined, about 10 seconds.

2. Add yogurt and olive oil; process until blended, about 10 seconds. Stop machine and scrape down inside work bowl with plastic spatula.
3. Using a fork or small whisk, beat yeast mixture briefly. Turn machine and pour yeast mixture through feed tube. Process for 50 seconds. (Dough will form a mass and is kneaded by spinning in machine for this period of time.) At this point, dough should feel smooth, elastic, and just slightly sticky to the touch. If dough feels wet, gradually add reserved flour 1 tablespoon at a time and process for 5 seconds after each addition until dough is the proper consistency.
4. Transfer dough to a clean, dry work surface. Knead until dough in smooth and satiny, about 2 minutes. Shape dough into a ball.

ELECTRIC MIXER AND HAND METHOD

1. In a large mixer bowl, put 1½ cups bread flour or unbleached flour; reserve remaining ½ cup. Add all the whole wheat flour and salt. Run machine at low speed for 30 seconds to combine.
2. Using a fork or small whisk, beat yeast mixture briefly and pour into flour mixture. Add yogurt and oil; blend at low speed until moistened, about 30 seconds. Turn machine off and scrape inside bowl with rubber spatula. Turn speed to medium and beat until smooth, about 2 minutes. At this point dough will be extremely sticky. Clean off any sticky dough attached to beaters and add to bowl. Remove bowl from stand. With your hand, gradually stir in reserved flour a little at a time (starting with ¼ cup and then 2 tablespoons at a time) just until the dough is a soft mass and pulls away from the sides of bowl.
3. Transfer dough to a lightly floured work surface. Rub a little flour on your hands and knead the dough until smooth, elastic, and satiny, about 8 to 10 minutes. If dough still feels sticky after 5 minutes of kneading, sprinkle 1½ teaspoons of the remaining flour on board under dough. Lightly flour hands once again and continue kneading until dough is the proper consistency. Shape dough into a ball.

FIRST RISING

1. Adjust rack to center of oven, set oven to lowest temperature for 2 minutes, and then turn off. If you have a gas oven with a gas pilot light, no preheating is necessary.
2. Lightly grease bottom and sides of a deep 2½-quart bowl with ½ teaspoon olive oil. Place dough in greased bowl, turning ball to coat entire surface with oil. Cover bowl with plastic wrap. Place bowl in center of a bath towel and fold ends loosely over top to cover. Transfer to oven and let dough rise until double in bulk, about 70 minutes.

SHAPING AND SECOND RISING

1. Lightly grease bottom and sides of an 8½- by 4½- by 3-inch loaf pan; set aside.
2. Using a closed fist, punch risen dough down in center. Gently pull the outside edges of dough to center.
3. Transfer dough to a clean, dry work surface. Knead dough gently for 30 seconds. Shape into a ball and cover with a dish towel. Let dough rest for 10 minutes before shaping into loaf (letting the dough rest briefly will make rolling and shaping easier).
4. Gently pat dough down with fingertips to flatten into a rectangle. Roll dough into a sheet about 10 inches long by 8 inches wide. Starting at far narrow edge, roll up jelly roll fashion toward you, sealing with your thumbs as you roll. Pinch seam and ends of dough firmly with fingertips to seal well. Place seam side down in greased pan. Lightly cover with plastic wrap and place a dish towel loosely on top. Return to turned off oven and let dough rise again until doubled, about 1 hour. (Dough should be just level with top rim of pan when doubled.)

TO BAKE

1. Leave rack in center of oven and preheat to 375 degrees.
2. With a single-edge razor blade or the metal blade from the food processor, cut a slash about ¼ inch deep down center top of loaf.
3. Bake in preheated oven until the top is well browned, about 35 to 40 minutes. Remove loaf from pan to wire rack and tap the bottom with your knuckles. If the bread sounds hollow and hard it is done;

if not, return loaf to oven, without its pan, for an additional 3 to 5 minutes; test again. Transfer to wire rack and cool to room temperature before serving, storing, or freezing.

Basic Sweet Dough

This is a basic sweet dough, which can be used as a base for other sweet breads. Recipes for four such breads follow on pages 300–303.

YIELDS 3 LOAVES

3 tablespoons plus 1 teaspoon sugar

¾ cup warm water (105 degrees F. to 115 degrees F.)

One ¼-ounce package active dry yeast

2¾ to 3 cups unbleached all-purpose flour

2 tablespoons nonfat dry milk powder

½ teaspoon salt

2 tablespoons unsalted margarine at room temperature, cut into 8 pieces

1 extra large egg at room temperature

2 teaspoons pure vanilla extract

In a 2-cup glass measure, stir 1 teaspoon sugar into warm water. Sprinkle yeast over water and stir briefly until completely dissolved. Set aside until foamy, about 5 to 10 minutes.

FOOD PROCESSOR METHOD

1. Fit food processor with metal blade. Put 2¾ cups flour in work bowl; reserve remaining ¼ cup. Add dry milk, the remaining 3 tablespoons sugar, and salt; process for 10 seconds to combine. Add margarine and process for 10 seconds. Stop machine and scrape inside work bowl with plastic spatula.
2. With a fork or small whisk, beat yeast mixture briefly. Turn ma-

chine on and pour yeast mixture through feed tube; process until blended, about 10 seconds. Stop machine and scrape down inside work bowl with plastic spatula.

3. Put whole egg and vanilla in a glass measure and beat lightly with a fork. With machine running, slowly drizzle egg mixture through feed tube. Process for 50 seconds. (Dough will form a mass and is kneaded by spinning in machine for this period of time.) At this point, dough should feel smooth, elastic, and just slightly sticky to the touch. If dough feels wet, gradually add reserved flour, 1 tablespoon at a time, and process for 5 seconds after each addition until dough is the proper consistency.

4. Transfer dough to a clean, dry work surface. Knead until dough is smooth and satiny, about 2 minutes. Shape dough into a ball.

ELECTRIC MIXER AND HAND METHOD

1. In large mixer bowl, put 2½ cups flour; reserve remaining ½ cup. Add dry milk, the remaining 3 tablespoons sugar, and salt; run machine at low speed for 30 seconds to combine.

2. Using fork or small whisk, whisk yeast mixture briefly and pour into flour mixture. Add margarine, egg, and vanilla; blend at low speed until moistened, about 30 seconds. Turn machine off and scrape inside bowl with rubber spatula. Turn speed to medium and beat until smooth, about 2 minutes. At this point dough will be extremely sticky. Clean off any sticky dough attached to beaters and add to bowl. Remove bowl from stand. With your hand, gradually stir in reserved flour a little at a time (starting with ¼ cup and then 2 tablespoons at a time), just until the dough is a soft mass and pulls away from the sides of the bowl.

3. Transfer dough to a lightly floured work surface. Rub a little flour on your hands and knead the dough until smooth, elastic and satiny, about 8 to 10 minutes. If dough still feels sticky after 5 minutes of kneading, sprinkle about 1½ teaspoons flour on board under dough. Lightly flour hands once again and continue kneading until dough is the proper consistency. Shape dough into a ball.

FIRST RISING

1. Adjust rack to center of oven, set oven to lowest temperature for 2 minutes, and then turn off. If you have a gas oven with a gas pilot

light, no preheating is necessary.

2. Lightly grease bottom and sides of a deep 2½-quart bowl with ½ teaspoon unsalted margarine, softened. Place dough in greased bowl, turning ball to coat entire surface with margarine. Cover bowl loosely with plastic wrap. Place bowl in center of bath towel and fold ends loosely over top to cover. Transfer to turned off oven and let dough rise until double in bulk, about 1 hour.

Mini Cinnamon Raisin Breads

No better way to start the day than a slice of this sweet loaf with its spiral cinnamon raisin filling.

Basic Sweet Dough, prepared through first rising	3 tablespoons sugar
	1½ teaspoons ground cinnamon
1 cup dark raisins	1½ teaspoons unsalted margarine, softened
1 cup boiling water	

1. While dough is rising, place raisins in a small bowl and cover with boiling water to plump for about 2 minutes. Transfer to strainer and refresh under cold water; squeeze out excess moisture with your hands and blot dry with paper towel; set aside.
2. In a small bowl, combine sugar and cinnamon; set aside.
3. Lightly grease bottom and sides of three 5- by 2½- by 2-inch loaf pans; set aside.

SHAPING AND SECOND RISING

1. Using a closed fist, punch risen dough down in center. Gently pull the outside edges of dough to center.
2. Transfer dough to a clean dry work surface. Divide dough into 3 equal pieces; knead each piece briefly Shape each into a ball and cover with a dish towel. Let dough rest for 10 minutes before shaping into loaves (letting the dough rest briefly will make rolling and shaping easier).
3. Take one piece of dough and leave remaining pieces covered with a towel. Gently pat down dough with fingertips to flatten into

rectangle, Roll dough into a sheet about 9 inches long by 5 inches wide. Spread ½ teaspoon softened margarine over entire surface of dough. Leaving a ¼-inch margin on all 4 sides, sprinkle dough with ⅓ cup raisins. Using your fingertips, press raisins into dough. Sprinkle 1½ tablespoons of sugar-cinnamon mixture over raisins.

4. Starting at far narrow edge, tightly roll toward you, jelly roll fashion, sealing with your thumbs as you roll. Pinch seam and ends of dough firmly with fingertips to seal well. Place seam side down in greased pan; repeat with remaining pieces of dough and filling. Lightly cover each pan with plastic wrap. Return to turned off oven, placing pans 1 inch apart. Loosely cover all three with one dish towel. Let dough rise again until doubled, about 50 to 60 minutes. (Dough should be about ½ inch above rims of pans when doubled.)

TO BAKE

1 egg	1 tablespoon water

1. Leave rack in center of oven and preheat to 350 degrees.
2. With a single-edge razor blade or the metal blade from the food processor, cut a slash about ¼ inch deep down center top of each loaf. Do not be concerned if some of the filling shows through after slashing.
3. In a small bowl, beat egg with water. Lightly brush glaze on top of each loaf.
4. Bake in preheated oven until the tops of loaves are well browned, about 25 to 30 minutes. Remove loaves from pans to wire rack and tap the bottom of each with your knuckles. If the loaves sound hollow and hard, they are done; if not, return loaves to oven without their pans for an additional 3 to 4 minutes; test again. Transfer to wire rack and cool to room temperature before serving, storing, or freezing.

≪≪

Apple Cinnamon Swirl Loaves

Basic Sweet Dough,
prepared through first
rising

2 medium-sized Golden
Delicious apples (10
ounces total weight),
peeled, halved, and cored

¼ cup light brown sugar

2 teaspoons ground
cinnamon

1½ teaspoons minute tapioca
or cornstarch

1½ teaspoons unsalted
margarine, softened

1. Prepare dough as directed through first rising. Punch dough down, divide into three pieces, and while dough is resting prepare apple filling. (Do not prepare ahead of time or apple filling will get soggy.)
2. Grate apples with the coarse side of a grater or in food processor fitted with shredding disc. In a bowl, combine brown sugar, cinnamon, and tapioca or cornstarch. Lightly toss apples with sugar mixture.
3. Roll each piece of dough as directed in Step 3 (page 300) for Cinnamon Raisin Breads. Spread each rectangle of dough with ½ teaspoon softened margarine. Sprinkle ⅓ of the apple mixture over each rectangle of dough, leaving a ½-inch margin on all four sides. Press mixture firmly into dough with fingertips before rolling up tightly. Follow same procedure for shaping, second rising, and baking as directed for Cinnamon Raisin Breads.

Fruited Loaves

Basic Sweet Dough
(substitute 1 tablespoon
grated orange rind for
vanilla), prepared through
first rising

½ cup candied fruit

½ cup white raisins

¼ cup Grand Marnier or
dark rum (preferably
Myers's)

1½ teaspoons unsalted
margarine, softened

1. While dough is rising, prepare filling. In blender or food processor fitted with metal blade, place candied fruit and raisins. Add Grand

Marnier or rum and run machine nonstop until finely chopped, about 30 seconds. Transfer to bowl and let stand at room temperature for at least ½ hour to soften.

2. After first rising, punch dough down, divide into three pieces, and let dough rest for 10 minutes. Roll each piece as directed Step 3 (page 300) for Cinnamon Raisin Breads. Spread each rectangle of dough with ½ teaspoon softened margarine. Spread ⅓ cup of the fruit filling over each rectangle of dough, leaving a ¼-inch margin on all four sides. Press mixture firmly into dough with fingertips before rolling up tightly. Follow same procedure for shaping, second rising, and baking as directed for Cinnamon Raisin Breads.

Nut Loaves

Basic Sweet Dough, prepared through first rising
¾ cup toasted pecans or walnuts
¼ cup dark brown sugar
1 teaspoon ground cinnamon
½ teaspoon freshly grated nutmeg
1½ teaspoons unsalted margarine, softened

1. Prepare dough as directed through first rising. Punch dough down, divide into three pieces, and while dough is resting prepare nut filling.
2. Coarsely chop pecans or walnuts (can be chopped in food processor fitted with metal blade). In a bowl, combine brown sugar, cinnamon, and nutmeg. Toss nuts with sugar mixture.
3. Divide dough into three pieces and roll as directed in Step 3 (page 300) for Cinnamon Raisin Bread. Spread each rectangle of dough with ½ teaspoon softened margarine. Sprinkle ⅓ of the nut mixture over each rectangle of dough, leaving a ¼-inch margin on all four sides. Press mixture firmly into dough with fingertips before rolling up tightly. Follow same procedure for shaping, second rising, and baking as directed for Cinnamon Raisin Breads.

⫷⫷⫷

QUICK BREADS

≪←

QUICK BREADS

Glazed Apple Loaf 308

Applesauce Raisin Loaf 311

Apricot Pineapple Loaf 313

Banana Pecan Loaf 315

Cranberry Nut Bread 317

Lemon-glazed Prune Loaf 320

MUFFINS

Basic Muffins 323

    Applesauce Muffins 324

    Blueberry Muffins 325

    Cranberry Muffins 325

    Date Muffins 325

    Strawberry Surprise Muffins 325

Cornmeal and Wheat Muffins 326

Raisin Bran Muffins 328

Whole Wheat Cinnamon Muffins 330

SPREADS

The simplest baked goods to prepare are quick breads. They range from fruity, cakelike loaves to tender, moist muffins. What distinguishes this variety of baked goods is that no yeast is used in their preparation. Quick breads are referred to by a wide assortment of names: batter breads, sweet breads, fruity breads, breakfast or dessert breads. The distinct advantage they all possess is that they can be served interchangeably for breakfast, brunch, lunch, dinner, dessert, or just plain snacking.

For tender, well-shaped loaves or muffins, it is most important to process or beat the mixture just until the flour is moistened and barely disappears into the batter. The batter should be lumpy, not smooth. The small lumps left in the batter disappear during baking. If using the food processor method, be especially careful not to overprocess batter to a smooth consistency or the loaves or muffins will be tough.

The following pages contain family favorites and adaptations of classic quick bread recipes. Directions and baking times are given for whole loaves as well as small loaves. I make large loaves only if I am entertaining or during the holiday season, since most of these will yield 16 to 20 slices. During the rest of the year, I prefer to make several small loaves; these fruit breads are wonderful to have on hand for unexpected guests and always make welcome, inexpensive hostess gifts.

QUICK BREADS
⫷⫷

Glazed Apple Loaf

Everyone from youngsters to oldsters likes this moist, old-fashioned apple loaf, which is especially good as a dessert. Ingredients are listed in sequence for food processor; if you use an electric mixer, they will be combined in a different sequence.

YIELDS 1 MEDIUM-SIZED LOAF OR 4 SMALL LOAVES

2 cups unbleached all-purpose flour

1 tablespoon double-acting baking powder

¼ teaspoon baking soda

1 teaspoon ground cinnamon

¾ cup sugar

1 extra large egg white at room temperature

1 extra large egg at room temperature

¼ cup (½ stick) unsalted margarine at room temperature (cut into 8 pieces for food processor method only)

½ cup low-fat yogurt at room temperature

1 teaspoon pure vanilla extract

2 medium-sized Golden Delicious apples (8 ounces total weight), peeled, halved, cored, and edges cut flat (for food processor) or thinly sliced

Adjust oven rack to center of oven; preheat to 350 degrees. Grease the bottom and sides of an 8½- by 4½- by 3-inch loaf pan or four 5- by 2½- by 2½-inch loaf pans. Dust pan(s) lightly with flour; shake out excess and set aside.

FOOD PROCESSOR METHOD

1. Put flour, baking powder, baking soda, and cinnamon in work bowl fitted with metal blade. Process for 5 seconds. Transfer dry ingredients to another bowl. Put sugar, egg white, and whole egg in work bowl; process for 1 minute. Add margarine and process for 30 seconds. Add yogurt and vanilla; process for 10 seconds. Stop machine and scrape down inside work bowl with plastic spatula. Add dry ingredients and blend by turning machine on/off 3 to 4 times just until incorporated and flour is moistened (do not overprocess). Transfer batter to a bowl.
2. Wash and dry work bowl. Insert medium serrated slicer. Arrange apples vertically in feed tube and slice using firm pressure.

ELECTRIC MIXER METHOD

1. In a shallow bowl, sift together flour, baking powder, baking soda, and cinnamon; set dry ingredients aside.
2. With electric mixer on medium speed, cream margarine and sugar until fluffy, about 2 minutes. Add egg white and whole egg and beat until smooth. Turn speed down to low and add dry ingredients alternately with yogurt in two batches, scraping down with rubber spatula after each addition, and beating just until ingredients are blended but batter is still slightly lumpy. Stir in vanilla extract.

TO BAKE

Turn batter into prepared pan(s) and smooth top with a narrow metal spatula. Tap pan(s) gently on work surface to break any air bubbles. For single loaf, press apple slices into batter, leaving about ¼ inch of each slice showing. For small loaves, press apple slices right down to bottom of pan. Bake in preheated oven until golden on top and a cake tester inserted in center comes out clean, about 60 minutes for large loaf and 30 to 35 minutes for small loaves. Let loaf or loaves cool in pan(s) on a rack for 10 minutes. Invert onto rack, remove pan(s), and invert again onto second rack.

Glaze

½ cup apricot preserves

1. In a small saucepan, melt apricot preserves over low heat, stirring constantly. Strain preserves in a strainer set over a bowl, pressing firmly with the back of a spoon.
2. While loaf or loaves are still warm, brush glaze over top and sides of loaf or loaves. Cool completely on rack.

NOTE: For storing or freezing, cool bread to room temperature, wrap in plastic wrap, place in plastic bag, and seal tightly. May be kept in freezer up to 2 months. To defrost, unwrap completely and bring to room temperature.

⫷⫷⫷

Applesauce Raisin Loaf

The raisins and applesauce makes this an especially moist flavorful bread. It is fine at breakfast, lunch, or snack time, and it goes extremely well with Poached Chicken with Apricot Sauce (page 176). Ingredients are listed in sequence for food processor; if you use an electric mixer, they will be combined in a different sequence.

YIELDS 1 MEDIUM-SIZED LOAF
OR 4 SMALL LOAVES

1 cup dark raisins
1 cup boiling water
2 cups unbleached all-purpose flour
1 tablespoon double-acting baking powder
½ teaspoon baking soda
1 teaspoon ground cinnamon
½ teaspoon freshly grated nutmeg
1¼ cups applesauce, preferably unsweetened

¾ cup lightly packed light brown sugar
1 extra large egg white at room temperature
1 extra large egg at room temperature
¼ cup (½ stick) unsalted margarine at room temperature (cut into 8 pieces for food processor method only)

1. Put raisins in a small bowl and cover with boiling water to plump for 2 minutes. Pour into strainer and refresh under cold water; squeeze out excess moisture with your hands and set aside.
2. Adjust oven rack to center of oven; preheat to 350 degrees. Grease bottom and sides of an 8½- by 4½- by 3-inch loaf pan or four 5- by 2½- by 2½-inch small loaf pans. Dust pan(s) with flour; shake out excess and set aside.

FOOD PROCESSOR METHOD
Put flour, baking powder, baking soda, cinnamon, and nutmeg in work bowl fitted with metal blade. Process for 30 seconds; transfer dry ingredients to another bowl. Put applesauce and brown sugar

in work bowl and process for 30 seconds. Add egg white and whole egg; process mixture for 1 minute; stop machine once and scrape inside work bowl with plastic spatula. Add margarine and process for 30 seconds. Add dry ingredients and blend by turning machine on/off 3 to 4 times just until the flour is moistened (do not over-process the batter). Transfer batter to bowl; fold raisins in with spatula.

ELECTRIC MIXER METHOD

1. In a shallow bowl, sift together flour, baking powder, baking soda, cinnamon, and nutmeg; set dry ingredients aside.
2. With electric mixer on medium speed, cream margarine and brown sugar until fluffy, about 2 minutes. Add egg white and whole egg; beat until smooth. Turn speed down to low and add dry ingredients alternately with applesauce in two batches, scraping down with rubber spatula after each addition, just until ingredients are blended; batter should be lumpy. Fold raisins into batter with spatula.

TO BAKE

Turn batter into prepared pan(s) and smooth top with a narrow metal spatula. Tap pan(s) gently on work surface to break any air bubbles. Bake in preheated oven until golden on top and a cake tester inserted in center comes out clean, about 50 to 60 minutes for large loaf and 35 to 40 minutes for small loaves. Let loaf or loaves cool in pan(s) on a rack for about 10 minutes. Invert onto rack, remove pan(s), and invert again onto second rack. Cool completely on rack before slicing.

NOTE: For storing or freezing, cool loaf to room temperature, wrap in plastic wrap, place in plastic bag, and seal tightly. May be kept in freezer up to 2 months. To defrost, unwrap completely and bring to room temperature.

⋘

Apricot Pineapple Loaf

The apricots give this loaf an unusual tangy flavor, while the pineapple adds moist texture. This fruit loaf makes a welcome, inexpensive hostess gift or a popular dessert when served with lemon sorbet or frozen vanilla yogurt. Ingredients are listed in sequence for food processor; if you use an electric mixer, they will be combined in a different sequence.

YIELDS 1 LARGE LOAF OR 4 SMALL LOAVES

One 6-ounce package (1 cup) dried apricots

1 ½ cups water

One 8-ounce can crushed unsweetened pineapple

2 ½ cups unbleached all-purpose flour

1 tablespoon double-acting baking powder

½ teaspoon baking soda

¾ cup sugar

1 extra large egg white at room temperature

1 extra large egg at room temperature

¼ (½ stick) cup unsalted margarine at room temperature (cut into 8 pieces for food processor method only)

2 teaspoons pure vanilla extract

1. Put apricots in a small saucepan and cover with water. Bring to a boil, covered, over high heat. Cook until apricots are slightly softened, about 1 minute. Transfer to strainer and refresh under cold water; drain thoroughly. Using a pair of kitchen shears, snip apricots into ½-inch pieces; transfer to a small bowl.
2. Drain pineapple in a strainer set over a bowl. Using the back of a wooden spoon, firmly press pineapple to extract as much juice as possible. You should have ½ cup of juice after draining pineapple. If you don't, make up the difference in liquid by adding a little water; reserve juice. Combine pineapple with apricots; set aside.
3. Adjust oven rack to center of oven; preheat to 350 degrees. Grease the bottom and sides of a 9- by 5- by 3 ½-inch loaf pan or four 5- by 2 ½- by 2 ½-inch small loaf pans. Dust pan(s) lightly with flour; shake out excess.

FOOD PROCESSOR METHOD

Put flour, baking powder, and baking soda in work bowl fitted with metal blade. Process for 5 seconds. Transfer dry ingredients to another bowl. Put sugar, egg white, and whole egg in work bowl; process for 1 minute. Add margarine and process for 1 minute. Stop machine once and scrape inside work bowl with plastic spatula. Add reserved pineapple juice and vanilla extract; process for 10 seconds. Add dry ingredients and blend by turning machine on/off 3 to 4 times, just until moistened. Do not overprocess; batter should be lumpy. Add pineapple-apricot mixture and process with 3 to 4 quick on/off turns to combine.

ELECTRIC MIXER METHOD

1. In a shallow bowl, sift together flour, baking powder, and baking soda; set dry ingredients aside.
2. With electric mixer on medium speed, cream margarine and sugar until fluffy, about 2 minutes. Add egg white and whole egg; beat until smooth. Turn speed down to low and add dry ingredients alternately with reserved pineapple juice in two batches, scraping down with rubber spatula after each addition, just until ingredients are blended; batter should be lumpy. Stir in vanilla extract. Fold pineapple-apricot mixture into batter with rubber spatula.

TO BAKE

Turn batter into prepared pan(s) and smooth top with a narrow metal spatula. Tap pan(s) gently on work surface to break up any air bubbles. Bake until golden on top and a cake tester inserted in center comes out clean, about 1 hour for large loaf and 35 to 40 minutes for small loaves. Let loaf or loaves cool in pan(s) on a rack for 10 minutes. Invert onto rack, remove pan(s), and invert again onto second rack. Cool to room temperature before slicing.

N O T E : For storing or freezing, cool loaf to room temperature, wrap in plastic wrap, place in plastic bag, and seal tightly. May be kept in freezer up to 3 months. To defrost, unwrap completely and bring to room temperature.

Banana Pecan Loaf

The bananas should be well ripened to add a sweet moist texture to this tempting loaf. For a quick dessert, try serving thin slices of this golden-hued bread with a scoop of strawberry sorbet. The ingredients are listed in sequence for the food processor method; if you use an electric mixer, the ingredients will be combined in a different sequence.

YIELDS 1 MEDIUM LOAF OR
4 SMALL LOAVES

¾ cup pecans
1 cup unbleached all-purpose flour
1 cup whole wheat flour
1½ teaspoons double-acting baking powder
¼ teaspoon baking soda
½ teaspoon freshly grated nutmeg
2 large ripe bananas (12 ounces total weight), peeled and cut into ½-inch pieces
¾ cup sugar

1 extra large egg white at room temperature
1 extra large egg at room temperature
¼ cup (½ stick) unsalted margarine at room temperature (cut into 8 pieces for food processor method only)
½ cup low-fat yogurt at room temperature
2 teaspoons pure vanilla extract

1. Adjust oven rack to center of oven; preheat to 350 degrees.
2. Place pecans on a cookie sheet and toast in preheated oven until lightly golden, about 5 to 7 minutes. Remove from oven and let cool to room temperature. Break into ½-inch pieces for food processor method or coarsely chop for electric mixer method; set aside.
3. Leave oven at same temperature.
4. Grease the bottom and sides of an 8½- by 4½- by 3-inch loaf pan or four 5- by 2½- by 2½-inch small loaf pans. Dust pan(s) lightly with flour; shake out excess and set aside.

FOOD PROCESSOR METHOD

Place both flours, baking powder, baking soda, and nutmeg in work bowl fitted with metal blade. Sprinkle nuts over dry ingredients and process until nuts are coarsely chopped, about 10 seconds (adding nuts last will keep them from being overprocessed). Transfer mixture to another bowl. Put bananas in work bowl and run machine nonstop until you have a smooth purée, about 1 minute. Stop machine once and scrape inside work bowl with plastic spatula. Add sugar, egg white, and whole egg; process for 1 minute. Add margarine and process for 30 seconds. Add yogurt and vanilla; process for 10 seconds. Add flour-nut mixture and blend by turning machine on/off 3 to 4 times just until moistened. Do not overprocess; batter should be lumpy.

ELECTRIC MIXER METHOD

1. In a shallow bowl, sift both flours, baking powder, baking soda, and nutmeg; set dry ingredients aside.
2. In a small bowl, mash bananas with a fork to a smooth purée; set aside.
3. With electric mixer on medium speed, cream margarine and sugar until fluffy, about 2 minutes. Add egg white and whole egg; beat until smooth. Turn speed down to low and add dry ingredients alternately with yogurt in two batches, scraping down with rubber spatula after each addition, just until ingredients are blended. Add mashed bananas, beating briefly until blended; batter should be lumpy. Stir in vanilla. Fold nuts into batter with spatula.

TO BAKE

Turn batter into prepared pan(s) and smooth top with a narrow metal spatula. Tap pan(s) gently on work surface to break any air bubbles. Bake in preheated oven until golden on top and a cake tester inserted in center comes out clean, about 60 to 70 minutes for large loaf and 35 to 40 minutes for small loaves. Let loaf or loaves cool in pan(s) on a rack for about 10 minutes. Invert onto rack, remove pan(s), and invert again onto second rack. Cool to room temperature before slicing.

N O T E : For storing or freezing, cool loaf to room temperature, wrap in plastic wrap, place in plastic bag, and seal tightly. May be kept in freezer up to 3 months. To defrost, unwrap completely and bring to room temperature.

Cranberry Nut Bread

Cranberries, orange, pecans, and whole wheat flour flavor this holiday favorite. For easier slicing, bake one day before serving. This bread is an excellent accompaniment to Peachy Drumsticks with Orange Sauce (page 185) or Glazed Rock Cornish Game Hen (page 188). Ingredients are listed in sequence for food processor; if you use an electric mixer, they will be combined in a different sequence.

YIELDS 1 LARGE LOAF OR 4 SMALL LOAVES

½ cup pecans
2½ cups fresh whole cranberries
1½ cups unbleached all-purpose flour
1 cup whole wheat flour
1 tablespoon double-acting baking powder
½ teaspoon baking soda
1 cup sugar
Thin outer peel of 1 medium-sized thick-skinned navel orange (6 ounces), removed with a zester for food processor method or finely grated to make 1½ tablespoons for electric mixer method

1 extra large egg white at room temperature
1 extra large egg at room temperature
¼ cup (½ stick) unsalted margarine at room temperature (cut into 8 pieces for food processor method only)
¾ cup fresh orange juice, strained

1. Adjust oven rack to center of oven; preheat to 350 degrees.
2. Place pecans on a cookie sheet and toast in preheated oven until lightly golden, about 5 to 7 minutes. Remove from oven and let cool to room temperature. If using electric mixer method, coarsely chop.
3. Leave oven at same temperature.
4. Pick over cranberries, discarding any bits of stems and bruised berries; wash berries in cold water. Thoroughly drain in strainer and blot dry with paper towel. If using electric mixer method, coarsely chop and add to nuts.
5. Grease the bottom and sides of an 9- by 5- by 3½-inch loaf pan or four 5- by 2½- by 2½-inch small loaf pans. Dust pan(s) lightly with flour; shake out excess and set aside.

FOOD PROCESSOR METHOD

Put both flours, baking powder, and baking soda in work bowl fitted with metal blade. Process for 5 seconds; transfer dry ingredients to another bowl. Put whole cranberries and nuts in work bowl. Coarsely chop cranberries and nuts by turning machine on/off 7 to 8 times; transfer to another bowl. Add sugar and orange peel to work bowl and run machine nonstop until peel is minced, about 1 minute; stopping machine once or twice to scrape inside work bowl with spatula. Add egg white and whole egg; process mixture for 1 minute. Add margarine and process for 1 minute. Stop machine once and scrape inside work bowl with plastic spatula. Add orange juice; process for 10 seconds. Add dry ingredients and blend by turning machine on/off 3 to 4 times, just until the flour is moistened. Add cranberry-nut mixture to batter and process by turning machine on/off 4 to 5 times or just until cranberry mixture is blended into batter. Do not overprocess; batter should be lumpy.

ELECTRIC MIXER METHOD

1. In a shallow bowl, sift both flours, baking powder, and baking soda; set dry ingredients aside.
2. With electric mixer on medium speed, cream margarine and sugar until fluffy, about 2 minutes. Add egg white and whole egg; beat until smooth. Turn speed down to low and add dry ingredients

alternately with orange juice in two batches, scraping down with rubber spatula after each addition, just until ingredients are blended. Batter should be lumpy. Stir in grated orange rind. Fold cranberry-nut mixture into batter with spatula.

TO BAKE

Turn batter into prepared pan or pans and smooth top with metal spatula. Tap pan(s) gently on work surface to break any air bubbles. Bake in preheated oven until golden on top and a cake tester inserted in center comes out clean, about 70 to 80 minutes for large loaf and 40 to 45 minutes for smaller loaves. Let loaf or loaves cool in pan(s) on a rack for 10 minutes. Invert onto rack, remove pan(s) and invert again onto second rack. Cool completely on rack before slicing.

NOTE: For storing or freezing, cool loaf to room temperature, wrap in plastic wrap, place in plastic bag, and seal tightly. May be kept in freezer up to 3 months. To defrost, unwrap completely and bring to room temperature.

⫷⫷⫷

Lemon-glazed Prune Loaf

For brunch, tea, luncheon, or just snacking, this tangy loaf always disappears as quickly as it is baked in my household. For easier slicing, bake one day before serving. This is an adaptation of one of the many recipes developed by my cousin Lorraine. No Christmas would be complete without a visit from Lorraine and a gift of no less than six different types of bread. Ingredients are listed in sequence for the food processor; if you use an electric mixer, the ingredients will be combined in a different sequence.

YIELDS 1 LARGE LOAF OR 4 SMALL LOAVES

1 cup (about 20) large pitted prunes, well packed

1¾ cups unbleached all-purpose flour

1 tablespoon double-acting baking powder

½ teaspoon baking soda

¾ cup old-fashioned oats, preferably Quaker

¾ cup sugar
Thin outer peel of 1 medium-sized lemon (3 ounces), removed with a zester for food processor method or finely grated to make 1½ teaspoons for electric mixer method

1 extra large egg white at room temperature

1 extra large egg at room temperature

¼ cup (½ stick) unsalted margarine at room temperature (cut into 8 pieces for food processor method only)

½ cup low-fat buttermilk or sour milk at room temperature (see Note)

1 teaspoon pure lemon extract

1. Place prunes in a 1½-quart saucepan with enough water to cover by 1 inch. Cover pot and bring to a boil. Cook until prunes are slightly softened, about 1 minute. Transfer to a strainer and refresh under cold water; drain thoroughly. Using a pair of kitchen shears, snip prunes into ½-inch pieces; set aside.

2. Adjust oven rack to center of oven; preheat to 350 degrees. Grease the bottom and sides of a 9- by 5- by 3½-inch loaf pan or four 5-

by 2½- by 2½-inch small loaf pans. Dust pan(s) lightly with flour; shake out excess and set aside.

FOOD PROCESSOR METHOD

Put flour, baking powder, and baking soda in work bowl fitted with metal blade. Process for 5 seconds. Transfer dry ingredients to another bowl, and stir oats into dry ingredients. Put sugar and lemon peel in work bowl and run machine nonstop until peel is minced, about 1 minute, stopping machine once or twice to scrape inside work bowl with plastic spatula. Add egg white and whole egg; process for 1 minute. Add margarine and process for 1 minute. Stop machine once and scrape inside work bowl with spatula. Add buttermilk or sour milk and lemon extract; process for 10 seconds. Add flour-oat mixture and blend by turning machine on/off 3 to 4 times just until moistened. Do not overprocess the batter; it should be lumpy. Add prunes and process with 3 to 4 quick on/off turns just to combine.

ELECTRIC MIXER METHOD

1. In a shallow bowl, sift together flour, baking powder, and baking soda. Stir oats into dry ingredients.
2. With electric mixer on medium speed, cream margarine and sugar until fluffy, about 2 minutes. Add egg white and whole egg and beat until smooth. Turn speed down to low and add flour-oat mixture alternately with buttermilk or sour milk in two batches, scraping down with rubber spatula after each addition, just until ingredients are blended; batter should be lumpy. Stir in lemon extract and grated lemon rind. Fold prunes into batter with spatula.

TO BAKE

Turn batter into prepared pan(s) and smooth top with a narrow metal spatula. Tap pan(s) gently on work surface to break any air bubbles. Bake until golden on top and a cake tester inserted in center comes out clean, about 1 hour for large loaf and 35 to 40 minutes for smaller loaves. Let loaf or loaves cool in pan(s) on rack for 10 minutes. Invert onto rack, remove pan(s), and invert again onto second rack. Place loaf or loaves on rack over a large piece of aluminum foil and prepare glaze.

Glaze

¼ cup lemon juice, strained   ¼ cup sugar

1. In a small saucepan, combine lemon juice and sugar. Cook over low heat, stirring once or twice, until sugar is completely dissolved, about 1 minute.
2. While loaf or loaves are still warm, pierce top and sides thoroughly with cake tester or toothpick. Brush glaze over top and sides of loaf or loaves several times until completely absorbed; cool completely on rack before slicing.

N O T E S : If you have no buttermilk or sour milk on hand, mix 1 tablespoon lemon juice with ½ cup low-fat or skimmed milk and let stand until curdled, approximately 5 minutes.

For storing or freezing, cool bread loaf to room temperature, wrap in plastic wrap, place in plastic bag, and seal tightly. May be kept in freezer up to 2 months. To defrost, unwrap completely and bring to room temperature.

≪≪←

MUFFINS

⇇⇇

Basic Muffins

Homemade muffins fresh from the oven are always a special treat on their own or when served as part of the meal. Whether mixed in a food processor or electric mixer, they are all a snap to prepare. See variations at bottom of recipe.

YIELDS 8 LARGE
SERVES 8

1¾ cups unbleached
   all-purpose flour
2 teaspoons double-acting
   baking powder
⅓ cup sugar
1 extra large egg, room
   temperature

2 tablespoons unsalted
   margarine at room
   temperature, cut into 4
   pieces
½ cup low-fat or skimmed
   milk at room temperature

Adjust rack to center of oven; preheat to 400 degrees. Lightly grease the bottom and sides of an 8-section muffin pan with 2½-by 1-inch cups; set aside.

FOOD PROCESSOR METHOD
Place flour and baking powder in work bowl fitted with metal blade and process for 5 seconds. Transfer dry ingredients to another bowl. Put sugar and egg in work bowl; process for 1 minute. Add margarine and process for 30 seconds. Stop machine and scrape inside work bowl with spatula. With machine running, pour milk into feed tube. Add dry ingredients and blend by turning machine on/off 3 to 4 times, just until mixture is moistened. Do not overprocess the batter. Batter should be very lumpy.

ELECTRIC MIXER METHOD

1. In a shallow bowl, sift together flour and baking powder; set dry ingredients aside.
2. With electric mixer on medium speed, beat sugar, egg, and margarine until creamy and smooth, about 1 minute. Stop machine and scrape down with rubber spatula. Turn speed down to low and add dry ingredients alternately with milk in two batches, scraping down with rubber spatula after each addition and beating just until ingredients are blended. Batter should be very lumpy.

TO BAKE

Spoon batter into prepared muffin cups, filling each about three-fourths full. Bake until golden on top, about 20 to 25 minutes. Turn muffins onto a rack and let cool for 10 minutes before serving.

NOTE: For storing or freezing, cool muffins to room temperature, place in plastic bag, and seal tightly. Store in refrigerator up to 3 days or freeze up to 2 months. If freezing, remove from plastic bag ½ hour before serving. Muffins may be warmed in a preheated 300-degree oven (or a toaster oven) for 10 minutes.

VARIATIONS

Applesauce Muffins

Basic Muffin batter   4 tablespoons applesauce

Prepare batter as directed for basic muffins, and spoon into prepared muffin cups. Using the back of a teaspoon, make a well in center of batter in each muffin cup about 1 inch wide by ½ inch deep. Spoon 1½ teaspoons applesauce into each cavity. Bake as directed for basic muffins.

Transfer muffins onto cooling rack by lifting out with a pair of metal tongs or two forks so that applesauce will not spill out of cavities after baking.

Blueberry Muffins

Basic Muffin batter

1 cup fresh blueberries,
washed and thoroughly
drained

Prepare batter as directed for basic muffins. If you use food processor method, transfer batter to bowl. Using a rubber spatula, gently fold blueberries into batter. Bake as directed for basic muffins.

Cranberry Muffins

Basic Muffin batter
2 teaspoons finely grated
orange rind

1 cup coarsely chopped
cranberries, picked over,
washed, and thoroughly
drained

Prepare batter as directed for basic muffins. If you use food processor method, transfer batter to bowl. Using a rubber spatula, gently fold orange rind and cranberries into batter. Bake as directed for basic muffins.

Date Muffins

Basic Muffin batter

1 cup pitted dates, cut in
¼-inch dice

Prepare batter as directed for basic muffins. If you use food processor method, transfer batter to bowl. Using a rubber spatula, fold diced pitted dates into batter. Bake as directed for basic muffins.

Strawberry Surprise Muffins

Basic Muffin batter

8 teaspoons strawberry
preserves

Prepare batter as directed for basic muffins. Spoon 1 ½ tablespoons batter into each prepared muffin cup. With the back of a teaspoon, make an indentation in center of batter in each muffin cup. Spoon 1 teaspoon strawberry preserves into each cavity. Cover with remaining batter. Bake as directed for basic muffins.

Cornmeal and Wheat Muffins

Incredibly easy to prepare. Excellent with any meal and especially good served with any of the hearty soup recipes in this book.

YIELDS 8 LARGE
SERVES 8

1 cup yellow cornmeal
¾ cup whole wheat flour
2 teaspoons double-acting baking powder
¼ cup sugar
1 extra large egg at room temperature

2 tablespoons unsalted margarine at room temperature, cut into 4 pieces
¾ cup low-fat buttermilk at room temperature

Adjust oven rack to center of oven; preheat to 375 degrees. Lightly grease the bottom and sides of an 8-section muffin pan with 2 ½-inch by 1-inch cups; set aside.

FOOD PROCESSOR METHOD
Place cornmeal, whole wheat flour, and baking powder in work bowl fitted with metal blade. Process for 5 seconds. Transfer dry ingredients to another bowl. Put sugar and egg in work bowl; process for 1 minute. Add margarine and process for 30 seconds. Stop machine and scrape inside work bowl with plastic spatula. With machine running, pour buttermilk into feed tube. Add dry

ingredients and blend by turning machine on/off 3 to 4 times, just until mixture is moistened. Do not overprocess the batter; it should be lumpy and slightly grainy.

ELECTRIC MIXER METHOD

1. In a shallow bowl, sift together cornmeal, whole wheat flour, and baking powder; set dry ingredients aside.
2. With electric mixer on medium speed, beat sugar, egg, and margarine until creamy and smooth, about 1 minute. Stop machine and scrape down with rubber spatula. Turn speed down to low and add dry ingredients alternately with buttermilk in two batches, scraping down with rubber spatula after each addition and beating just until ingredients are blended. Batter should be lumpy and slightly grainy.

TO BAKE

Spoon batter into prepared muffin cups, filling each about three-fourths full. Bake until golden on top, about 20 to 25 minutes. Turn muffins onto a rack and let cool for 5 minutes before serving.

NOTE: For storing or freezing, cool muffins to room temperature, place in plastic bag, and seal tightly. Store in refrigerator up to 3 days or freeze up to 2 months. If freezing, remove from plastic bag ½ hour before serving. Muffins may be warmed in preheated 300-degree oven (or a toaster oven) for 10 minutes.

Raisin Bran Muffins

These classic muffins have been a favorite on my breakfast table for years. They are so easy to make that I am sure you will want to serve them as often as I do.

YIELDS 8 LARGE
SERVES 8

1 cup whole bran cereal
¾ cup low-fat yogurt
1 cup unbleached all-purpose flour
2 teaspoons double-acting baking powder
1 teaspoon ground cinnamon

⅓ cup well packed light brown sugar
1 extra large egg at room temperature
2 tablespoons unsalted margarine, softened
½ cup dark raisins

1. Place bran in a small deep bowl. Add yogurt and mix thoroughly to moisten cereal. Let mixture stand at room temperature until bran is softened, about 10 minutes.
2. Adjust rack to center of oven; preheat to 375 degrees. Lightly grease the bottom and sides of an 8-section muffin pan with 2½-by 1-inch cups; set aside.

FOOD PROCESSOR METHOD

Place flour, baking powder, and cinnamon in work bowl fitted with metal blade. Process for 5 seconds. Transfer dry ingredients to another bowl. Put brown sugar, egg, and margarine in work bowl; process mixture for 30 seconds. Stop machine and scrape inside work bowl with plastic spatula. Add the softened bran-yogurt mixture; process until blended, about 5 seconds. Add dry ingredients and blend by turning machine on/off 2 to 3 times, just until mixture is moistened. Do not overprocess the batter; it should be lumpy. Add raisins and process with 2 to 3 quick on/off turns to combine.

ELECTRIC MIXER METHOD

1. In a shallow bowl, sift together flour, baking powder, and cinnamon; set dry ingredients aside.
2. With electric mixer on medium speed, beat sugar, egg, and margarine until creamy and smooth, about 1 minute. Turn speed down to low and add bran-yogurt mixture; beat until blended, about 20 seconds. Stop machine and scrape down with rubber spatula. Add dry ingredients and beat at low speed just until ingredients are blended; batter should be lumpy. Fold raisins into batter with spatula.

TO BAKE

Spoon batter into prepared muffin cups, filling each about three-fourths full. Bake until golden on top, about 25 minutes. Turn muffins onto a rack and let cool for 10 minutes before serving.

NOTE: For storing or freezing, cool muffins to room temperature, place in plastic bag, and seal tightly. Store in refrigerator up to 3 days or freeze up to 2 months. If freezing, remove from plastic bag ½ hour before serving. Muffins may be warmed in a preheated 300-degree oven (or a toaster oven) for 10 minutes.

⫷⫷⫷

Whole Wheat Cinnamon Muffins

These muffins have a slightly nutty flavor. They are great for breakfast, brunch, lunch, or just plain snacking.

YIELDS 8 LARGE
SERVES 8

¾ cup unbleached all-purpose flour
¾ cup whole wheat flour
2 teaspoons double-acting baking powder
1½ teaspoons ground cinnamon
½ cup well packed light brown sugar

1 extra large egg at room temperature
2 tablespoons unsalted margarine at room temperature, cut into 4 pieces
½ cup low-fat buttermilk at room temperature

Adjust oven rack to center of oven; preheat to 375 degrees. Lightly grease bottom and sides of an 8-section muffin pan with 2½- by 1-inch cups; set aside.

FOOD PROCESSOR METHOD

Place both flours, baking powder, and cinnamon in work bowl fitted with metal blade. Process mixture for 5 seconds. Transfer dry ingredients to another bowl. Put brown sugar and egg in work bowl; process mixture for 1 minute. Add margarine and process for 30 seconds. Stop machine and scrape inside work bowl with plastic spatula. With machine running, pour buttermilk into feed tube. Add dry ingredients and blend by turning machine on/off 3 to 4 times, just until mixture is moistened. Do not overprocess the batter; it should be lumpy.

ELECTRIC MIXER METHOD

1. In a shallow bowl, sift both flours, baking powder, and cinnamon; set dry ingredients aside.

2. With electric mixer on medium speed, beat sugar, egg, and margarine until creamy and smooth, about 1 minute. Stop machine and scrape down with rubber spatula. Turn speed down to low and add dry ingredients alternately with buttermilk in two batches, scraping down with spatula after each addition and beating just until ingredients are blended. Batter should be lumpy.

TO BAKE

Spoon batter into prepared muffin cups, filling each about three-fourths full. Bake until golden on top, about 20 to 25 minutes. Turn muffins onto a rack and let cool for 10 minutes before serving.

NOTE: For storing or freezing, cool muffins to room temperature, place in plastic bag, and seal tightly. Store in refrigerator up to 3 days or freeze up to 2 months. If freezing, remove from plastic bag ½ hour before serving. Muffins may be warmed in a preheated 300-degree oven (or a toaster oven) for 10 minutes.

SPREADS
〈〈〈‑

Raisin Spread

Use this spread for Basic Muffins (page 323) or any of the muffin variations that do not contain fruit. Also excellent on toasted homemade Whole Wheat Bread (page 292), or Old-fashioned Sesame Oatmeal Bread (page 289). See variations at bottom of page.

YIELDS ¾ CUP

1 cup golden raisins	½ teaspoon finely grated
¼ cup applesauce	lemon rind
	1 teaspoon fresh lemon juice

1. In a 1½-quart saucepan, combine raisins with 1 cup water. Cover pan and bring to a boil over high heat. Cook just until raisins are plumped, about 30 seconds. Transfer to a strainer and refresh under cold water. Set strainer over a bowl and with the back of a wooden spoon press raisins to get rid of excess liquid; discard liquid.
2. Place raisins and remaining ingredients in blender or food processor fitted with metal blade. Run machine nonstop until you have a smooth paste. Stop machine once and scrape down inside workbowl with plastic spatula. Transfer to a small jar and refrigerate for at least 3 hours or until needed. (Raisin spread may be stored in refrigerator up to 1 month.)

〈〈〈‑

Apricot or Prune Spread

Substitute 1 cup dried apricots or prunes (well packed) for the raisins. Cook apricots or prunes for 2 minutes before draining. Follow same procedure as directed for Raisin Spread.

⋘

DESSERTS

I can still remember the old icebox we had when I was a child. The iceman came down our street every day; if we wanted ice, we put a sign in our window and he would stop. The ice was a huge block, covered with a large piece of burlap. I was always amazed at how deftly he used an ice pick to chizzle away from the block a piece of ice that always fit perfectly into our ice compartment. During the summer months it was always fun to get some of the ice shavings as he chipped away. I am sure many of you can still remember the drip tray at the bottom of the icebox, which had to be emptied daily.

Chilled desserts were very limited in those days because of refrigeration. While desserts were never the highlight of a meal, I never failed to ask as I was sliding into my chair at the dinner table, "What's for dessert?" The answer was always the same: "Fruit," or occasionally "Jell-O." When company was coming, desserts were usually very special, but there were also times when a variation of one or another of the quick breads in this book were made for simple entertaining.

I vividly recall the first dessert I ever made. I was six years old, and it was Jell-O. This could only be made once a week—when the iceman delivered the ice—because only then would the Jell-O chill properly. The day our first electric refrigerator was delivered will stay in my memory forever. I can still see my mother, my sister Louisa, and myself with our hands clasped as we danced around the sparkling new "G.E." My biggest thrill was not having to wait for a special day each week to prepare my famous culinary creation—I made Jell-O every day for two weeks straight.

Today I rarely serve any dessert for my husband and myself other than fresh fruit or an impromptu fruit salad—how history repeats itself. But I refuse to make Jell-O!

Most human beings have an irrespresible appetite for something sweet at the end of a meal. Taking today's tastes into consideration, I have developed recipes that are not only delicious but use sugar sparingly and substitute part-skim ricotta cheese and low-fat yogurt for heavy cream. As you read through the following pages, you will find that while my desserts are all fruit-based, they provide a wide variety of selections, including crisps, custards, clafoutis, meringues, mousses, parfaits, dessert pancakes, and others. Simple recipes for fruit sauces that can be served with sorbets for a quick dessert, variations on crunchy fruit cups, and of course the quick breads in the previous chapter, will expand your repertoire of final sweet touches to your perfect meal.

⫷

Apple Meringue

For best flavor, serve this dessert warm or at room temperature.

SERVES 2

2 large Golden Delicious apples (12 ounces total weight), peeled, quartered, cored, and sliced crosswise into ½-inch pieces to make 2 cups, well packed

⅓ cup unsweetened apple juice

1 extra large egg white at room temperature

Pinch of salt

Pinch of cream of tartar

2 tablespoons plus 1 teaspoon sugar

¼ teaspoon pure vanilla extract

1. In a 10-inch skillet, combined sliced apples and apple juice. Cover pan and bring to a boil over high heat. As soon as juice reaches a boil, turn heat down to medium. Cook, uncovered, spooning juice over apples, until they are barely tender when tested with a fork, about 3 minutes. Transfer apples to a strainer set over a bowl; reserve juice. Spoon drained apples into two 6-ounce ovenproof custard cups. Spoon 1 tablespoon of the reserved juice over each; set aside.
2. Adjust rack to center of oven and preheat to 375 degrees.
3. Beat egg white until foamy. Add salt and cream of tartar, and continue beating until whites hold soft peaks. Gradually add sugar; continue beating until stiff and glossy. Add vanilla and beat just until blended. Spoon meringue over apples. Using a rubber spatula, spread meringue to the inside edges of cups.
4. Place baking cups on a small baking sheet (the oven tray from a toaster oven works well). Bake in preheated oven until meringue is lightly golden, about 8 to 10 minutes. Transfer to cooling rack and cool for at least 30 minutes before serving, or serve at room temperature.

≪≪

Apricot Custard

An excellent do-ahead winter dessert. The texture of this dessert is more like a light cheesecake than a custard. It can be served either at room temperature or well chilled. If serving chilled, unmold for a beautiful presentation.

SERVES 2

2 tablespoons diced dried apricots (cut into ½-inch dice)
¾ cup low-fat yogurt
1 extra large egg, lightly beaten

2 tablespoons sugar
½ teaspoon pure vanilla extract

1. Adjust rack to center of oven and preheat to 350 degrees. Lightly grease two 6-ounce ovenproof custard cups; set aside.
2. Place apricots in a small bowl. Add enough boiling water to cover and let stand for 10 minutes to soften. Transfer to strainer and drain thoroughly. Place 1 tablespoon diced apricots in bottom of each prepared custard cup.
3. Place yogurt, beaten egg, and sugar in a deep bowl. Beat with a wire whisk until smooth and creamy. Stir in vanilla. Pour mixture into cups over apricots. Place custard cups in a deep ovenproof baking dish. Add enough boiling water to baking dish to reach ⅔ of the way up the sides of cups.
4. Bake in preheated oven until slightly puffed, very lightly golden around edges, and a cake tester inserted in center comes out clean, about 35 to 40 minutes. Immediately remove from water bath and place on a rack to cool to room temperature. This dessert can be served at room temperature or well chilled (chill in refrigerator for at least 3 hours before unmolding). To unmold, insert the tip of a knife between the custard and the side of the custard cup. Run knife around inside edge to loosen, unmold onto individual dessert plates, and serve.

⫷⫷⫷

Banana Flambé

Select a perfect, unblemished yellow banana that is slightly tinged with green for this spectacular dessert.

S E R V E S 2

½ pint vanilla ice milk or frozen vanilla yogurt	2 tablespoons honey, preferably orange blossom
1 large yellow banana (6 ounces) tipped with green	1 tablespoon crème de cacao liqueur
2 teaspoons unsalted margarine, cut into ½-inch cubes	3 tablespoons Cognac, warmed

1. Scoop ice milk or frozen yogurt onto individual serving plates and place in freezer until needed.
2. Peel banana and cut in half lengthwise, then crosswise.
3. In a 10-inch skillet, melt margarine over medium-high heat; add honey and swirl pan so that it is evenly coated. Continue cooking and swirling pan until honey-margarine mixture is a light caramel color, about 30 seconds. Add liqueur and swirl in pan to combine.
4. Add banana quarters to sauce and turn heat up to high. Using a serving fork and spoon, keep turning and basting quarters in sauce until lightly glazed, about 30 seconds. Add warmed Cognac, shake pan, and ignite. Remove from heat and keep basting until the flame goes out.
5. To serve, place two sections of banana, curved side up, on either side of ice milk or frozen yogurt. Spoon sauce over each portion and serve immediately.

<<<-

Crunchy Blueberry Cups

A satisfying finale for lunch or dinner when fresh blueberries are in season. This dessert is best served lukewarm while the streusel topping is still crisp. See variations at bottom of recipe.

SERVES 2

1¼ cups blueberries
½ teaspoon finely grated
　lemon rind
2 teaspoons lemon juice,
　strained

2 teaspoons sugar
½ teaspoon cornstarch

1. Adjust rack to center of oven and preheat to 350 degrees. Lightly grease two 6-ounce ovenproof custard cups; set aside.
2. Pick over blueberries to remove any stems. Place blueberries in a strainer and wash thoroughly under cold water. Blot dry with paper towel and transfer to a deep bowl.
3. In a small bowl, combine remaining ingredients and stir with a spoon until cornstarch is completely dissolved. Pour lemon mixture over blueberries. Toss berries to coat thoroughly with lemon mixture. Spoon blueberry mixture into prepared custard cups; set aside.

Streusel Topping

2 tablespoons light brown
　sugar
1½ tablespoons unbleached
　all-purpose flour
1½ tablespoons wheat germ
¼ teaspoon ground
　cinnamon

1 tablespoon unsalted
　margarine, well chilled
　and cut into 12 pieces
½ teaspoon sifted
　confectioner's sugar (for
　dusting)

1. Place brown sugar, flour, wheat germ, and cinnamon in a small bowl. Stir with fork to combine thoroughly. Add margarine and

blend with your fingertips until mixture resembles coarse (pea-size) crumbs. Spoon crumb mixture over blueberries.

2. Place custard cups on a small baking sheet (the oven tray from a toaster oven works well). Bake in preheated oven until the blueberry mixture is bubbling around the edges of the custard cups and the crumbs are golden, about 20 minutes.

3. Transfer to rack and cool to lukewarm, about 25 minutes. Dust with confectioner's sugar just before serving.

VARIATIONS

Crunchy Apple Cups

For a winter dessert, substitute 1¼ cups of peeled and diced Golden Delicious apple (½-inch dice) for the blueberries. Bake as directed for Crunchy Blueberry Cups, increasing baking time to about 25 minutes total.

Crunchy Peach Cups

For another summer dessert, you can substitute 1¼ cups well packed peeled and diced ripened peaches (½-inch dice) for the blueberries. Bake as directed for Crunchy Blueberry Cups.

⋘

Cran-raspberry Mousse

This memorable dessert looks and tastes as if you had labored on it all day.

SERVES 2

1½ teaspoons unflavored
    gelatin
¼ cup fresh orange juice,
    strained
One 8-ounce can Ocean Spray
    cran-raspberry sauce
¼ cup whipped part-skim
    ricotta cheese (page 37)

1 extra large egg white at
    room temperature
Pinch of salt
Pinch of cream of tartar
2 tablespoons sugar

1. In a small bowl, sprinkle gelatin over orange juice and let stand until gelatin is softened, about 3 minutes.
2. Put cran-raspberry sauce in a 1½-quart saucepan. Cook over low heat, stirring constantly with a whisk until melted, about 2 minutes. Stir in gelatin mixture and cook, stirring constantly, until sauce has dissolved and mixture just starts to come to a boil, about 2 minutes. Remove from heat and transfer to a deep bowl. Cool to room temperature. Chill, stirring once or twice, until mixture is the consistency of unbeaten egg whites, about 1 hour and 15 minutes.
3. Using a rubber spatula, fold ricotta into gelatin mixture.
4. Beat egg white until foamy. Add salt and cream of tartar; continue beating until egg white holds soft peaks. Gradually add sugar; continue beating until stiff and glossy. Using a rubber spatula, fold gently but thoroughly into gelatin mixture. Ladle into two 8-ounce dessert bowls, preferably glass, or 8-ounce wine glasses. Refrigerate until firm, about 5 hours or overnight.

<<<

Poached Nectarines with Blueberry Sauce

One of the great, all-time favorite desserts to serve during the summer months.

SERVES 2

2 large, unblemished
nectarines (12 ounces total
weight)
1 cup water
½ cup sugar

1 small lemon (3 ounces),
ends trimmed and sliced
into 6 even rounds
4 tablespoons Blueberry
Sauce (page 360)

1. Wash and dry nectarines. Using a small knife, halve one nectarine lengthwise through stem end. Grasp both halves firmly and twist in opposite directions until one side pulls free of the pit. If you cannot easily pry the pit from the other half with your fingers, cut the pit out neatly with a serrated knife. Repeat with other nectarine.
2. Place water and sugar in a heavy 2½-quart saucepan. Bring to a boil over medium heat, stirring constantly with a wooden spoon until all the sugar is dissolved. Turn heat to low and cook syrup for 2 minutes.
3. Add the lemon slices to syrup. Place nectarine halves skin side down in syrup. Cover pan and simmer until the nectarines are barely tender when tested with a cake tester, about 3 minutes. Using two spoons, gently turn each nectarine half skin side up in syrup. Continue simmering, covered, until the fruit is slightly softened when tested again with cake tester, about 2 minutes.
4. Using a slotted spoon, transfer nectarines to a large, flat plate, skin side up, to cool a little. When cool enough to handle, carefully peel the skin from each half with a small knife. Place peeled halves back on same plate, cut sides down.
5. Discard lemon from syrup. Spoon 1 tablespoon of syrup over each half; cover with plastic wrap and refrigerate until ready to serve.

(Nectarines may be poached up to 4 hours before serving.) Discard remaining syrup.

6. When ready to serve, drain nectarines and discard any remaining syrup on plate.

7. Place two nectarine halves on each dessert plate, cut sides down. Carefully spoon 2 tablespoons of blueberry sauce around nectarine halves on each plate and serve.

Nectarine Clafouti

This quick-to-prepare homestyle dessert looks like a puffed fruit pancake when finished and is best served lukewarm. See variations at bottom of recipe.

SERVES 2

2 medium-sized ripe unpeeled nectarines (8 ounces total weight), halved, pitted, and sliced lengthwise into ¼-inch slices to make 1½ cups
One 5½-ounce can apricot nectar
1 large egg, lightly beaten

2 tablespoons sugar
¼ teaspoon ground cinnamon
3½ tablespoons unbleached all-purpose flour
½ teaspoon sifted confectioner's sugar (for dusting)

1. Adjust rack to center of oven and preheat to 350 degrees. Lightly grease a shallow 2½-cup ovenproof baking dish.

2. Arrange nectarine slices in a slightly overlapping pattern in two layers in prepared dish.

3. Place apricot nectar, egg, sugar, cinnamon, and flour in blender or food processor fitted with metal blade. Run machine nonstop until batter is smooth, about 1 to 1½ minutes. (It is important that machine run for at least one minute so that clafouti will puff in

baking.) Slowly pour batter over nectarines.

4. Bake in preheated oven until surface is golden and slightly puffed, about 30 to 35 minutes. The clafouti is done when the batter has set into a custardlike mass on surface and a cake tester comes out clean when inserted in center.

5. Remove from oven and transfer to a cooling rack. Let clafouti cool on rack until lukewarm, about 35 minutes. Dust surface of lukewarm clafouti with confectioner's sugar. Spoon onto individual dessert plates and serve.

VARIATIONS

Apricot Clafouti

Substitute 4 ripe unpeeled apricots (about 8 ounces total weight), halved, pitted, and sliced lengthwise into ¼-inch slices to make 1½ cups for the nectarines. Prepare and bake as directed for nectarine clafouti.

Peach Clafouti

Substitute 2 ripe peaches (10 ounces total weight), blanched, peeled, halved, pitted, and sliced lengthwise into ½-inch slices to make 1½ cups for the nectarines. Prepare and bake as directed for nectarine clafouti, decreasing baking time 5 minutes (bake about 25 to 30 minutes).

⫷⫷

Orange Compote with Liqueur

A light, sweet finale to any meal; particularly good after a fish or seafood dinner.

SERVES 2

2 large navel oranges (1¼ pounds total weight)
1 tablespoon confectioner's sugar

2 tablespoons Grand Marnier or mandarine liqueur

1. Cut a slice from top and bottom of oranges to expose the fruit. Peel the oranges and remove all the white membrane with a vegetable peeler. Cut out each orange segment, removing its protective membrane as you cut. Place orange sections in strainer set over a bowl to drain thoroughly. Place in refrigerator to chill for at least 1 hour or until ready to serve.
2. When ready to serve, place orange sections in a bowl and toss with confectioner's sugar. Spoon sections into two dessert dishes, preberably glass. Sprinkle 1 tablespoon liqueur over each dessert and serve.

Peach Cream

Select clingstone peaches for this dessert; they have a firmer flesh adhering to the stone and are better for cooking than the freestone variety, which have a juicier pulp and are better for eating.

S E R V E S 2

2 large ripe cling peaches (14 ounces total weight)
2 tablespoons sugar
2 teaspoons fresh lemon juice, strained
1 tablespoon dark rum, preferably Myers

½ cup whipped part-skim ricotta cheese (page 37)
2 teaspoons confectioner's sugar
⅛ teaspoon ground cinnamon

1. Blanch peaches in 4 cups boiling water for 2 minutes. Transfer to a strainer and rinse under cold water. When cool enough to handle, peel skins, cut peaches in half, discard stones and coarsely chop fruit. (You can chop peaches in the food processor fitted with metal blade. For an even chop, quarter peaches before placing in processor and chop with 3 to 4 quick on/off turns.)
2. In a 1½-quart saucepan, combine peaches, 2 tablespoons sugar, and lemon juice. Bring to a boil over high heat. As soon as mixture reaches a boil, turn heat down to medium-low. Cook, stirring frequently with wooden spoon, until very little liquid is left in pan and peaches just start to stick to bottom of pan when stirred with spoon, about 10 to 12 minutes. Transfer to bowl. Cool to almost room temperature and stir in rum. Cover with plastic wrap and refrigerate until well chilled, about 1½ hours.
3. In a small bowl, combine whipped ricotta, 2 teaspoons confectioner's sugar, and cinnamon. Blend thoroughly with fork or small whisk. Using a rubber spatula, fold ricotta mixture into peach mixture.
4. Spoon peach cream into two 8-ounce wine glasses and chill for at least 2 hours before serving.

Dessert Pancakes with Peach Filling

Part-skim ricotta cheese and whole wheat flour contribute a light texture to the batter, adding a delicate flavor to the pancakes. See variations on fillings and toppings at bottom of recipe.

SERVES 2

Peach Filling

- 2 medium-sized ripe peaches (10 ounces total weight), peeled, halved, pitted, and coarsely chopped to make 1 cup well packed (peaches can be chopped in food processor fitted with metal blade; cut into quarters before placing in work bowl)

- 3 tablespoons dark raisins
- 1 tablespoon light brown sugar
- ¼ teaspoon ground cinnamon
- 1 tablespoon fresh orange juice, strained

In a 1½-quart saucepan, combine all of the filling ingredients. Bring to a boil over high heat. Turn heat to low and cook, stirring frequently until peaches are soft and filling is slightly thickened, about 8 minutes. Transfer to bowl and cool to room temperature. (Filling may be made 1 day ahead, covered with plastic wrap, and refrigerated. Return to room temperature 1 hour before making pancakes.)

Pancakes

¼ cup part-skim ricotta
  cheese, or whipped
  part-skim ricotta cheese
  (page 37)
1 extra large egg

1 teaspoon sugar
1½ teaspoons vegetable oil,
  preferably corn oil
2 tablespoons whole wheat
  flour

1. Place ricotta cheese, egg, sugar, and vegetable oil in a deep bowl. Beat with a whisk until thick and creamy, about 30 seconds. Add flour and beat until well combined. (Batter may be made up to 2 hours before cooking pancakes. Cover with plastic wrap and leave at room temperature. Stir with whisk to combine before spooning batter onto hot skillet.)
2. Lightly grease a 12-inch skillet, or spray with cooking spray. Heat skillet over medium-high heat. Spoon 2 tablespoons of batter into skillet. Repeat with remaining batter to make a total of 4 pancakes, leaving 2-inch spaces between pancakes. When pancakes are lightly golden on the underside and bubbles appear on the surface, turn and brown lightly on second side. Transfer pancakes to plate.
3. To serve, place one pancake on each plate and spread each with 2 tablespoons of peach filling. Top with remaining pancakes and spoon remaining filling on top of each; serve immediately.

VARIATIONS

Apple Filling

Substitute for the peaches 1 large Golden Delicious apple (8 ounces), peeled, halved, cored, and coarsely chopped to make 1 cup well packed. Substitute 2 teaspoons lemon juice for the orange juice. Cook as directed for peach filling. Filling may be made 1 day ahead, covered with plastic wrap, and refrigerated. Return to room temperature 1 hour before making pancakes.

«‹‹

Strawberry Filling

Place 1 cup thinly sliced strawberries in a small bowl. Lightly toss berries with 1 tablespoon confectioner's sugar, ½ teaspoon grated lemon rind, and 1 tablespoon Grand Marnier. Cover bowl and leave at room temperature for ½ hour before making pancakes.

Blueberry Sauce Topping

Stack pancakes and spoon 2 tablespoons Blueberry Sauce (page 360) over each portion.

Strawberry Sauce Topping

Stack pancakes and spoon 2 tablespoons Strawberry Sauce (page 361) over each portion.

Poached Sliced Pears with Marmalade Sauce

Especially good for late fall or during the winter months when Bosc pears are abundant.

SERVES 2

2 cups water	2 large, firm, unblemished
1 cup sugar	Bosc pears (about 14 ounces
¼ cup fresh lemon juice	total weight)

1. In a 10-inch sauté pan, combine sugar, water, and juice. Bring to a boil over high heat, stirring frequently until sugar is completely dissolved. Turn heat down to low, cover pan, and cook syrup for about 8 minutes while preparing pears.

2. Remove core and stem from each end of pears. Peel fruit with a vegetable peeler. Cut the pears in half lengthwise. Using a melon ball scoop, remove the center core. Cut away the fibrous line leading from the core to the stem end. Slice each halved pear lengthwise into 3 even pieces.
3. Place pear slices in syrup. Simmer, uncovered, spooning syrup over slices until they are tender when tested with a fork, about 5 minutes (time will vary depending on ripeness of pears). Remove from heat, cover pan, and let pears cool in syrup to room temperature or until ready to serve.

Marmalade Sauce

¼ cup orange marmalade   1 tablespoon Grand Marnier

1. Put marmalade in a small saucepan. Stir in about 1 to 1½ tablespoons of the pear syrup, or just enough to barely loosen marmalade (amount will depend on how thick marmalade is). Cook over low heat, stirring constantly, just until marmalade has melted. Remove from heat and stir in Grand Marnier.
2. Using a pair of tongs, lift pear slices from syrup. With narrow ends facing inward, arrange 6 pear slices on each dessert plate in a circular pattern. (Syrup may be reserved for additional poaching or discarded.) Spoon warm sauce over pears and serve immediately.

Pineapple Sorbet with Sambuca

This quick and easy dessert is delectable for any occasion. A thin slice of zesty Lemon-glazed Prune Loaf (page 320) would prove a perfect partner.

S E R V E S 2

½ pint Dole's pineapple
  sorbet (see Note)

2 tablespoons Sambuca
  liqueur

Place one scoop of sorbet in each dessert bowl, preferably glass, or in 8-ounce wine glasses. Drizzle 1 tablespoon liqueur over each portion and serve immediately.

  N O T E : If pineapple sorbet is unavailable, substitute pineapple sherbert.

Plum Crisp

A great-tasting dessert that's easy on the budget in late summer or early fall when Italian purple prune plums are in season. This dessert is best served lukewarm. See variations at bottom of recipe.

S E R V E S 2

½ teaspoon finely grated
  lemon rind
2 teaspoons lemon juice,
  strained
2 tablespoons sugar
1 teaspoon minute tapioca

8 Italian purple prune plums
  (8 ounces total weight),
  washed, dried, halved,
  pitted, and sliced into
  ½-inch pieces

1. Adjust rack to center of oven and preheat to 350 degrees. Lightly grease a shallow 2½-cup ovenproof baking dish; set aside.
2. Place lemon rind, juice, sugar, and tapioca in a deep bowl. Stir with fork to combine. Add plums and toss to coat thoroughly with lemon mixture. Spoon plum mixture evenly into prepared dish.

Topping

2 tablespoons light brown sugar

1½ tablespoons unbleached all-purpose flour

1½ tablespoons old-fashioned oats, preferably Quaker

¼ teaspoon ground cinnamon

1 tablespoon unsalted margarine, well chilled and cut into 12 pieces

½ teaspoon sifted confectioner's sugar (for dusting)

1. Put brown sugar, flour, oats, and cinnamon in a small bowl. Stir with a fork to combine thoroughly. Add margarine and blend with your fingertips until mixture resembles coarse (pea-size) crumbs. Sprinkle crumb mixture over plums.
2. Bake in preheated oven until the plum mixture is bubbling around the edges of the baking dish and crumbs are golden, about 25 minutes.
3. Transfer to rack and cool to lukewarm, about 35 minutes. Dust with confectioner's sugar just before serving.

VARIATIONS

Apple Crisp

Substitute 2 Golden Delicious apples (10 ounces total weight) for the plums. Peel, halve, and core apples, and slice into ½-inch pieces. Prepare and bake as directed for plum crisp.

⫷⫷⫷

Peach Crisp

Substitute 2 large ripe peaches (about 12 ounces total weight) for the plums. Blanch peaches in boiling water, drain, and peel when cool enough to handle. Halve peaches, remove pits, and slice into ½-inch pieces. Prepare and bake as directed for plum crisp, decreasing baking time 5 minutes, for a total of about 20 minutes.

Star-spangled Parfait

Since so many of the commercial low-fat yogurts tend to be watery, drain thoroughly before assembling this distinctive red, white, and blue dessert.

SERVES 2

1 cup low-fat yogurt
2 teaspoons grated lemon rind
8 large ripe strawberries, washed, hulled, blotted dry with paper towel, and thinly sliced to make 1 cup
1 cup blueberries, picked over, washed, drained, and blotted dry with paper towel

2 tablespoons honey, preferably orange blossom
2 strawberries, washed and hulled (garnish)

1. Line a fine mesh strainer with a double thickness of dampened cheesecloth and set it over a bowl. Spoon yogurt into lined strainer and place, uncovered, in refrigerator to drain thoroughly for at least 2 hours. (Yogurt will exude as much as 4 tablespoons of liquid, and after draining it should be the consistency of whipped heavy cream.) Discard liquid. Using a rubber spatula, scrape yogurt from cheesecloth into a small bowl and stir in lemon rind.
2. Put strawberries and blueberries in separate bowls. Drizzle 1 tablespoon honey over each and toss gently with a rubber spatula.

3. Spoon sweetened strawberries into two 8-ounce parfait glasses or 8-ounce wine glasses. Carefully spoon 3 tablespoons of yogurt mixture into each glass over strawberries; spread evenly with a rubber spatula. Carefully spoon sweetened blueberries over yogurt mixture. Place a dollop of the remaining yogurt mixture on top of each dessert and chill for 2 hours before serving. (Do not chill any longer or berries will start to exude their juices.) Garnish with whole strawberries just before serving.

Frozen Strawberry Cream Parfaits

It is essential to work quickly when preparing this easy, fast dessert. When served, the strawberry cream will still be partially frozen. See note for variations.

SERVES 2

One 10-ounce package frozen sliced strawberries in syrup, unthawed
1 tablespoon Grand Marnier

¼ cup plus 2 teaspoons whipped part-skim ricotta cheese (page 37)
2 mint leaves (garnish)

1. Working quickly, cut the block of frozen strawberries into 1½-inch pieces.
2. In blender or food processor fitted with metal blade, place strawberries and liqueur. Run machine nonstop until mixture appears slushy, about 30 seconds. Scrape down inside work bowl with plastic spatula. Evenly distribute ¼ cup ricotta over strawberries. Process until ricotta is well incorporated and strawberry cream is a smooth consistency, about 30 seconds.
3. Spoon into 1-cup glass goblets and garnish each with 1 teaspoon of ricotta and a sprig of fresh mint; serve immediately.

NOTE: You may substitute a 10-ounce package of frozen raspberries or mixed fruit in syrup for the strawberries.

Prune Whip

A stunning way to cap a winter meal without the calories and cholesterol of traditional recipes.

SERVES 2

One 8-ounce can Sunsweet or
　other premium pitted
　prunes
¼ cup whipped part-skim
　ricotta cheese (page 37)
1 extra large egg white at
　room temperature

Pinch of salt
Pinch of cream of tartar
2 tablespoons sugar
1 teaspoon finely grated
　lemon rind

1. Using a pair of kitchen shears, cut prunes into ¼-inch dice. Place in a 1½-quart saucepan. Add 1 cup water, cover, and bring to a boil. Cook just until prunes are softened, about 2 minutes. (If you use the brand suggested above, they will be soft in 30 seconds.) Transfer to strainer and drain thoroughly. Place prunes in bowl and cool to room temperature. Cover with plastic wrap and refrigerate until well chilled, about 1½ hours.
2. Using a rubber spatula, fold ricotta into prunes.
3. Beat egg white until foamy. Add salt and cream of tartar; continue beating until egg white holds soft peaks. Gradually add sugar; continue beating until stiff and glossy. Add lemon rind and beat just until combined. Using a rubber spatula, fold gently but thoroughly into prune mixture. Ladle into two 8-ounce dessert bowls, preferably glass, or 8-ounce wine glasses, and refrigerate until well chilled, about 2 hours.

⋘

Lemon Sherbet with Fruit and Strawberry Sauce

A spectacular, light dessert to make whenever you can find fresh strawberries and kiwi fruit at the market.

SERVES 2

6 medium-sized ripe
strawberries (3 ounces)
1 large kiwi fruit (about 2
ounces)
1 tablespoon sugar
½ teaspoon grated lemon rind

1 tablespoon Grand Marnier
½ pint lemon sherbet
(preferably tangy, if
available)
4 tablespoons Strawberry
Sauce (page 361)

1. Rinse berries in cold water, thoroughly drain in strainer, and blot dry with paper towel. To core the berries, gather up the leaves of each stem cap and with the tip of a small knife cut a ¼-inch circle around the base of the cap. Pull the leaves and the white core will come out as well. Quarter berries and transfer to a small bowl.
2. Cut about ¼ inch from top and bottom of kiwi fruit. To remove the fuzzy brown skin, peel lengthwise with a vegetable peeler using a zigzag motion. Slice into ¼ inch-rounds; slice each round in half crosswise.
3. Transfer kiwi to bowl with berries; combine with sugar and lemon rind. Cover with plastic wrap; refrigerate for 2 hours.
4. When ready to serve, remove fruit from refrigerator; combine with Grand Marnier. (Strawberries will get too soggy if marinated with liqueur in advance.)
5. Place one scoop of sherbet into individual bowls, preferably glass. Arrange fruit around sherbet. Spoon 2 tablespoons strawberry sauce over each portion; serve immediately.

〈〈〈

SAUCES

⋘

Blueberry Sauce

One of summer's most tantalizing treats is the sauce made from fresh blueber-ries. An excellent sauce for Poached Nectarines (page 345), or Dessert Pancakes (page 350), it also adds a regal touch to lemon sherbet, pineapple sorbet, vanilla ice milk, or frozen vanilla yogurt.

YIELDS 2 ½ CUPS

1 pint blueberries	1 teaspoon lemon rind
½ cup plus 2 tablespoons water	2 tablespoons fresh lemon juice, strained
½ cup sugar	1 teaspoon cornstarch
1 cinnamon stick about 2 inches long	

1. Pick over blueberries, wash thoroughly, and drain in colander.
2. In a 5-quart saucepan, combine ½ cup water, ½ cup sugar, and cinnamon stick. Bring to a boil and cook, stirring constantly until sugar is completely dissolved, about 4 minutes.
3. Add blueberries, lemon rind, and lemon juice. Cook, stirring con-stantly over high heat, just until blueberries start to pop, about 2 minutes.
4. Place cornstarch and 2 tablespoons water in a small cup; stir with spoon until cornstarch is completely dissolved. Turn heat down to medium and stir cornstarch mixture into blueberries. Cook, stir-ring constantly until sauce is thickened, about 2 minutes. Transfer sauce and cinnamon stick to a 1½-pint jar and cool to room tem-perature. Store in refrigerator until needed. (Blueberry sauce will keep up to 1 month in refrigerator.)

⋘

Strawberry Sauce

This sauce may be prepared up to one week before using. Leftover sauce enhances any combination of fresh fruits and is equally delicious when spooned over pineapple or lemon sorbet. Also, it makes a crowning topping for Dessert Pancakes (page 350).

Y I E L D S   1   C U P

One 10-ounce package Birds
   Eye frozen strawberry
   halves in syrup
2 tablespoons seedless red
   raspberry jam

1 tablespoon fresh lemon
   juice, strained
1 tablespoon Grand
   Marnier

1. Thaw berries in strainer set over a bowl; reserve juice.
2. Put berries in blender or food processor fitted with metal blade. Run machine nonstop until you have a smooth purée, about 30 seconds. Transfer to a small bowl.
3. Place reserved juice in a 1½-quart saucepan. Add jam and lemon juice; stir to combine. Bring to a boil over high heat, stirring constantly with wire whisk until jam is dissolved. Turn heat to low and cook syrup for 6 minutes. At this point syrup will still be thin. Pour hot syrup over the puréed berries and whisk to combine. Cool to room temperature and stir in Grand Marnier. Transfer sauce to a 10-ounce jar and refrigerate until well chilled and slightly thickened, about 3 hours.

SEASONAL MENUS

≪←

For most people today, time is at a premium, and they do not want to spend hours in the kitchen preparing a meal. This is why the seasonal menus I present are particularly appealing. Many of these can be prepared well in advance; most should take no longer than one hour to assemble. They are the essence of simplicity without sacrificing elegance. While all the menus suggested will be for two, any recipe can be increased for entertaining.

As you read through the book, you will find many one-dish meals that are not listed in the following suggested menus, meals such as soups, pasta, stir-fry dishes, salads, and stews. Suggestions for simple accompaniments are recommended with each of these recipes. I have often used many of these one-dish meals for informal entertaining as well.

We all know how disappointing a poorly conceived meal served in dull, unpleasant surroundings can be. Esthetically, food either pleases or fails to stir the senses. The impression that one receives is most important. Menu and mood really matter. In planning meals, remember that it matters not only how the food looks, smells, and tastes, but how the combination of colors and textures relate to one another. In planning a meal, even for two, create an atmosphere through your choice of music, china, napery, wine, and other embellishments.

The simple yet impressive seasonal menus that follow are designed with today's sensible approach to food, and are dedicated to your good health.

Winter Menus

Grated Potato Soup

Roast Chicken with Rosemary

Peas and Mushrooms

Wheat and Yogurt Bread

Poached Sliced Pears with Marmalade Sauce

Green Noodles with Carrots and Parsnips

Chicken Breast with Lemon Caper Tarragon Sauce

Cucumber and Radish Salad

Frozen Strawberry Cream Parfaits

Oven-barbecued Chicken Thighs

Bulgur Pilaf

Spinach Salad

Apricot Pineapple Loaf

Chicken Breast with Artichoke Hearts

Brown Rice Pilaf

Parsleyed Baby Carrots

Apple Crisp

Minestrone Soup

Lettuce and Carrot Salad

Mini Dill Bread

Crunchy Apple Cups

Lentil and Brown Rice Soup

Mixed Green Salad with Mustard Vinaigrette

Old-fashioned Sesame Oatmeal Bread

Apricot Custard

Oven-fried Beef and Spinach Patties

Brown Rice with Red Kidney Beans

Broccoli with Garlic and Lemon

Glazed Apple Loaf

Spaghettini with Creamy Artichoke Heart Sauce

Veal Scallops with Mushrooms

Spinach Salad

Cran-raspberry Mousse

Stuffed Pork Chops

Savoy Cabbage and Potatoes

Cucumber and Radish Salad

Three-grain Rolls

Prune Whip

Glazed Roast Pork with Fruit Stuffing

Brown Rice with Carrots and Tarragon

Baked Acorn Squash Rings

Pineapple Sorbet with Sambuca

Spaghettini with Shrimp and Lemon Sauce

Poached Fish Rolls in Tomato Wine Sauce

Orange and Kiwi Salad

Apple Meringue

Oven-fried Fillet of Sole

Barley and Mushroom Casserole

Shredded Zucchini with Garlic

Lemon-glazed Prune Loaf

Spaghettini with Spinach-Ricotta Pesto

Sautéed Scallops with Mushroom Herb Sauce

Mixed Green Salad with Mustard Vinaigrette

Orange Compote with Liqueur

Spring Menus

Chicken Breast with Potatoes and Red Pepper

Romaine au Gratin

Wheat Germ Bread

Prune Whip

Curried Braised Chicken with Tomato, Green Pepper, and Raisins

Simmered White or Brown Rice

Two-minute Mushrooms

Apple Crisp

Shells with Peas and Herbs

Turkey Cutlets with Tomato Sauce

Marinated Eggplant

Lemon Sherbet with Fruit and Strawberry Sauce

Artichokes with Green Dipping Sauce
Veal Piccata
Rice with Zucchini
Apricot Custard

Vermicelli with Asparagus
Sweet and Sour Veal Chops
Spinach Salad
Apricot Pineapple Loaf

Spaghettini with Parsley-Ricotta Pesto
Pork Scaloppine
Shredded Zucchini with Garlic
Frozen Strawberry Cream Parfaits

Chicken Soup with Herbs
Oven-fried Pork Chops
Asparagus and Tomatoes
Apple Meringue

Rack of Lamb
Rice with Peas
Parsleyed Baby Carrots
Lemon Sherbet with Fruit and Strawberry Sauce

Linguine with Scallops and Parsley Sauce
Poached Red Snapper with Tomato Dill Sauce
Green Beans with Carrots and Tarragon
Orange Compote with Liqueur

Poached Salmon with Dill Sauce
Lemony Rice
Grapefruit Salad with Watercress Dressing
Cran-raspberry Mousse

Asparagus Soup
Broiled Flounder with Thyme
Brown Rice with Carrots and Tarragon
Banana Flambé

Summer Menus

Chilled Tomato Mint Soup
Poached Chicken with Apricot Sauce
Rice Salad
Basic Muffins
Lemon Sherbet with Blueberry Sauce

Spaghettini with Basil-Ricotta Pesto
Chicken Breast with Piquant Vinegar Sauce
Minted Green Beans
Crunchy Peach Cups

Julienned Vegetable Soup
Peachy Drumsticks with Orange Sauce
Fruity Brown Rice Salad
Dessert Pancakes with Strawberry Filling

Broiled Rock Cornish Game Hen
Herbed Rice
Baked Tomatoes Provençale
Peach Clafouti

Grilled Filet Mignon

Herbed Potato Salad

Green Beans with Carrots and Tarragon

Star-spangled Parfait

Grilled Veal Chops

Tabbouleh

Vegetable Kebabs

Nectarine Clafouti

Grilled Pork Chops with Rosemary

Pasta Salad with Green Beans and Pimientos

Poached Nectarines with Blueberry Sauce

Chilled Cucumber Salad

Shrimp and Snow Pea Salad

Wheat Germ Bread

Peach Crisp

Swordfish and Cucumber Kebabs with Basil Dressing
Grilled Potatoes
Vegetable Kebabs
Apricot Clafouti

Spaghettini with Shrimp and Lemon Sauce
Broiled Halibut Steaks with Herbs
Red Onion and Tomato Salad
Peach Cream

Cold Melon Soup
Chicken Salad With Yogurt Mint Dressing
Whole Wheat Cinnamon Muffins
Crunchy Blueberry Cups

Fall Menus

Linguine with Broccoli

Turkey Cutlets with Mushrooms and Tarragon

Cucumber and Radish Salad

Crunchy Apple Cups

Pumpkin Apple Soup

Glazed Rock Cornish Game Hen

Barley Pilaf with Raisins

Green Bean and Zucchini Salad with Tarragon Dressing

Apple Meringue

Spicy Broiled Chicken Strips

Simmered White or Brown Rice

Broccoli with Garlic and Lemon

Apricot Custard

Linguine with Marinara Sauce

Veal Cutlets with Parmesan Topping

Two-minute Mushrooms

Apple Crisp

Pork Tenderloin with Apples and Prunes
Candied Yams with Pecans
Parsleyed Baby Carrots
Orange Compote with Liqueur

Julienned Vegetable Soup
Yummy Pork Chops
Shredded Zucchini with Garlic
Whole Wheat Bread
Plum Crisp

Cauliflower Soup with Parsley
Broiled Lamb Steaks with Thyme
Celery au Gratin
Three-grain Rolls
Poached Sliced Pears with Marmalade Sauce

Broiled Monkfish with Mustard and Chives
Rice with Zucchini
Orange and Kiwi Salad
Banana Pecan Loaf

Linguine with Scallops and Parsley Sauce

Speedy Shrimp Scampi

Peas and Mushrooms

Pineapple Sorbet with Strawberry Sauce

Broiled Swordfish Steaks

Lemony Rice

Green Bean and Zucchini Salad with Tarragon Dressing

Prune Whip

Raw Mushroom Soup

Baked Trout with Shallots, Orange, and Watercress

Baked Acorn Squash Rings

Apple Meringue

INDEX

About the Author

ANNE CASALE is the director of Annie's Kitchen Cooking School, which she founded in 1963, and author of *Italian Family Cooking Like Mama Used to Make,* a Columbine book (Ballantine Books).

She is currently president of the New York Association of Cooking Teachers and is also an Institutional and Certified Teacher of the International Association of Cooking Professionals.

Ms. Casale has worked in sales and marketing and as a lecturer, consultant, and designer for restaurants, gourmet shops, and cooking schools. She has taught in cooking schools throughout the United States and has appeared on numerous television and radio programs. She makes her home with her husband, John, in New Jersey.